The Miracle that was Macedonia

Nicholas G.L. Hammond

SIDGWICK AND JACKSON
LONDON

ST MARTIN'S PRESS
NEW YORK

To Macedonians past and present

First published in Great Britain in 1991
by Sidgwick & Jackson Limited, Cavaye Place, London SW10 9PG
and in the United States of America in 1991
by St. Martin's Press, 175 Fifth Avenue, New York, N.Y. 10010

ISBN 0-312-06586-8 St. Martin's Press
ISBN 0-283-99910-1 Sidgwick and Jackson

Typeset by Florencetype Ltd, Avon

Printed by Mackays, Kent

Library of Congress Cataloging-in-Publication Data

Hammond, N.G.L. (Nicholas Geoffrey Lamprière), 1907–
   The miracle that was Macedonia.
      p.   cm. —(Sidgwick and Jackson great civilization series)
   Includes bibliographical references and index.
   1. Macedonia—History—To 168 B.C.   I. Title. II. Series:
Sidgwick & Jackson great civilization series.
DF261.M2H36   1991   91-3255
938'.1—dc20   CIP

The illustration on the jacket shows a section of the Royal
Hunt Fresco of Tomb II at Vergina. The rider, Philip II,
who was blind in the right eye, is turning his head to see
with his left eye and strike the lion. It was the king's
prerogative to dispatch a lion.

Contents

List of Figures

Note: Figs 1 and 16 were drawn by N.G.L. Hammond. Acknowledgement is made to Oxford University Press for permission to reproduce Figs 2, 3, 4, 6, 7, 13, 14 and 17–20; to Bristol Classical Press for permission to reproduce Figs 5 and 9–12; and to Professor M. Andronicos in connection with Fig. 14.

List of Plates

Illustrations in colour will be found in M. Andronicos, *Vergina: the Royal Tombs* (Athens, 1984); the Catalogue *Sindos* of the Museum of Thessaloniki; and *Macedonia*, ed. M.B. Sakellariou (Athens, 1983).

Introduction

'Alexander *is* a Macedonian,' cried an Australian Macedonian during a demonstration by rival ethnic bands of 'Macedonians' in Sydney. There was some truth in his cry; for Alexander lives as a symbol not only of ancient Macedonia and its military prowess but also of the ecumenical ideas and practice which were then and are today of the greatest importance. In that sense, Alexander is and will continue to be a living force. But that was not what was in the demonstrator's mind. He wished to imply that Tito's 'Macedonia' in southern Yugoslavia did not date merely from the 1940s but was and is the home of the great Alexander. Demonstrators of other ethnic origins might have uttered the same cry, to imply that Alexander was and is a Greek of Greek Macedonia, or that Alexander was Illyrian in blood and is correctly portrayed as an Albanian on the Albanian 'lek', a coin which might indeed have taken its name from Alexander.

Controversy about Macedonia is not new. The identity of the ancient Macedonians and the significance of their achievements in world history were viewed differently by Demosthenes and Livy on the one hand and by Isocrates and Arrian on the other. Those modern writers of ancient history who give their highest accolade to the Greek city-state and its classical culture have always tended to see the victory of the Macedonian army as marking the end of the free city-state and as introducing a new period, in which the influences of city-state culture, albeit somewhat diluted, penetrated Egypt and Asia and created the civilization of what they call 'the Hellenistic world'. But they are looking at only one facet of a complex situation. Macedonia was a completely separate entity, both as a monarch-ical state in which the ruler had very wide powers, and as a kingdom within which many races were melded into a strong community. As such Macedonia was the earliest example in Europe of that form of monarchical rule and of that form of multi-racial kingdom which were to be the hallmarks of the period after Alexander's conquests, of the later Roman Empire, of the Byzantine Empire and of the many kingdoms of mediaeval and later Europe. Macedonia, not Athens, was the model for most of the political systems of posterity for many centuries. In his book *The Glory that was Greece* J. C. Stobart gave to his last chapter the title 'The Macedonian World'. He was correct; for the so-called Hellenistic kingdoms were in all respects Macedonian kingdoms of the traditional Macedonian type, and the diffusion of Greek culture within that Macedonian world was comparable to the spread of European culture within the British Empire and Common-wealth.

As we shall see, Macedonia was both within Greece and yet outside it. The royal house was Greek in origin. The kings maintained some links with their homeland, Argos in the Peloponnese; and they stressed their descent from Heracles, son of Zeus, through the royal house of Argos. But they were thoroughly Macedonian in spirit and conduct; for they alone had ruled in Macedonia during the three centuries which preceded the acces-sion of Philip, father of Alexander, and they identified themselves with the fortunes and interests of the Macedonian people as closely as our Hanoverian house identifies itself with our fortunes and interests. Some Macedonian institutions, especially in matters of religion and of city life, were markedly Greek, even as the language of the Macedonian State was Greek; and it has become apparent from recent archaeological discoveries that Macedonian art and architecture had much in common with contem-porary Greek art and architecture. But some purely Macedonian institutions were of crucial importance: monarchical control, court ceremonial, companion cavalry, royal pages, primitive kinds of assembly and of treason trial, and an attachment to primitive forms of Dionysiac, Orphic and other religious beliefs. And our conventional ideas that Macedonian art and architecture were derived from Greece have been revolutionized by the amazing discoveries of Professor M. Andronicos at Vergina in and after 1977 and of other archaeologists elsewhere in Macedonia. We realize now that Macedonia in the reign of Philip was the leading centre of painting, mosaic, palace construction and tomb architecture, and that it led the world in the production of arms and armour and in the making of exquisite jewellery in gold, silver, ivory and bronze.

The explosion of interest in ancient Macedonia came at a time when I had completed a full-scale history of Epirus, a neighbouring and in some respects similar region, and was beginning a comparable history of Mace-donia. The basis of any such history is personal knowledge of the country. One conclusion which emerged from my topographical studies was my identification of the site at Vergina with the early capital, Aegeae, where the kings of Macedonia were said to have been buried. At that time, in 1968, the Institute of Balkan Studies in Thessaloniki organized the first International Conference on Ancient Macedonia and I was able to announce there my belief – at that time peculiar to myself – that Vergina was the ancient Aegeae and would one day yield up the bones of Macedonian kings. Disbelief was vehemently expressed, not least by the excavator of Vergina, Professor Andronicos. But in 1976, with characteristic generosity, he informed me that he was now of my persuasion and would excavate the Great Mound in 1977. His results left no doubt about the placing of Aegeae at Vergina. During these and subsequent years my three-volume *History of Macedonia* – the first in any language – was being published (Volume I in

1972; Volume II, written jointly with G. T. Griffith, in 1979; and Volume III, with F. W. Walbank, in 1988) and a separate book, *The Macedonian State*, was published in December 1989. Meanwhile a spate of articles has been published in the proceedings of four conferences on Ancient Macedonia, in connection with the exhibition of treasures from Vergina under the title 'In Search of Alexander', and in many learned periodicals and Festschrifts.

The invitation to write this book came at a time when I appreciated the extent to which *The Miracle that was Macedonia* had a right to be placed alongside *The Glory that was Greece* and *The Grandeur that was Rome*. It seemed that I had the appropriate background to accept the invitation, because I had travelled, mainly on foot, through much of Macedonia (especially western Macedonia in 1943), all of Epirus, and parts of central Albania, southern Yugoslavia and western Bulgaria; and because I had co-ordinated the results of these travels in a book, *Migrations and Invasions in Greece and Adjacent Areas*. Participation in guerrilla warfare has some relevance to an understanding of ancient warfare. Living under wartime conditions with Macedonian peasants gives one an insight into some aspects of life in ancient Macedonia. Let me quote a remark by E. Howell, an escaping prisoner-of-war, who walked through Chalcidice in the winter of 1943–4 and saw nomadic shepherds constructing an enclosure for their herd of sheep to keep out predators. 'They were very quick at this,' he wrote, 'cutting the wood and driving it into the ground with the certainty of long practice.' It must have been in just this manner that a Macedonian army on a campaign fortified its camp each evening with a palisade of stakes, whereas the soldiers of a settled community such as Athens lacked the expertise and camped unfortified.

I

The Land and the People

The origins of the Macedonians

The earliest surviving statement about the Macedonians and their habitat was made by the Greek poet Hesiod, writing c.700 BC. He cast the traditions about the peoples of his time into the form of genealogies, in which the eponymous ancestors of ethnic groups were related to one another. Thus Deucalion, living in Thessaly, had a son, Hellen, and a daughter, Thyia. The sons of Hellen, the eponymous ancestor of the Hellenes, were Dorus, Xouthus and Aeolus, these being the ancestors of the three dialect groups into which the Hellenes as speakers of the Greek language were divided – namely Doric, Ionic (Ion being a son of Xouthus) and Aeolic. Of Deucalion's daughter Thyia, Hesiod wrote:

> She conceived and bore to Zeus, whose joy is the thunderbolt,
> Two sons, Magnes and Macedon who goes to war in a chariot,
> And they had their dwellings around Pieria and Mount Olympus.

Thus the Magnetes and the Macedonians in Hesiod's opinion, were very closely related to the Hellenes and it follows that they also were speakers of the Greek language. By way of comparison we may cite the genealogy of Illyrius, the eponymous ancestor of the Illyrians, who was blessed with six sons and more than three daughters, the nine who are named being the ancestors of the Encheleeis, Autarieis, Dardanoi, Maidoi, Taulantioi, Perrhaiboi, Parthinoi, Dassaretioi and Darsioi. In this genealogy a Greek writer has applied to these tribes the common name 'Illyrian', taken probably from a tribe, 'Illyrii', which lived on the northern Albanian coast and came very early into contact with Greek seafarers. The basis of the relationship of these (and other unnamed) tribes was that they all spoke 'Illyrian'.

The area in which, according to Hesiod, the Magnetes and the Macedonians lived is exceptionally beautiful. Mount Olympus, the home of the Greek gods, dominates the scene with its lofty peak (2911 metres) and sheer, north-facing precipices, and its northerly outlier, the Pierian range, is remarkable for its rich pastures and stands of fine timber. When one walks from inland and reaches the high Pierian ridge, one looks down for the first time on the sparkling sea and the fertile lowlands of light-coloured soils. In

1

the early time of which Hesiod wrote, the mountains belonged to the Magnetes and the Macedonians, and the lowlands to people of a different speech, the Thracians, who were famous for their music; it was in the lands around Dium in Pieria that the Thracian singer Orpheus, the founder of the Orphic religion, was commemorated and that 'the Pierian Muses' sang by the sacred spring Pipleia.

Because the Magnetes and the Macedonians held the high ground, they must have lived by herding sheep and goats and by logging timber, and they must have rented pastures in the lowlands from the Thracians; for in the climatic zone which covers western Macedonia, Epirus and Albania there is only one form of large-scale herding – that known as transhumant pastoralism, in which the herds are led to the mountain pastures in the spring and to the lowland pastures in the autumn. It was in the summer that the shepherds met one another, as the two shepherds met on Mount Cithaeron in Sophocles' play, *Oedipus the King*:

> We spent together three whole six-month seasons,
> From spring until the rising of Arcturus.
> Then with the coming on of winter, I
> Drove my flocks home, he his, to Laius' folds.

The great merit of Mount Olympus and Pieria for the shepherds was the immediate proximity of the summer pastures to the winter pastures; for in most of this climatic zone the herds had to migrate from the coast to the central range of Pindus, travelling 100 miles even as the crow flies, and very much farther as the goat or sheep grazes. One consequence of the proximity was the isolation of the local shepherds from the shepherds of, for instance, central Pindus. In our era, when the Vlachs have practised this form of transhumant pastoralism on a large scale, the Vlachs of Mount Olympus and Pieria have developed a marked dialect of the Vlachic language peculiar to themselves, because their self-sufficiency in respect of summer and winter pastures has kept them isolated. It was the same with the Magnetes and the Macedonians, for the latter certainly developed their own distinct dialect of the Greek language.

Were there any memories of this very early period of transhumant pastoralism? The lays of ancient Rome or the tales of King Arthur and his Knights expressed posterity's belief of what their ancestors had been like and how they had lived. The stories which the Macedonians retailed about their ancestors had much to do with the pastoral way of life. One tells of the coming to Macedonia of three brothers who were descended from Temenus, king of Argos in the Peloponnese but who had become refugees. They came from inland to Lebaea ('Cauldron-town') and entered the service of the king of the Macedonians for pay: one tending the horses, another the cows, and the youngest, Perdiccas (meaning 'Partridge'), the smaller cattle (i.e. goats

2

and sheep). The queen cooked for them. When she baked bread, the loaf intended for Perdiccas swelled to twice the size of the other loaves. The queen informed the king, who saw it as a portent, so he summoned the brothers and told them to leave his country. They said 'We have a right to our pay; when we receive it we shall go.' It happened that sunlight was coming through the smoke-hole and shining on the floor of the house. The king pointed at the sunlight and said, 'That's the pay you deserve. I give it to you.' The older brothers stood motionless, aghast. The youngest, who happened to be holding a knife, said, 'We accept, O king, what you give us'; and he drew a ring round the patch of sunlight on the floor of the house, swept it three times into the fold of his cloak, and they departed, he and his brothers. When they had gone, one of the king's advisers warned him that the young boy had acted with intent and that his action was significant. Horsemen were sent in pursuit; but they were halted by a river which rose in spate just after the boys had crossed into another country. The portent was fulfilled in the course of time. Perdiccas became king of the Macedonians, and his descendants thereafter offered sacrifice to the river-god as their saviour.

The setting of the story is familiar to anyone who has visited Vlach shepherds or their Greek equivalent, the Sarakatsani, in one of their encampments. The cauldron for boiling the milk; men herding the animals and women baking bread; the one-roomed hut with a smoke-hole in the roof; and the importance of the herder of 'the smaller cattle'. Where was Lebaea? In 1984 Photios Petsas reported a similar name, 'Aleb(?e)a', on an inscribed stone in the hill-country near the western frontier of the canton later called Pieria, and it is possible that the king's summer capital was there.

Another indication of this way of life is contained in an early oracle mentioning goats, which are the leaders when they pasture with a herd of sheep. When the same Perdiccas wished to enlarge his kingdom, he consulted Apollo at Delphi and received this answer: 'The noble descendants of Temenus hold royal sway over a wealth-producing land; for it is the gift of aegis-bearing Zeus. But arise, hasten to Bouteis, rich in sheep, and where you may see gleaming-horned, snow-white goats sunk in sleep, sacrifice to the gods and found the city of your state on the levels of yonder land.'

In another version Perdiccas was led by a she-goat to the spot where he was to found his city. In gratitude for the service of the she-goat he called his city 'Aegeae', supposedly from the Greek word for goats, *aiges*. As that word is onomatopoeic – giving the sound of the goat's cry – Aegeae can be translated as 'Bleaters'. This explanation of the name was probably used by Euripides in his play *Archelaus*, for he too had a she-goat lead the way. In later times she-goats went in front of the Macedonian army on the march, even as a goat precedes the Welch Regiment on parade; and the goat was portrayed frequently on Macedonian coins.

3

The characteristics of transhumant pastoral peoples

The long period of transhumant pastoralism left a very strong mark on the Macedonian people, the nature of which can be inferred from what has been observed in recent times of the Vlachs and the Sarakatsani. Where pastures are good, as they are in Pieria, a transhumant group consists of up to 500 persons (men, women and children), and the entire group moves with its goats, sheep, mules, horses and sometimes cattle from the summer pastures to the winter pastures; they are nomadic in the sense that they move with the seasons and live in hastily constructed huts or bothies and not in permanent dwellings. The group or 'company' (the Greek term being *parea*) is close-knit. Men, women and children are all actively engaged in the group's activities. They own in common – not by family or individually – the animals, the summer pastures, the timber and all the products of their activities. They marry within the company or with members of a related company. Each company is self-sufficient, in that it grows its own food, makes its own clothing, builds its own bothies and defends its own livestock. Defence is in the hands of the armed men, who have to contend with brown bears, wolves, lynx and fox, and in ancient times with mountain lions, panthers and leopards, as well as with human predators and organized enemies. A company on the move was described by G. Weigand in 1899 as a column of horses and mules heavily laden with rugs, utensils, children and women, preceded and followed by a number of strong, well-armed men, while the sheep, divided into flocks by age and sex, were guarded as they grazed by armed men and ferocious dogs. They regarded the settled peoples with suspicion and indeed with scorn, for they thought of their own nomadic life as adventurous and superior.

The administration of the company, consisting as it does of families, is strictly patriarchal, although the women play a much more active part than they would in an urban situation. The men elect from their own number a *tshelniku*, 'head shepherd', who has almost unlimited authority in directing the company's movements, renting winter pastures, disposing of surplus produce and organizing defence (see Plate 2). When three or four companies combine to form a larger unit, as happened at the founding of Samarina as a summer village in the mountains, a head shepherd is elected by the armed men to take charge and his successors are sometimes from the same family. Here we see the antecedent to a hereditary monarchy with wide powers, and also the need of the monarch to be on the best of terms with the armed men who have elected him and who hunt and fight under his direction. Each company may be called a clan, and a cluster of clans such as we see at Samarina may be called a tribe; and it was these clans and tribes which, on the basis of traditional relationships or shared localities, made up a larger group, in ancient Greek an *ethnos*.

4

We can now imagine the conditions under which the king or head shepherd of the Macedonians was living. He led a cluster of tribes which had a shared name, 'Macedones', and he himself belonged to a clan called the Argeadae within the cluster, so that he and his clansmen were 'Argeadae Macedones' (we may compare 'Imphees Perrhaiboi' or 'Orestai Molossoi'). These Argeadae, being the descendants of Argeas, son of Macedon, were the royal tribe, into which Perdiccas and his brothers were adopted when he became king (how, we do not know). From then on son succeeded father as king for seven generations from Perdiccas I to Alexander I, so that, on reckoning a generation as thirty years, we find that Perdiccas became king c.650 BC. At that time the Magnetes, having migrated southwards, were in eastern Thessaly, and the Macedonians alone held the highlands of Olympus and Pieria. The lowlands were still held by the Thracians, and the rich plain to the north by the Bottiaeans.

Were the Macedonians Greek-speaking?

The language spoken by these early Macedonians has become a controversial issue in modern times. It seems not to have been so in antiquity. As we have seen, Hesiod made Magnes and Macedon first cousins of the Hellenes, and he therefore regarded them as speakers of a dialect (or dialects) of the Greek language. That he was correct in the case of the Magnetes has been proved by the discovery of early inscriptions in an Aeolic dialect in their area of eastern Thessaly. Then late in the fifth century a Greek historian, Hellanicus, who visited the court of Macedonia, made the father of Macedon not Zeus but Aeolus, a thing which he could not have done unless he knew that the Macedonians were speaking an Aeolic dialect of Greek. A remarkable confirmation of their Greek speech comes from the Persians, who occupied Macedonia as part of their conquests in Europe c.510–480: in the list of their subjects 'in lands beyond the sea' they mention 'the Greeks wearing the shield-like hat', who are unlikely to be any people other than the Macedonians, well known for their wearing of sun-hats. Moreover, the place-names of Olympus and Pieria are predominantly Greek. They are likely to have been attributed to the mountains, rivers and springs of 'the rich land' (Pieria) by Greek-speaking inhabitants in very early times.

Disagreements over this issue have developed for various reasons. In the second half of the fifth century Thucydides regarded the semi-nomadic, armed northerners of Epirus and western Macedonia as 'barbarians', and he called them such in his history of events in 429 and 423. The word was understood by some scholars to mean 'non-Greek-speakers' rather than 'savages'. They were shown to be mistaken in 1956, when inscriptions of 370–68, containing lists of Greek personal names and recording in the Greek language some acts of the Molossians, were found at Dodona in

Epirus. This discovery proved beyond dispute that one of Thucydides' 'barbarian' tribes of Epirus, the Molossians, was speaking Greek at the time of which he was writing. Demosthenes too called the Macedonians 'barbarians' in the 340s. That this was merely a term of abuse has been proved recently by the discovery at Aegeae (Vergina) of seventy-four Greek names and one Thracian name on funerary headstones inscribed in Greek letters. Since the headstones date from c.350 onwards and record many patronymics, it follows that the Macedones were Greek-speaking in the late fifth century BC. Another source of disagreement arose from the distinction which ancient authors made between the royal family, the Temenidae, who were aristocratic Hellenes, and the Macedonians, who were not Hellenes at all. This was thought to be a distinction between Greek-speakers and non-Greek-speakers, whereas it differentiates the descendants of Hellen from the descendants of Thyia, as in the genealogy provided by Hesiod.

The strongest opposition has come from philologists. Their concern has been with the 153 or so words which may be attributed to the Macedonians specifically. Some were clearly Greek and others, equally clearly, were not Greek. If one made the assumption that the Greek words came in with the Greek language c.340 (as could have been argued before the discovery of the inscriptions at Dodona and the funerary names at Aegeae), then the non-Greek words were the survivors of a non-Greek Macedonian language. But the opposite assumption was equally reasonable: that the non-Greek words came from the many non-Greek peoples who were living within the Macedonian kingdom of Philip II, and that the Greek words were those of the Macedones themselves. The choice between the rival assumptions has been settled outside the specialist field of philology, by discoveries which have revealed that the Molossi and the Macedones were speaking Greek and using Greek nomenclature in the latter part of the fifth century BC – i.e. at a time when they had very little contact with the southern Greeks.

The conclusion, then, is certain that when ancient authors wrote of Macedonians speaking Makedonisti they were referring to a dialect of Greek and not to a non-Greek language. That dialect was very different from the standard Greek (koine) which spread from the early fourth century onwards throughout all Greek-speaking areas, including Macedonia – as standard English has spread in this century even into Scotland. But the dialect persisted alongside the standard Greek, especially in the King's Army, where the regional pride of the original Macedones was as deeply rooted as the regional pride of the Scots Guards in Her Majesty's forces. The king himself might use the dialect in speaking to his own soldiers, and they might show their affection for a non-Macedonian commander by addressing him in the dialect.

How did the Macedonian kingdom differ from the Greek city-state?

We have already touched on some points of difference between the Macedonian kingdom and the Greek city-state. The Macedonians were still semi-nomadic in the seventh century, whereas the Greeks had formed settled communities with an urban centre. Accordingly, the Macedonians were always armed, for purposes of hunting and war; the tradition was maintained that a man who had not killed an enemy should wear a halter, and a man who had not killed a wild boar without using a net should eat standing. The king himself set the example. He led the charge against enemy forces and in the hunt had the prerogative of despatching a lion with his spear. No surprise was expressed when Alexander the Great killed a corrupt governor with his own hand. In a Greek city-state men went unarmed about their daily business and hoped for a peaceful life, or for a fairly safe form of warfare in a phalanx of well-armoured men; and hunting by Greek aristocrats was as safe and as socially divisive as fox-hunting. Again, the Macedonian Assembly killed a man condemned for treason with spears or with stones. In Athens executions were carried out at a fixed place, the Barathron or pit, into which the condemned man was hurled. The Macedonians, living outdoors or in bothies and having a climate of which the seasons were more extreme, wore very different clothing of heavy felt material and shield-like hats. They carried much of their wealth on their persons, both men and women having bronze pendants, beads, belt-ornaments, armlets and bracelets (see Plate 1). Dress and jewellery in Greek city-states were light by comparison, while the ladies had sophisticated hairstyles. The Macedonians had no slaves, whereas the Greeks left many manual tasks to their slaves. Thus, in manner of life and in conduct the Macedonians were poles apart from the citizens of contemporary Athens or Corinth. Their affinities were with other pastoral peoples in the Balkans, whether Greek, Illyrian or Thracian. It was therefore not surprising that Thucydides wrote of the Molossians and the Macedonians as 'savages'.

Monarchy, so firmly established in Macedonia, was anathema to the Greek city-states (Sparta excepted). Greeks, like many Americans and some Australians, were aggressively republican and regarded their own exercise of republicanism as the hallmark of civilized progress. One-man rule, whether exercised by a king or a dictator, was to them a negation of liberty; and their victory over the Persian emperor – the epitome of despotism – proved them right in their sense of their own superiority. In this tradition the Athenian people voted to bestow a crown on the assassin of Philip, the head indeed of an allied state but in their view a despot. Aristotle, who lived through the reigns of Philip and Alexander and taught Alexander at the court, had little regard for monarchy. In his view the Greeks of the city-state world, being both spirited and intelligent, were able to govern themselves. But the barbarians, being 'servile by nature', or spirited but stupid, or both servile and stupid, could not govern themselves and therefore submitted to monarchy. In the same way, the self-governing city-states were superior to the tribal states (*ethne*), found especially in colder regions and in Europe, which were full of spirit but deficient in intelligence and skill. It is clear that Aristotle would have put the Macedonian State in this last category.

The Macedonians had confidence in their own form of state and in their monarchical system. They had no desire to become part of the world of city-states, or indeed to be thought of as Hellenes in a city-state sense. Their way of life made them independent, versatile and warlike, and transhumant pastoralism accustomed them to hard manual work and not, as Aristotle strangely supposed, to idleness. Their destiny too was to prove very different from that of the city-states.

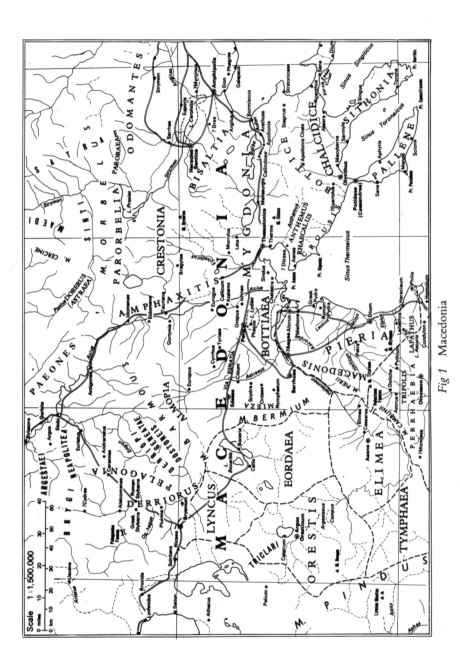

Fig 1 Macedonia

II

The Growth of the Macedonian State, c.650–475

The expulsion of neighbouring peoples

When Perdiccas came to the throne c.650 BC, the southern neighbours of the Macedonians were similar to the Macedonians in their way of life and customs. The *Magnetes*, who had shared the homeland of the Macedonians, lived in the mountains of north-east Thessaly, where they cut timber and practised transhumant pastoralism; their dialect was Aeolic, their war-dances were like those of the Macedonians, and they and the Macedonians celebrated a festival which was called by each people 'The Companion Festival' (*Hetairideia*). The *Perrhaebi* lived in the hill-country south-west of Mount Olympus. Like the Macedones, they were a cluster of tribes which engaged in transhumant pastoralism; and they went far inland to their summer pastures on the Pindus range, where one group was known as 'the nomadic Perrhaebi'. They too were Greek-speaking. Both the Magnetes and the Perrhaebi needed winter pastures in the Thessalian plains, and in consequence they were often politically dependent on the rich city-states of the north Thessalian plain, especially Larissa. The western neighbours of the Macedones, the *Elimeotae*, were engaged in pastoralism but also in agriculture on good arable land in the middle valley of the Haliacmon river. They were akin to the Molossians and spoke a dialect of West Greek; but they traded mainly southwards with the city-states of north-west Thessaly, to which access was easy. To the east, the Thracian-speaking *Pieres* held the coastal lowlands. They engaged in agriculture and stock-raising, and they let their winter pastures to the Macedones. They were a gifted and warlike people, but they were vulnerable in that their land was far from the lands of other Thracian tribes.

On the Pierian coast there were two natural harbours, suitable for small ships, and each was held by settlers who had come from city-states of southern Greece. The more northerly, Methone, was occupied c.730 by Eretrians from Euboea. Pydna, situated on a defensible hill 8 kilometres to the south, received Greek settlers of unknown origin but probably from Euboea; for other colonies were founded by Euboeans, led by Eretria and Chalcis, on the eastern side of the Thermaic Gulf and on the three peninsulas of 'Chalcidice', so named from the men of Chalcis. These Euboeans were daring seafarers with merchantmen under sail and small

11

warships under oar; they were well equipped with bronze armour, out-fought the local people and fortified their sites with masonry walls. They were racially exclusive, regarding the local people as savages. What attracted them was the fine timber of Pieria, suitable for ship-building, which was in great demand; and they hoped to export to the mainland and the islands any surplus of cereals or animal products of the hinterland. The dialect of their Greek speech, Ionic, differed from the dialect of the Macedonians and had no effect upon it.

To the north, the coastal plain west of the Axius (Vardar) and its hinterland formed an exceptionally rich and well-watered area, suitable for cereals and fruit and also providing winter pastures, because the flood-waters of the uncontrolled rivers left swampy meadows. The dominant power for some three centuries, down to c.800 had been the *Phrygians*, both of whose two chief cities were called Edessa, meaning 'water' in their language. One retained its name and is still called Edessa. The other was renamed Aegeae, and it was here, down in the plain, that the leading Phrygians were buried in a great cemetery of some 300 tumuli, each some 20 metres in diameter. When these Phrygians migrated to Asia c.800, they founded Gordium (near Ankara) and buried their kings and nobles in even greater tumuli. This talented people was said to have excelled in the working of iron and bronze, and during the occupation of Macedonia its wealth was attributed to the exploitation of iron (available in the Pierian mountains, in Almopia and east of Mount Paiko). This tradition was confirmed by the quantity and quality of the iron weapons and by the extremely numerous bronze ornaments and plaques in the 100 tumuli below modern Vergina which were excavated by Manolis Andronicos and by Photios Petsas between 1951 and 1961. The former noted that the bronze objects, locally made, had been shaped by hammering and not by the use of a mould. The richest period of the Phrygians was 900–800, and it was enshrined in the memory of the highland Macedones. They told Herodotus the traditional story of how the Phrygian king, Midas, son of Gordias, captured Silenus, a satyr who served the god Dionysus, in the royal gardens, where roses grew of their own accord, each with sixty petals (the rose in modern Greek is a 'thirty-petaller'). They told him also that their ancestors had lived with the Phrygians (whom they called *Briges* in their dialect). It was no doubt from them that the Macedonians learnt metallurgy (important for nomadic peoples), music and a worship of Dionysus.

The Phrygians seem to have been on good terms with the inhabitants of the rich plain, Emathia, who called themselves *Bottiaei* and claimed that they had come from Crete during what we call the Late Bronze Age. Their claim has been supported by the discovery of a rod carrying three double-axes of bronze, all cast in one piece, in five burials of women in tumuli at Vergina. Each burial had unusually rich offerings. The rod was fitted as a pendant to an elaborate headdress. Both the double-axe and the headdress were typical of Minoan Crete (the headdress being worn by a girl-tumbler in the bull-ring). The women were evidently priestesses of a Minoan cult, which had survived into the Greek-speaking period at Cnossus and had been taken overseas in a diaspora of Cretans c.1300. Confirmation of the tradition may be seen in an inscription yet to be published by Iulia Vokotopoulou, which proves that the Bottiaei were speakers of Greek when they moved from the rich plain into the hinterland of Chalcidice.

We turn now to the expansion of the Macedonian kingdom. When Perdiccas became king, he organized the Macedonians, defeated the Thracian Pieres in battle and drove them overseas to settle in a coastal strip west of the river Strymon. Next, the Macedonians conquered the Bottiaeans and drove them out from the gardens of Midas and from most of the coastal plain west of the Axius; and the Bottiaeans fled to the hinterland of Chalcidice. The capital city of Perdiccas, Aegeae, was now at the centre of a kingdom, which included a relatively large area of excellent arable land. These spectacular successes confirmed the authority of the Temenid kings, and Perdiccas or his son directed various tribal 'companies' to abandon transhumant pastoralism, settle in towns and practise agriculture. The towns were called *poleis* (plural), but they differed in some respects from contemporary Greek *poleis*: they were not independent city-states but units within a kingdom, their territory was not flexible but fixed by the king, and the population of each *polis* (singular) consisted of small interrelated pastoral groups. Thus, unlike the Greek *poleis*, they had an inner cohesion, a social uniformity and a lack of foreign policy. The seeds of the *stasis* (revolutionary strife), which wrecked so many Greek *poleis*, were lacking in the Macedonian *polis*. Moreover, there was no subject population, and no bought slaves. All Macedonians worked in freedom, whether as pastoralists, peasants or artisans.

The next expansions were northwards into Almopia and westwards into Eordaea, areas then richer in timber and pasture than in arable land, and again the survivors of the defeated peoples were expelled and fled as refugees to lands east of the Axius. These conquests were completed by 510 approximately.

The Macedonians now faced some different neighbours. To the west and north-west the *Orestae* and the *Lyncestae*, like the Elimeotae, were related to the Molossians and spoke the dialect known as West Greek. Their way of life was pastoral. Land on both sides of the Axius down to the sea was held by the *Paeones*, the collective name of numerous related tribes with their own language. They were the most powerful people in the central Balkan region, for they controlled much of the catchment area of the Axius and the Strymon, and they had well-established cities in the Axius basin, such as Pella and Ichnae, and in the Strymon basin, such as Sirris (modern Serres).

At this time the Persians appeared on the scene. The masters of a great empire in Asia, they defeated the Paeonians, who had the temerity to offer

13

resistance, and expelled them from the Strymon basin. The Macedonians took advantage of the disasters of the Paeonians to win Pella and Ichnae c.505; and, led on by the Argeadae, the royal tribe, they crossed the river, destroyed a fortified site, Amydon, on the east bank, and occupied part of the area called Amphaxitis. But the future lay with the Persians. An embassy demanded and received submission from Amyntas, the king of the Macedonians. As a loyal subject of Persia, he gave his daughter in marriage to the Persian commander, and he was awarded the possession of Anthemus, a fertile valley on the east side of the Thermaic Gulf. The peoples of Amphaxitis and Anthemus were not expelled but lived alongside the Macedonians. This new policy was due to Amyntas, perhaps at the suggestion of Persia. The Persians also favoured the Thracians, who had rallied to their side. The leading Thracian tribe, the Edones, occupied Crestonia and Mygdonia up to the delta of the Axius, thus becoming formidable neighbours to the Macedonians.

'Macedonia' now had two meanings, both recorded by Herodotus. The original homeland, bounded on the south by the Tempe Pass and by Perrhaebia, and on the north by the river Haliacmon, was still 'the Macedonian land', and the Pierian mountain was 'the Macedonian mountain'. But the territory over which the king of the Macedonians ruled by 505 was also called Macedonia, although it included some people in Amphaxitis and Anthemus who were not Macedones by race. Thus Aeschylus, writing in 472, described 'the territory of Macedones' as including the ford of the Axius in Amphaxitis. What united the Macedones and the non-Macedones was the rule of the king; and as we shall see later it was the king and not the Macedones who owned 'the spear-won land'. For it was through his command in war that the limits of the original territorial kingdom had been expanded.

The period of Persian relations, c.510–477

The Persian conquest of the eastern Mediterranean shores from Cyrenaica in the south to Macedonia in the north between 545 and 510 BC opened up new horizons for the Balkan peoples. There was a great demand in Asia and Egypt for the unusually pure silver which was mined in South Illyria, Paeonia, Chalcidice, Thasos, the Strymon basin, the upper Strymon valley, Mount Pangaeum and Philippi. It was exported both as bullion and as heavy coin (see Plate 7a). Only some of the coins carried the name of the issuing authority (a tribe, a city or a king). It was in Greek letters, for Greek was the only alphabet in use in Europe. It is an indication of the range of exchange that most of these heavy coins have been found in hoards in Asia and Egypt. The emblems on the coins were religious, portraying for instance a Silenus (a kind of Satyr) courting a Nymph, a Centaur abducting a Nymph, a bearded god between two oxen, an armed hero holding a prancing horse, or a god of war. The choice of emblems and the crude vigour of the workmanship came from the native peoples. Ten or so Greek city-states on the coasts of the Thermaic Gulf and the Chalcidic peninsulas also issued large silver coins at this time. The emblems included a variety of animals and objects, such as the amphora, and the workmanship was more artistic. Tribute to Persia was paid in precious metals, and large Persian forces which served in the Balkan area provided a market for surplus foodstuffs. Timber too was much in demand for the building of ships, transport wagons and bridges; for the Persians relied on sea-transport and on an all-weather road system in Europe.

'The King of Kings', as the Persian Emperor styled himself, preferred to deal with kings, such as Amyntas and his son Alexander and the kings of Thracian tribes. If they were loyal, he rewarded them with additional territory. Thus, as we have seen, Amyntas was given Anthemus. In the late 480s, when Xerxes was preparing to invade Greece with an enormous army and fleet, he decided to strengthen the defences of the launching area, Macedonia, by subjugating part of its hinterland – namely the lands of the Elimeotae, Orestae, Lyncestae and Pelagones (see Plate 4). These peoples had no option but to submit. Xerxes placed them under the rule of Alexander. Thenceforth they were known as Elimeotae Macedones, Orestae Macedones, etc., and their lands were called *Upper Macedonia*, even though their subjection to the Macedonian king was often to be purely nominal. For the invasion, Xerxes conscripted troops from his Balkan subjects: from east of the Axius Thracians, Paeonians, Eordi, Bottiaei, Pieres, Brygi and Chalcidian Greeks, and from west of the Axius Macedones. The last comprised both cavalry and infantry, and they were under the command of their king; for Alexander sent Macedonians, evidently cavalry-men, ahead of the main army to take over some of the Boeotian city-states and protect them from marauders, and later during the manoeuvres which preceded the battle of Plataea a unit of Macedonian infantry was posted opposite the Athenian hoplites (heavily armed infantrymen). Alexander himself stood high in the favour of Persia. He was chosen by Mardonius, the Persian commander in 479, to offer easy terms to Athens and to split the Greek resistance.

The Persian presence gave to the peoples of Thrace and Macedonia a period of peace and protection which lasted for a generation – a very rare, perhaps unique experience for these warring tribes – and the Persian Empire provided large, profitable markets for their goods. The increase in wealth was seen not only in the production of silver bullion and coin but also in the courts of the kings; for they took the lion's share of any profits. An insight into their situation has been provided by the excavation of several royal cemeteries. At Duvanli in central Thrace some burials of the Persian period were accompanied by gold and silver vessels and jewellery,

15

bronze helmets and cuirasses, and gold pectorals and earrings, often with motifs derived from Persian art. At the most westerly point of Thracian occupation, modern Sindos near the Axius river, some royal tombs of the Persian period contained many objects of gold and silver (see Plates 5a–6b). These included gold death-masks, gold mouthpieces (which had been tied over the mouth and sometimes over the eyes of the corpse), gold and silver jewellery, and gold facings on clothing. The men were accompanied by helmet, sword, two spears and occasionally a bronze shield. Equally remarkable tombs were found outside the Persian sphere at Radolishte, Delogozda and Trebenishte, north of Lake Ochrid, where it seems that two royal houses were in league. The richest cemetery, at Trebenishte, had gold death-masks, gloves, sandals and mouthpieces, and gold and silver jewellery; and the men were buried with helmet, sword and spears. Thracian influences were strong at Sindos and Trebenishte; but there was evidence also of Greek imports, especially bronze vessels from Corinth and Corinthian colonies.

It seems that the rulers at Sindos controlled the chief harbour for merchandise at the head of the Thermaic Gulf. On the other hand, the area of the Macedonian kingdom did not impinge on the main trade-route, which went up the east side of the Axius valley and then either continued northwards towards the Danube or turned westwards via the head of Lake Ochrid to reach two Corinthian colonies on the Adriatic coast, Dyrrachium and Apollonia. Similar forms of wealth, though less lavish, appeared in southern Macedonia. Burials in pit-graves with fine gold and silver objects, such as were found at Sindos, have been discovered recently at Aegeae and at Elimea (Aiane), the capitals of the king of the Macedones and of the king of the Elimeotae. These burials are dated within the Persian period.

The gold was not imported from the East. The rulers of Trebenishte obtained silver from a nearby mine at Damastium, and their gold came from Metohija and Kosovo (in southern Yugoslavia), which were part of their kingdom. The rulers of Sindos controlled the washing of gold in the river Edonus (named after the Thracian royal tribe) – the modern Gallikos – and the mining of gold in Crestonia; and their silver was probably obtained from a mine in the Kumli valley. On the other hand, the kingdoms of the Macedones and of the Elimeotae had no deposits of gold or silver at all, and their kings did not issue any coinage.

Free trade seems to have prevailed between the countries of the Persian Empire and those outside it, such as Greece, except when hostilities imposed a local ban. There was also freedom of movement. During the reign of Amyntas as a client-king of Persia, his son Alexander competed twice in the Olympic Games. On the first occasion the qualifications of 'Alexander the Macedonian', as he was called, were questioned but ratified by the special judges (*Hellanodicae*), who ensured that only Greeks were admitted. The Macedonians in general, being regarded as barbarians, were

16

not eligible; but Alexander, as a descendant of Temenus, was a Greek of aristocratic descent, and it was easy to check at Argos the affinity of the Macedonian royal family. On the second occasion, c.495, his victory in the pentathlon was celebrated in an ode by Pindar, who visited the Macedonian court then or later; a fragment survives in which Pindar addresses Alexander as 'bold-scheming son of Amyntas'. The epithet was well chosen; for Alexander played a double game with great skill during the invasion of Greece. He had prepared the ground by a special service for Athens, which named him as her friend, representative (*proxenus*) and benefactor, very probably because he provided the timber for building the new fleet which was said to be for war against Aegina but in the event defeated the Persian fleet decisively at the Battle of Salamis. When the Greeks planned to hold the Pass of Tempe, Alexander sent envoys to advise them to withdraw. The advice was taken. It could have been argued that the withdrawal suited Xerxes also. Then at Plataea in 479 Alexander himself crossed no-man's-land at night, informed the Athenian commander, Aristides, of an impending attack, and returned unobserved to his post in the Persian lines. It was presumably a calculated risk; for he probably foresaw the defeat of Persia and hoped to earn the gratitude of the victors.

Whether or not Alexander had such foresight, he made the most of Persia's defeat as soon as her forces evacuated Macedonia and withdrew to hold the line of the Strymon. He attacked the Thracian royal tribe, the Edones, drove them east of the Strymon, and annexed the land between the Axius and the Strymon, where he ruled over the pro-Persian Thracians and the Bisaltae, a powerful tribe of Thracian speech. He took as his personal possessions the gold of the valley of the Edonus, which now received a Greek name, Echedorus ('Holder of Gifts'), the mine in the Kumli valley which yielded a talent of silver a day, some gold near Lete in Mygdonia, and more gold at Nigrita in the Strymon basin.

Alexander was able at last to issue a coinage in large denominations. At first he used the emblems and types of the Bisaltic coins with the substitution of his name for that of the Bisaltae, and later he made his own innovations. Perhaps in 477 he felt strong enough to capture Nine Ways at the crossing of the Strymon (the site of Amphipolis), and he dedicated gold statues of himself – probably lifesize – at Delphi and Olympia as 'the firstfruit of spoils from captive Medes'. Thus he advertised himself to the Greeks as their champion against Persia in the cause of liberty; but he managed to maintain friendly relations with the Persian court through his nephew, Amyntas, who enjoyed the favour of the King of Kings. This high-water mark of Macedonian achievement was not to be surpassed for more than a century.

Amyntas and Alexander had shown remarkable ability in exploiting the favourable circumstances which developed with the expansion of Persia into Europe and ended with the rise of Athenian naval power. It was not enough to submit passively to Persia. They engaged actively in the promotion of Persia's interests. Amyntas attacked the Paeonians in the rear when they were at war with Persia, and he and his son remained loyal to Persia when the Greek city-states of Asia Minor were in revolt (499–3). Faithful service was amply rewarded. Persia, as overlord of her European province, awarded part of Amphaxitis and Anthemus to Amyntas, entrusted the control of the strategic ford over the Axius to the Macedonians, and extended the authority of Alexander as her client-king over the lands of Upper Macedonia – thereby doubling the extent of the king's territory and the number of his subjects.

The Persian presence was of great economic benefit. The Persian armies developed communications leading to the kingdom and within the kingdom, where few, if any, had existed. At least two bridges were built over the Strymon (the roadway being laid on very numerous wooden piles, which have been found by excavation in the old riverbed). All-weather roads, suitable for wheeled transport, were built from the Strymon to the Axius. One ran direct through the natural sink, containing two lakes, to Therme at the head of the Thermaic Gulf (this being the predecessor of the Via Egnatia). Another turned inland up the Kumli valley and descended down the Gallikos valley to modern Sindos beside the swampy delta of the Axius; this road passed through wild, undeveloped country in which mountain lions preyed upon the camels of the Persian supply train. Another road followed the coast southwards, passed over the necks of the three peninsulas and traversed the coast of Crousis and Anthemus to reach Therme. Large supply-dumps, requiring the construction of granaries, were laid down at suitable places on the roads. Provision was made also for the very large fleet of Xerxes. A canal wide enough to permit two merchantmen to pass one another was dug through the neck of the Athos peninsula, in order to avoid the dangerous rounding of Mount Athos (see Fig. 1). The few harbours on the coast of the Macedonian kingdom were improved, and one such harbour, that of the Greek city Pydna, was placed under the control of Alexander. In the south of the kingdom the Macedonian city Heracleum, no doubt fortified, withstood the probing of the Greek forces at Tempe in 480. When Xerxes inspected the Pass of Tempe, he realized the need to build a road further inland over the Petra Pass through undeveloped, forested country. One-third of his army completed the task. A subsidiary road was probably built further west over the Volustana Pass, leading from Elimeotis to Perrhaebia.

For the first time in the history of the kingdom, Amyntas and Alexander were able to trade directly by sea and by land with eager customers. In the past Greek city-states – Pydna, Methone, Dicaea and Aenea – had acted as intermediaries and garnered the profits, but now Alexander had harbours at Anthemus, Pydna and probably Methone. At the head of the Gulf the king had his own harbour in Anthemus. Thus, if Alexander supplied great quantities of ship-building timber to Athens c.483, he could demand his own price and deliver the timber direct to Athenian agents; and this was true of the Persians and other purchasers, such as the Aegean islanders and the Ionian Greeks of the Asiatic coast. Within the kingdom there was a sure market for surplus foodstuffs, because Persian forces were stationed in this border province. Equally important was the development of trade overland throughout the Balkan area, which was made possible by the imposition of peace. We have seen signs of it in the royal cemeteries of Trebenishte, Sindos and Duvanli; and many other examples of gold objects have been found in burials in Thrace, Paeonia, the vicinity of Thessaloniki, at Aegeae and at Elimea; and not least the great prosperity of the Greek city-states on the Thracian coast, in Chalcidice, and on the offshore island of Thasos.

The remarkable increase in the size and the prosperity of the Macedonian kingdom was due as much to the Macedonians as to their kings. The majority had changed their way of life from transhumant pastoralism to settled life in cities and to the cultivation of a fertile countryside. In so doing they had retained in each city the social cohesion which had been a mark of the pastoral 'company', and when we have evidence of their institutions we find that each had its own citizenship and administration and treated anyone who came from even a nearby city as a foreigner or as a resident alien (*katoikos* or *metoikos*). Above all, they were fine fighters; for it was in war that they defeated their neighbours before the arrival of the Persians, and it was no doubt their record in war which won the approval of the Persian commanders who called them up for service. What they needed to achieve success was the undisputed leadership of a capable king – a need which was met by Amyntas and Alexander in this critical period, when intelligent opportunism was an essential part of statesmanship.

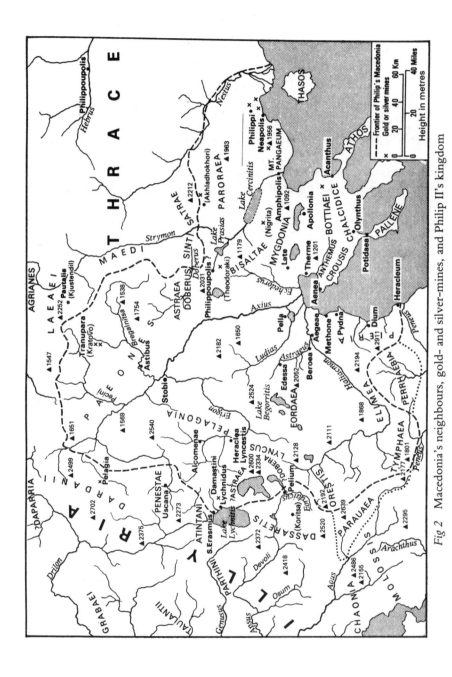

Fig 2 Macedonia's neighbours, gold- and silver-mines, and Philip II's kingdom

III

Periods of Adversity and Defeat, 476–359

Pressures from Balkan neighbours and from Athens

The extension of the kingdom which was made possible by the favour of Persia and then by the flight of the Persian forces brought the Macedonians into contact with some new neighbours and into closer contact with old neighbours. Let us consider them, beginning in the area known as Upper Macedonia (see Fig. 1). There the Elimeotae, new subjects of the king, enjoyed easy access to their southern neighbours, the city-states of the western Thessalian plain, of which Tricca was the most important. The danger was rather that the Elimeotae could find support there if they should wish to cast off the rule of Alexander, than that the city-states would invade Elimeotis. The other tribal states of Upper Macedonia were adjacent to those which lay outside the kingdom to the west – from south to north, the Tymphaei, the Parauaei and the Dassaretae. Both sets of tribal states were frequently in contact with one another, because they all used the summer pastures and the timber of the high country (see Plate 4). Known as North Pindus (Mount Smolika being 2639 metres and Mount Grammus 2520 metres), this vast area of virgin forest and alpine pasture was adequate for all the tribal states in their transhumant pastoralism, and the watershed formed a natural divide for the movement of flocks westwards or eastwards in pursuit of winter pastures. The Tymphaei took their name from Mount Tymphe (1801 metres), north of the Zygos Pass between Epirus and Thessaly; the Parauaei were named after the river Aous (also called Aeas), which draws its headwaters from West Pindus; and the Dassaretae, under a variant name 'Dexari', were associated by Hecataeus, an early geographer, with Mount Amyrus (modern Mount Tomor, 2418 metres), which dominates the forested area between the rivers Osum and Devoll before they join to form the Semeni (Apsus). All these tribal states on either side of the watershed spoke the West Greek dialect and were related to two powerful tribal states in Epirus, the Molossi and the Chaones. They were often ready to combine, whichever side of the watershed they came from; thus in 429 the forces of the Orestae and the Parauaei served under the king of the latter. Their way of life was similar to that which the Macedones themselves had practised before they expanded into the Emathian plain.

21

The most northerly tribal state of Upper Macedonia, that of the Pelagones, was neighboured on the west by three Illyrian tribal states: the Enchelees, associated with Lake Lychnitis (Lake Ochrid); the Atintani, north of the Lake's basin; and the Penestae. However, the Pelagones were not immediate neighbours to any of them, because a continuous mountain range, some 2000 metres high, lay between. The Enchelees owned the rich fisheries at the northern end of Lake Lychnitis, and it was probably they, the Atintani and a northern Illyrian tribe called the Dardanii, who combined to create the prosperity of which there was evidence at Radolishte and Trebenishte (see p. 16). One clue is found in the very heavy silver coins from this area, which must have been connected with the rulers of Trebenishte; for some carried in Greek letters the name 'Tynteni', which in the Ionic dialect was a shortened form of Atintani. These, and indeed all Illyrian tribes, were exceedingly bellicose (*machimoi*). It was fortunate that the tribes tended generally to fight, plunder and enslave one another. When a number of them did combine under a capable leader, as happened *c.*400–359, they were a scourge to the Greeks of Epirus and Upper Macedonia. The terror which Illyrian warriors – cavalry and infantry alike – inspired in the Macedonians was apparent in 423, when the mere news of their approach caused the Macedonian troops to cut and run. The warrior class ruled in Illyrian society, and in particular the aristocratic cavalrymen held 'the mastery which they gained only by their superiority in battle, a few governing many', as Thucydides remarked of the situation in 423.

As neighbours on the east the Pelagones had the Paeones, who cultivated the fertile basins of the Axius and its eastern tributaries, the Bregalnitsa and the Pecinj. There were other Paeonian tribes in the upper valley of the Strymon. Both groups of Paeonians had deposits of gold and silver, and they issued coins during and after the Persian period. The king of the western group had his capital at Astibus (modern Štip), and the royal tribe was probably called Derrones after their god of healing, Darron. Exceptionally heavy coins were issued in the name of this tribe in the Persian period; and the emblems included a god in association with very large oxen, domesticated specimens of the wild aurochs, for which Paeonia was famous. Although they had been weakened by the Persians, they were still a formidable and well-organized people.

In the Strymon basin Alexander was the neighbour of a royal Thracian tribe, the Edones. The enmity between them was continuous and damaging. The Thracian tribes generally were exceedingly warlike and considered it glorious to live by war and plunder, as Herodotus remarked, so much so that they despised those who practised agriculture. They were also very numerous. In the opinion of Herodotus, they were potentially the most powerful race in the Balkan area; but in practice they found it almost impossible to combine with each other. Thus in conflicts between the Macedonians, the Bisaltae and the Edones, for instance, there was usually an ebb and flow. The Edones alone were a match for the Macedonians; for they had large resources of gold and silver in the eastern part of the Strymon basin, and their king Getas issued exceptionally heavy silver coins in the 470s and 460s. It was only in 429 that a large number of Thracian tribes did combine. They were then able to invade the heart of the Macedonian kingdom – an event to which we shall come later.

These Balkan neighbours were usually more interested in loot than in trying to occupy Lower Macedonia. For the Illyrians and the Thracians were aptly described as 'being accustomed to live by rapine' (*rapto vivere assueti*), and they hoped to take home as many humans, animals and moveable goods as possible. In most of their raids they probably got no further than the cantons of Upper Macedonia in the west and the lowlands of Mygdonia in the east; but occasionally they joined forces with one or more tribal states which were nominally subject to the Macedonian king. This happened in 423. Illyrian warriors then joined the defeated forces of the Lyncestae, whom Perdiccas II was trying to reduce to obedience, and they drove out the combined armies of Perdiccas and the Spartan commander, Brasidas. In the latter part of Alexander's reign the Edones deprived him of the Bisaltic silver mine for some years, and after his death the Bisaltae broke away and their king coined in his own name, Mosses.

The Macedonian kingdom was the neighbour also of the three peoples who lived in the Chalcidic peninsula: the Crousaei, on the coast south of Anthemus; the Bottiaei in the interior; and the thirty or so Greek colonial city-states, of which the strongest was a colony of Corinth called Potidaea, controlling the approach to the Thermaic Gulf. All three peoples were Greek-speaking. They lived in small city-states and were fiercely independent. Indeed the inhabitants of the western peninsula, Pallene, rose successfully against the Persians in the winter of 480/79. On their own these peoples did not usually constitute a danger to the Macedonian kingdom; for they were divided among themselves and acted as individual city-states.

The most dangerous and economically much the most damaging enemy was Athens. As the proud possessor of 200 warships, she attracted the alliances of many maritime Greek city-states and thereby in 477 created a well-organized coalition, which was called 'Athens and her Allies' (or by most modern scholars, 'The Confederacy of Delos'). Athens held the hegemony – she alone exercised the executive powers of command. The forces of the coalition aimed to liberate their compatriots and 'to retaliate for what they had suffered by ravaging the territory of the Great King'. In 476 their combined forces landed at the mouth of the Strymon, defeated the pro-Persian Edones and laid siege to the Persian stronghold, which was then not at Nine Ways (which Alexander had held for less than a year) but at Eïon, just east of the river mouth. The Persian governor fought to the end, killing his family and then himself. The Athenian commander sold the population for what they would fetch as slaves and occupied the site in the

23

name of Athens and her Allies. Their next target was the small island of Scyros. Its Greek inhabitants, accused of practising piracy, were given the same treatment and the island was occupied by settlers from Athens only. These and other operations brought to Athens and her Allies a monopoly of sea-power in the northern Aegean.

It was therefore prudent for any maritime city-state in the region to join the coalition for various reasons: to have access to the sea-lanes for trade, to be protected from aggression or piracy and to share in any loot. Most of the city-states on the east side of the Thermaic Gulf and on the coast of Chalcidice entered the coalition. On the other hand, the Macedonians were regarded by the coalition as enemies, comparable to the Thracians, and as rivals for the possession of the Strymon basin; and Alexander showed his hostility by giving sanctuary in Pydna to Themistocles when Athens wanted him extradited for trial late in the 470s.

A colony was established at Eïon after its capture, but its life was short. In 465 Athens demanded from the wealthy islanders of Thasos a share in their commercial and mining interests on the opposite mainland, which lay east of Eïon, and when they refused and seceded from the coalition they were defeated at sea and put under siege. The chief aim of Athens and her Allies was revealed by the landing of 10,000 would-be settlers and supporting troops on the Thracian coast. They captured Nine Ways from the Edones and were establishing a colony there in 464, when an advance force of Athenians was annihilated by that rare event, a combination of all the Thracian tribes of the region. That project was abandoned; but Thasos fell, and Athens appropriated gold-mines and territory on the Thracian coast. The Athenian commander, Cimon, was later put on trial; one charge against him was that he had failed to advance from that base and 'cut off a large piece of Macedonia'. When Alexander died c.452, three Greek city-states on the east side of the Thermaic Gulf – Dicaea, Aenea and Strepsa – were already members of the Athenian coalition and could be used as bases for attack. In the western part of the Strymon basin a Greek city-state on the coast, Argilus, was already a member, and in 451 Berge, a village of the Bisaltae some 40 kilometres upriver, became a member and was probably near the site of a mixed settlement of 1000 Athenians and the Bisaltae. The aim of Athenian policy there was to gain some control of the gold at Nigrita and the silver-mine of the Bisaltae. Thus Athens did 'cut off a large piece' of the kingdom of Alexander. Athens's gains were finally confirmed by her founding and fortifying of a powerful city-state at the site of Nine Ways, renamed Amphipolis, on the east bank of the Strymon in 436. The immediate losers were the Edones; but its presence put an end to Macedonian hopes of subjugating the Bisaltae.

The effect of Athenian imperialism on the economy of the central Balkan peoples was disastrous. Because Athens in effect controlled all exports into the Aegean Sea and her terms for safe passage were stringent, there was a sharp decline in prosperity, and the movement of goods between the Aegean area and southern Yugoslavia almost ceased in the period 450–400. Thus the royal graves at Trebenishte were followed by the 'poor graves' after 470. Further north, at the same time, Greek goods ceased to be imported via the Black Sea and the Danube to the royal cemetery at Atenica near Cacak. There was stagnation in Upper Macedonia except in Derriopus, where small towns were developing; some imported goods have been found there, probably derived from Dyrrachium and Apollonia on the Adriatic coast. Even in Derriopus, at Saraj on the Erigon, a royal cemetery came to an end before the middle of the fifth century. In Lower Macedonia the royal cemetery at Sindos flourished until c.470. There were imports of Corinthian and Attic pottery, but less rich offerings in burials around the head of the Thermaic Gulf and at Aegeae. There were richer fifth-century graves with some gold and silver objects at Kozani in Elimeotis, which traded with Thessalian centres. The general decline in prosperity was made manifest by the coinage of Alexander, which sank to a low level of production c.459–2 and included then some light coins (tetrobols) of alloyed silver. Worse followed in the reign of Perdiccas II. Whereas Alexander issued heavy coins (octadrachms and tetradrachms) to the end of his reign, Perdiccas issued mainly tetrobols and those not continuously (see Plates 7a and 7b). In one period of stress he paid his troops in counterfeit tetrobols of plated copper.

Struggles for the survival of the Macedonian State

Decline was one thing. Survival was involved when a great power invaded Lower Macedonia, sometimes with support from defecting tribal states. In 434 BC Athens laid plans to conquer and hold the heartland of the Macedonian kingdom. She entered into alliance both with Philip, a brother of Perdiccas, who ruled over Amphaxitis, and with Derdas, king of the Elimeotae. In the surviving fragment of the treaty, Athens and her Allies revealed their normal practices when they promised not to harbour pirates and not themselves to plunder the territory of Philip and his allies. In 432 Athens sent two expeditionary forces. The first, consisting of 1000 hoplites and 30 triremes (warships, each with a crew of 200 men), joined the forces of their allies, captured Therme, which was Perdiccas' main port at the head of the Thermaic Gulf, and then switched their attack to Pydna on the Pierian coast. The second force, consisting of 2000 Athenian hoplites and 40 triremes, sailed direct to Pydna and joined in the siege of the city, which was some 30 kilometres from Aegeae as the crow flies. Had not Perdiccas taken countermeasures in advance, he would surely have lost his kingdom; for his poorly equipped infantrymen, not fighting in any formation, would have been outfought by the phalanx of bronze-clad hoplites (their shields, helmets, cuirasses and greaves all being of bronze) and by the 600 fine cavalry of Philip and Derdas. At the instigation of Perdiccas, the Chalcidian city-states, including Potidaea, and the Bottiaeans in the hinterland seceded from the coalition of Athens and her Allies, which had become a screen for Athens' imperialism. Perdiccas encouraged the Chalcidians to form a single state with its capital at Olynthus and to abandon some exposed sites on the coast, and he offered to Chalcidian evacuees the use 'of his own land' by Lake Bolbe for the duration of the war. He negotiated also with Sparta and her Allies (called 'the Peloponnesian League' by most scholars), and a force of 2000 Peloponnesian 'volunteers' entered Potidaea forty days after its secession. The timing of Perdiccas' diplomatic initiatives could hardly have been better.

The Athenian commanders thought it essential to intervene against Potidaea and the Chalcidians, but it was difficult to disengage their forces at Pydna, because they lacked transporters at sea. They therefore entered into alliance with Perdiccas; and covered by this alliance the military forces marched overland, leaving 'Macedonia' (in its original meaning) when they crossed the Haliacmon river. They broke the alliance by turning back to attack Beroea or some nearby place unsuccessfully, mustered all available forces (probably at Therme) and proceeded by land and sea towards Potidaea. Perdiccas had not waited until Athens committed a breach of the alliance. He appointed a deputy to command the kingdom, hastened with 200 cavalry to Potidaea, and there he was given command of the confederate cavalry forces. The Athenians won a battle in which the cavalry on either side took no part, invested Potidaea in autumn 432, and gained the alliance of Perdiccas, whose price was the restoration of Therme to himself. Potidaea fell by blockade in the winter of 430/29, the survivors being allowed to depart with one garment for men and two garments for women, and they found refuge with the Chalcidians and the Bottiaeans, who were undefeated. Athens occupied Potidaea with Athenian settlers. At some time between late summer 432 and summer 431 the other Greek city on the Pierian coast, Methone, joined the coalition of Athens and her Allies.

The next crisis arose in 429 when a huge army of Thracians invaded Lower Macedonia in collusion with Athens, which was secretly betraying her alliance with Perdiccas. The Thracian commander was Sitalces, king of the Odrysians, who had united under his rule the Thracian tribes and the Paeonian tribes from the Black Sea to the middle and upper Strymon valley, the Getae and other tribes on the south side of the Danube, and a number of Greek city-states on his coasts. At the head of an army reputedly of 150,000 men and accompanied by an Athenian general and Amyntas, son of Philip, whom he intended to place on the Macedonian throne, Sitalces entered Amphaxitis from the north, received the submission of most cities which were well disposed to Amyntas, took one city by assault and failed to capture Europus. The intention was that large

Athenian forces would join him from Methone and Potidaea, but they did not materialize. His army split into marauding groups which ravaged and pillaged the area round Cyrrus and Pella, Crestonia, Mygdonia, Anthemus, Chalcidice and Bottice (the interior of the Chalcidian peninsula). Since the Athenians still did not come and supplies were short for his huge numbers, Sitalces set off for home with the loot. The deluge had lasted for a month. No infantrymen opposed the Thracians. The Macedonian cavalry, from the original kingdom and from parts of Upper Macedonia, harassed the Thracians at first but soon desisted in the face of such numbers. Perdiccas owed his survival to the inactivity of Athens and to his own cunning; for Perdiccas made a secret offer of his sister and a rich dowry to Seuthes, the nephew of Sitalces, who then persuaded his uncle that it was time to withdraw. Moreover, Perdiccas honoured the undertaking, and on his accession in 424 Seuthes was friendly to Perdiccas.

Perdiccas reached his lowest ebb when he and Brasidas parted in anger after the débâcle with the Illyrians (see p. 23) and Brasidas was in league with the Edones, the Bottiaeans and the Chalcidians. Now isolated, Perdiccas sought protection with Athens in 423 and he obtained a form of alliance at Athens' price: an undertaking to supply troops to serve under Athenian command in operations of Athens' choice, and the inclusion of Heracleum in the south and Bormiscus in the east as tribute-paying members of the Athenian Alliance. Heracleum, the first Macedonian city to join the Alliance, controlled the entry from Thessaly into Pieria, while Bormiscus lay on the eastern side of the Pass of Rendina, leading into Mygdonia. Perdiccas must also have supported Athens in her control of Traïlus in Bisaltia, since Amphipolis had been captured by Brasidas. Athens wanted an obedient Perdiccas because with the loss of Amphipolis she needed ship-building timber from Macedonia at her own price. At this time too Perdiccas ceased to issue any coins, probably on a demand by Athens. In effect he was a subject of Athens, and Thucydides wrote of Perdiccas 'seceding' when he allied himself with Sparta and Argos secretly in 418 and openly in spring 417.

This was a false step; for Athens instituted a blockade of his coast from her bases at Heracleum, Methone, Potidaea and Bormiscus, and she landed a cavalry force of Athenians and émigré Macedonians at Methone which ravaged parts of Pieria. Once again, Perdiccas had to submit to Athens, probably in 415, to which year a fragmentary inscription should be dated. It records a treaty between Athens and Perdiccas, in which three kings of tribal states in Upper Macedonia are recognized as 'allies' of Perdiccas and as 'the kings with Perdiccas', and 'Arrhabaeus and his allies' appear as an independent block. The allies of Perdiccas were kings of Elimeotis, Orestis and a third canton (the name is missing); Arrhabaeus was king of Lyncus, and his allies probably included the Derriopes and the Pelagones. Thus Athens presided over the dissolution of the subject status of all these kings

27

to their nominal overlord, the king of the Macedones, and the cutting down of Perdiccas to rank as only one of such kings.

Perdiccas died in 413, the year of the Athenian disaster in Sicily. The tables were turned dramatically. Athens needed timber desperately but had no means of pressurizing the new king Archelaus, the son of Perdiccas. She won his favour by sending ships and troops to help him in a blockade of Pydna, the Greek city which she had tried to capture for herself in 432, and by letting him keep the prize. Whereas in 415 Athens had made Perdiccas swear to export oars only to herself, in 407–6 she honoured Archelaus and his sons as her representatives (*proxenoi*) and benefactors for supplying oars and ship-timber and (probably) for letting Athenian shipwrights build hulls of triremes in Macedonian ports. Archelaus was able to issue his own full-value silver coinage in didrachms (2-drachma pieces) and lesser denominations. However, in 399, when he was in his late forties, he was killed during a hunting expedition.

The next threat to the independence of the Macedonian kingdom came from the Illyrians. An able king, Bardylis, ruling *c.*400–356, brought about a combination of tribes, even as Sitalces had done in Thrace, and created a state which was powerful economically and militarily. His original kingdom was probably that of the Dardanii, whose territories included the gold and silver deposits in Metohija, Kosovo and Polog and the fertile agricultural plains of the last two regions; the Dardanii were described by Strabo as one of the three most powerful Illyrian tribal states (the others being the Autariatae and the Ardiaei, of whom we shall hear later). Expanding southwards, Bardylis brought into his state the Illyrian tribes in the region of Lake Lychnitis, where even the poor graves at Trebenishte ceased about 400, and he thereby gained control of the silver-mines, which had once issued the coins of the 'Tynteni' (Atintani). Now a prolific silver coinage in the name of a people, the Damastini, mainly in large denominations (tetradrachms) and having an ingot as one emblem, was issued *c.*395 and continued down to *c.*358. The pattern of distribution of the coins, found singly and in hoards, is indicative of a sphere of trade within the central Balkans, extending from the Adriatic coast north of Dyrrachium to Bulgaria and from the Morava valley in the north to Stobi (in southern Paeonia) in the south. They are most common in Metohija and in the eastern part of the upper valley of the Axius.

The controller of this coinage and of this sphere of trade was certainly Bardylis. His kingdom and his sphere of trade were remote from that of mainland Greece, from which hardly anything was imported in his time; but he was in friendly contact with Dionysius, the tyrant of Syracuse, who joined the people of Paros in founding colonies on the Dalmatian islands of Pharos and Issa and thus entered the Illyrian sphere of trade.

The Illyrians of Bardylis were formidable warriors. Whereas in 423 they had fought individually, man by man, now they were trained to fight in phalanx formation in the manner of Greek hoplite warfare; for c.385 Bardylis was given by Dionysius 500 sets of Greek hoplite armour, which were suitable only for that kind of fighting. Their cavalry too had a high reputation. Nor did they lack incentive; for Bardylis undertook his campaigns for slaughter and loot, and he was described by Theopompus, a contemporary Greek writer, as 'an Illyrian robber but one who divided the loot honourably'. In 393/2 Bardylis invaded Macedonia, had Amyntas deposed and replaced by a pretender, and two years passed before Amyntas was able to recover the kingdom. In 385/4 Bardylis invaded Epirus. His army, strengthened by the 2000 soldiers and the sets of armour sent by Dionysius, defeated the Molossians in battle and killed more than 15,000 men. His aim was to restore an exiled king to the throne as his puppet, but the Spartans came north and saved Epirus from subjugation by the Illyrians.

In 383/2 Bardylis invaded Macedonia again, defeated the army of Amyntas and occupied the country; but on this occasion Amyntas staged counterattacks and in three months of operations he recovered possession of the throne. Late in his reign, which ended c.370, Amyntas was defeated by the Illyrians and was forced to pay tribute to Bardylis. His successor, Alexander II, continued the payments and was forced to give the Illyrians his young brother, Philip, as a hostage. During the reign of Perdiccas III the Orestae abandoned any nominal tie with the Macedonian throne and enrolled themselves in the Molossian group of tribal states. In a war with the Illyrians, any Macedonian prisoners were held to ransom or killed, and in an Illyrian invasion of Epirus c.360 the Molossian king did not engage in a set battle but laid successful ambushes for the looting groups of Illyrians. Early in 359 the Illyrians invaded Macedonia. They won an outright victory, killing Perdiccas and 4000 soldiers, pillaged and plundered far and wide, and occupied the cities of Upper Macedonia. They were collecting large forces in 358 in order to give the *coup de grâce* to the Macedonian State, which had elected as its king an infant, Amyntas IV.

During this period of forty years, the independence of Macedonia was also infringed by other peoples. Sparta marched her armies to and from Asia through Macedonia, whether its king gave permission or not, between 400 and 394. When Amyntas was expelled by the Illyrians in 393–1, he enlisted the help of the Chalcidian League, but he had to pay by loaning to it some of his eastern territory, probably the rich land by Lake Bolbe. On regaining his throne he recovered that territory and entered into a defensive alliance with the Chalcidian League for fifty years. That treaty was not honoured; when Amyntas was driven out again in 383 and obtained sanctuary by loaning Anthemus to the League, although he recovered his throne without any assistance from the League, he was not only cheated of Anthemus but his kingdom was invaded by the Chalcidians, who captured his eastern territories, including the capital Pella, and confined him to the western part of Lower Macedonia.

In this desperate situation Amyntas invoked the help of Sparta, and from 382 to 379 Macedonia was the base of operations for Sparta and her Allies. Thus Amyntas became one of those 'Allies', required as they were to serve under Spartan command and to follow Sparta's policy. At the start the Spartan commander-in-chief urged Amyntas 'to hire mercenaries and give money to the nearby kings in the hope of winning their alliance', and he warned Derdas, king of the Elimeotae, that if he did not offer his services his lesser realm would suffer the fate of 'the greater realm, Macedonia'. In the course of the operations the cavalrymen of Derdas won distinction, Amyntas led 'a personal force', probably including mercenaries, and Sparta finally triumphed with the help also of Thessalian cavalry. The Chalcidian League was disbanded, Amyntas recovered his territory, and he and each Chalcidian city-state individually were perforce 'allies' of Sparta. The years of war had been very destructive, with looting, ravaging and cutting down of trees both in Macedonia and in Chalcidice.

The next great power to enter Macedonia was the League of Boeotian city-states, led by Thebes. The general in command of the army, Pelopidas, required Alexander II to enter into alliance and, as a guarantee of good faith, to surrender his young brother Philip (now returned from Illyria) and thirty sons of leading Macedonians, who were taken to Thebes as hostages. A year later, in 367, Pelopidas returned. He imposed a defensive and offensive alliance, and took away a son of Ptolemy, who was acting for the young king Perdiccas III, and fifty leading Macedonians. When the young king came of age in 365, he served the Boeotian League well, probably by supplying ship-timber for a Boeotian fleet, and he obtained the release of Philip, then aged sixteen or seventeen. But Athens, the enemy of the Boeotian League, sent a fleet into the Thermaic Gulf, which got possession of Pydna, Methone and Potidaea, raided nearby territory, brought many inland tribal states into alliance, and left Perdiccas isolated. In 364/3 he had to submit. He was made to provide troops which served under Athenian command against Olynthus, the capital of the re-formed Chalcidian League. He broke away from Athens but was defeated, and he was lucky to obtain an armistice. He was enjoying a brief interlude of independence when the Illyrians of Bardylis descended upon the weakened kingdom, of which the actual frontiers were much as they had been in the reign of Amyntas, the father of Alexander I. The ebbing tide must have seemed irreversible.

IV

The Institutions and the Qualities of the Macedonian State

The monarchy of the Temenidae

The original setting of monarchy was a single tribe. When a cluster of tribes formed under a common name (e.g. Macedones, Molossi, Paeones) and adopted one man to be king of the cluster, that man's tribe became the royal tribe: the Argeadae for the Macedones, the Peiales for the Molossians, the Derrones for the Paeonians and the Edones for a cluster of Thracian tribes. The full name of the royal tribe then became 'Argeadae Macedones', 'Peiales Molossoi' and 'Derrones Paeones'. A royal tribe had its own founding ancestor: Argeas for the Argeadae, and Peialus for the Peiales. In the case of the Argeadae Macedones, its geographical habitat as a single tribe was known: Orestis. When a king of different origin was elected, he and his family were adopted into the royal tribe. Thus when Perdiccas I became king, he and his successors in his family were Argeadae; similarly Neoptolemus, son of Achilles, and his successors were Peiales. At the same time the new royal family retained its hereditary name: Temenidae for Perdiccas and his successors until c.308, Aeacidae for Neoptolemus and his successors until c.232, and Bacchiadae for Arrhabaeus and his successors among the Lyncestae until 358.

Attempts were sometimes made to fuse together the genealogy of the royal tribe's ancestor with that of a subsequent royal house. This is seen clearly in Molossia, where Philoxenus, a historian of the third century BC, made Peialus a son of Neoptolemus; and in Macedonia early in the fourth century BC Caranus (meaning 'Billy-goat') was foisted into the Temenid line as a son sometimes of Poeanthes and sometimes of Pheidon. When the last Temenid died c.308, self-appointed kings and their successors tried to pass themselves off as true successors. Thus Philip V, a member of the Antigonidae, and Philip II, a member of the Temenidae, were both described in a late Sibylline oracle as 'Argeadae Kings'; and in a recently published inscription of the latter half of the third century BC a Ptolemy, a member of the Lagidae, and an Antiochus, a member of the Seleucidae, were addressed in a flattering manner as 'the descendants of Heracles' (like the Temenidae) and then additionally as 'Argeadae' (as members of the royal tribe), although they ruled respectively in Egypt and Syria.

31

The chief function of the king, whether of one tribe or of a cluster of tribes, was religious. He sacrificed daily to the appropriate deities, and each of his successors followed his example, so that specific sacrifices and rituals became 'customary', 'traditional' (*patria*) and 'ordained'. Thus sacrifices traditionally made for the Argeadae were maintained alongside the sacrifices which were offered by the Temenidae, particularly to 'Heracles Patrous' as their ancestor. When Alexander the Great was far away in Asia, he had need of a priestly server who was an expert in 'the Argeadic and the Bacchic rites'. And when Alexander the Great died, a will (fictitious but composed near the time) ordered 'the elected successor to preserve the area ruled by the Argeadae', and ordered 'the Macedones together with the successor to celebrate the customary rites for the Argeadae'.

The extreme conservatism of the Macedonians in religious rituals is seen also in the purification of the armed men each spring. 'The fore part of a dog was cut off and placed on the right side of the route, the hind part and the entrails on the left side, and the armed forces were led between the parts of the divided victim. The arms [? and insignia – text uncertain] of all the kings from the earliest beginnings of Macedonia were carried in front of the vanguard; then came the king himself and his children', and so on. 'The earliest beginnings' (*ultima origo*) preceded the coming of Perdiccas. They reached back into the purely pastoral stage of the Argeadae and the Macedones, when the fierce sheepdog ranked very high in importance, and when the purification was carried out as the armed men of the pastoral companies were preparing to move from the coast to the mountains in the spring (see p. 2). It is apparent that the names and the weapons of the kings were kept from generation to generation, and that the weapons were symbolic of the past kings being present and had some superhuman power for the living. It was for this reason that Alexander the Great equipped himself for his first battle in Asia with arms which had been dedicated, it was believed, to Athena of Troy during the Trojan War. In 323 the corpse of Alexander, accompanied by his arms and other insignia, was placed in the midst of the Assembly of the Macedones, 'so that his majesty might be a witness of their decisions'.

Because the living king was the intermediary between the Macedones and the gods, he too had some superhuman power. It did not matter in that context that the king might be an infant or an incompetent. The report was probably correct that in early times after a defeat the infant king was brought in his cradle into battle and the army was victorious. So too the infant king Amyntas IV was taken to an oracular shrine at Lebadea *c*.358, no doubt in order to ask advice on behalf of his people. Philip Arrhidaeus, who was not *compos mentis*, carried out state sacrifices both before and after he became king in 323. The numinous aura of a king was such that the Macedonians felt for him 'an inborn reverence' (*veneratio*). When a king proved by remarkable successes that the gods indeed favoured his people, they tended to view him as a god in life and to set up a worship of him after his death. Thus a statue of Philip II 'fit for a god' was carried behind the statues of the Twelve Olympian Gods in a procession on the day of his assassination in 336. Worship of an outstanding king after his death is attested in the cases of Archelaus and Amyntas III, and there may have been earlier examples.

In his religious persona the king presided over numerous festivals and ceremonies, which were conducted in the traditional manner. In 335 Alexander presided over a nine-day festival to the Muses, which was probably of great antiquity, and over a festival with a competition in drama which Archelaus had first established. He held banquets for his leading Macedonians and for envoys 'from the cities' (i.e of the kingdom); and he gave victims for sacrifice to those of his armed forces who were in attendance. Weddings and funerals in the royal family were religious occasions. The wedding of Cleopatra, daughter of Philip II and Olympias, was an occasion for dramatic and athletic competitions, religious processions and state banquets. The funeral of Philip II was attended by armed forces and by representatives from 'all Macedonia'; and there were competitive games, which sometimes included single combat between armed warriors. On all these occasions preliminary sacrifices were made, omens were interpreted by the priests, and the king decided whether or not to proceed. The king conducted numerous cults. One was in honour of the god of hunting, Heracles Cynagidas; for the hunting of lions, leopards, bears, boars, deer and aurochs with javelin, spear and bow and arrow was the sport of Macedonian kings and their Royal Pages. It was also a form of religious observance, and the rules of conduct were strict.

As the supreme commander of the armed forces, the king led them to battle and went first into action. The men swore individually an oath of loyalty, which, like all oaths, had religious sanctions. To break it was an act of sacrilege. The oath committed them to obey the orders of the king, to have the same friends and enemies as he, to defend him with their lives and never to desert him. The king alone could free a man from his oath and discharge him from the forces. In the field the king took all decisions, whether or not he consulted his staff officers in advance, and he issued orders which were relayed to unit commanders. He had complete powers of discipline, which included execution for breaking the oath of allegiance and flogging for misconduct. The king admitted recruits to his armed forces, made promotions and demotions, selected his deputies and his officers, and alone granted payments, bounties, leave and relief for parents and dependants of men killed in action.

When a king was elected, the infantrymen clashed their spears against their shields to indicate that 'they would sate themselves with the blood of those who had claimed a throne to which they had no right'. They acted thus when a man was found guilty of treason in accordance with a traditional procedure. The king acted solely as prosecutor. He laid the charge and produced the witnesses before the Assembly of the Macedones, meeting under arms. The accused man defended himself. The Assembly decided. If they found him guilty, they executed him forthwith, either by stoning him or with their spears. The family of the traitor was put to death, in order to avert the danger of revenge and to safeguard the life of the king; for the safety of the king was the safety of the State.

The king owned the land which was 'won by the spear' – i.e. by himself and his armed forces. He might give part of it to a foreign grandee (Amyntas offering Anthemus to an Athenian, Hippias, c.505), to a refugee community (the survivors of Mycenae in 468), to Macedonians to form a city and its territory, or to a leading Macedonian to own for his services. He himself owned all mineral deposits and all fine timber in the kingdom, and he kept hunting parks, stud farms and some estates as the property of the royal family. He received taxes from the cultivators of the land, from harbour dues and from letting royal lands and properties. Thus he held in his hands a very large part of the product of the kingdom, and he was immensely richer than any Greek city-state capitalist, even when the kingdom was in severe straits. His expenses were, of course, also of a very high order. In particular he armed, fed and maintained the armed forces in the field and at sea.

The right of appeal to the king was universal. Men and women delivered their appeal in person or in writing. As Plutarch remarked, 'nothing so befits a king as the work of justice'. Philip II was highly praised as a judge. A story was told of more than one Macedonian king that he said he had no time to hear an appellant, who was an old lady, and she shouted at him 'Then you have no business to be king'; whereupon he heard her case and other cases and gave his judgements.

The succession to the throne

Aristotle considered the grounds on which a man might be made king. One ground was merit, when a man of exceptional ability had conferred a great benefit on a community, for instance by settling a country or by acquiring territory, and he cited as examples the kings of the Spartans, the Macedonians and the Molossians. He evidently had in mind the accounts which Herodotus and Thucydides mentioned, in which the first Perdiccas acquired territory and settled Macedonians on it. But should the qualification of his successor be merit or heredity? A modern democratic thinker might be more inclined to favour meritocracy than nepotism; but that would be on secular grounds. Pindar, the poet who wrote of Alexander, son of Amyntas, will help us to understand one ancient answer to our question. A man has mighty power not by learning but 'by means of inborn valour', and he cites

Achilles, the son of a goddess and a man. The descendants of Achilles were called the Aeacidae. 'Their light has shone afar,' wrote Pindar, 'for they are thy blood, O Zeus.'

The belief is a religious one, that a god places exceptional ability in a man, and that this ability is inherited in his descendants not always but often. If that man as king wins divine favour which is shown in successful actions, then his descendants are likely to continue to obtain that divine favour. The family to which Perdiccas belonged was the Temenidae. Their ancestor was Heracles, the son of Zeus and a woman, and Pindar wrote of his descendants, the Heracleidae, 'the fame of their spear burst into bloom'; for they founded dynasties of kings. 'Happy is Lacedaemon, blessed is Thessaly; both of them are under the royal sway of a clan descended from Heracles, prince of warriors'. He might equally have said that Argos and Macedonia were happy in that their royal houses were descended from Heracles.

It was on similar religious grounds that the Macedonians chose their kings by heredity for some 300 years. When the early death of Alexander the Great might have led to a succession by merit, the Macedonian infantrymen chose Alexander's half-witted brother, rejoicing that 'the strength of the kingdom would stay in the same house and family'. The same adherence to the principle of heredity was seen in the long-lasting royal houses of Sparta and of Molossia, and the succession was by heredity in Balkan tribes such as the Dardanians and the Odrysians. Given that principle, it was essential that the king should have sons available to succeed him, and in the dangerous conditions of almost continuous warfare a number of sons had to be born. Polygamy was therefore practised by the kings of Macedonia and of Molossia; and the children born to the queens were all equally legitimate. This sometimes had the desired result; Alexander I, for instance, left five adult sons when he died. But it also produced strains within the royal family. Half-brothers might be hostile to one another, and the ten known grandsons of Alexander I in five collateral branches might consider themselves equally eligible for the throne, as indeed they were. It is no exaggeration to say that at any one time there were usually one or more members of the royal house who were pretenders to the throne.

In theory a law of succession might have determined the choice. It could have been ordained that the first-born male should succeed, or the son 'first born in the purple' – i.e. born when the father was reigning. But there was no such law in Macedonia. The Assembly of Macedones made its choice each time between the available males of the Temenidae. What guided that choice was their belief that the divine favour passed from father to son; and it resulted in the throne's passing from father to son for ten generations, from Perdiccas to Orestes, over a period of some 250 years. The three of whom we have information – Alexander, Perdiccas and Archelaus – were certainly very able men, and it may be conceded that the Assembly chose well in those instances. But let us consider the defects of the system and the troubles which ensued.

When Alexander died a violent death (details unknown) c.452, he left five adult sons by more than one wife (see genealogy, Fig. 3). Of these the Assembly appointed three as joint kings, presumably because each of the three had numerous supporters. Philip, probably the eldest, was given a realm which included Amphaxitis and the delta of the Axius, so that he controlled the main outlet for exports. Alcetas, it seems, held eastern Macedonia, where he quickly lost the Bisaltic silver-mine to the Bisaltae. Perdiccas received the old kingdom, centred on Pieria, which also exported ship-building timber; and he became Athens' 'ally and friend', no doubt for exporting it to her. After a period of decline the Assembly made a change c.435; Perdiccas was made sole king, Alcetas agreed to serve him, but Philip refused and absconded with a considerable number of supporters. As we have seen (p. 25), with Derdas and Athens, Philip came near to ousting Perdiccas. A potential ally for either was Sitalces, king of the Odrysians. Both Philip and Perdiccas courted him. In 429 Sitalces and Philip's son, Amyntas, whom Sitalces intended to install as puppet-king, invaded Macedonia with huge forces; and if Athens had joined him, as she had intended to do, Perdiccas would have been expelled (see p. 26). Much damage was done, but Perdiccas intrigued with Seuthes, who persuaded Sitalces to withdraw and no doubt to execute Amyntas and his younger brother, for the line of Philip died out.

A reigning king was able to reveal his choice of a successor in the order of precedence at court and in the swearing of oaths to a treaty. Thus c.415 Perdiccas took the oath first in the treaty with Athens, and he was followed by his half-brother Alcetas (who had been king) and then by his own son Archelaus. When Perdiccas died a natural death in 413, the Assembly did not accept that preference but elected Archelaus. But there were repercussions. Alcetas, one of Alcetas' sons, and a young half-brother of Archelaus met their deaths. These happenings were reported at Athens as examples of the villainy of a savage king, and lurid details were supplied by Plato in his dialogue *Gorgias* some twenty years later. The true facts are unknown. As far as the interests of Macedonia are concerned, it was a blessing that Alcetas did not follow the example of Philip. Steps were taken to dispose of Alcetas' three sons, and his line died out. Archelaus seems to have had no rival during his reign, which was a very successful one.

Archelaus met his death during a hunting expedition in 399. The Assembly elected Orestes, a minor, who was a son of Archelaus, and appointed Aëropus as his guardian. We may infer from later examples, when an uncle on the male side was chosen as guardian, that Aëropus was a half-brother of Archelaus and an uncle of Orestes. A year or so later Aëropus became king, and Orestes does not appear again in the very scanty

THE SONS OF ALEXANDER I (OB. *C*.452) AND THEIR DESCENDANTS

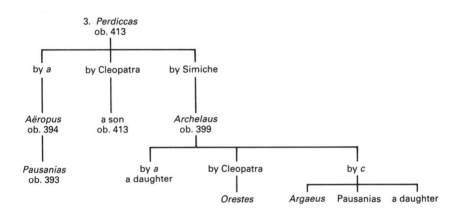

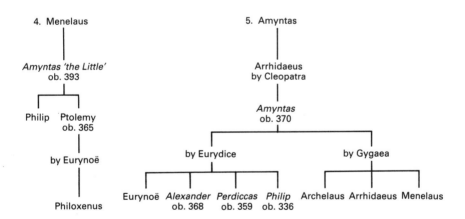

Note The sons of Alexander I are numbered 1 to 5. Those who became king are in italics.

Fig. 3 Sons and descendants of Alexander I.

record (in Diodorus). Aëropus died of disease in summer or autumn 394. The next king was Amyntas II, nicknamed 'the Little', a descendant not of Perdiccas, but of Menelaus, another son of Alexander I; but he was soon killed by Derdas, a Royal Page. The Assembly then chose a son of Aëropus, called Pausanias; he died soon afterwards, and the Assembly had recourse to a new line and in 393 elected Amyntas III, grandson of the fifth of Alexander I's sons. He was soon driven out of the kingdom by the Illyrians of Bardylis, whose puppet, the pretender Argaeus, ruled as king for two years, being probably a son of Archelaus. When Amyntas recovered the throne, he remained as king until 370.

The period 399–1 was the nadir of the hereditary principle; for after the death of Archelaus there were six kings, deriving from three collateral lines, in eight years. Only four of them issued coins. The confusion in loyalties and in the administration of the kingdom must have made it easier for the Illyrians to overrun Macedonia and put their puppet on the throne. There is no evidence to suggest that the Assembly made unwise choices. The point is rather that to abide by the hereditary principle was to create a dangerous discontinuity at the time and a legacy of pretenders.

The next successions followed the normal procedure. When Amyntas died in 370 he left at least two trios of sons by two wives. The Assembly elected the eldest of the six, Alexander; but he had to fight for his throne against a pretender, Ptolemy, a son of Amyntas the Little. The divided country was invaded by Pelopidas (see p. 30), who forced a reconciliation on the two and took hostages. In 368 Alexander was assassinated during a festival. The Assembly elected Perdiccas, the brother of Alexander, as king and, since he was a minor, his uncle by marriage, Ptolemy, as his guardian. In 367 two pretenders, Pausanias and Philip, sons respectively of Archelaus and Amyntas the Little, 'who enjoyed much support in Macedonia', invaded with a force of Greek soldiers and captured Anthemus and Therme. Their advance was halted with the help of an Athenian general, but this intervention brought Pelopidas back to Macedonia in 367 and the price of his support was another set of hostages and acceptance of the policy of the Boeotian League (see p. 30).

In 365 Perdiccas III came of age and Ptolemy died, perhaps by assass-ination. The Macedonian kingdom was now a storm centre. As Perdiccas was obedient to Boeotia, Athens supported the king of the Pelagones, who was hostile to Perdiccas. The Orestae joined the Molossians. There was conflict between Perdiccas and the Illyrians of Bardylis. Perdiccas was driven in and out of the arms of Athens twice. He gave his brother Philip, who had been released by Boeotia, a strategic area – probably Amphaxitis – to hold with a force of Macedonians. They were both afraid of various pretenders. Argaeus, who had been king for two years, was with Athens; Pausanias, who had captured Calindoea (a Bottiaean city south of Lake Bolbe), had the support of a Thracian king, Cotys; and there were the three half-brothers, whose cause might be promoted by the Chalcidian League. Then disaster struck. Perdiccas and 4000 Macedonians were killed by the Illyrians in 359. Perdiccas' only son was the infant Amyntas, named after his grandfather. Now, if ever, the crisis demanded the rule of a strong hand. Nevertheless, the Assembly of Macedones elected Amyntas IV as king, and appointed Philip, his uncle, as guardian.

When we look back over the events of 399–59, we are more aware of the defects of the Macedonian system of succession than of its merits. The defects need no enlarging. What were its merits? To elect kings only from the house of the Temenidae was to exclude anyone else from any hope of becoming king, no matter how high his status might be in Lower or Upper Macedonia. The only pretenders were Temenids; for they alone could hope for some support within the country. Thus the royal house was unusually secure in its position. Next, to elect a son to succeed his father was to favour youth. For example, Alexander I was elected to the throne in his late twenties, Alexander II at the age of twenty-one, Perdiccas III as a minor at sixteen and then of age at eighteen, Philip II in his early twenties, and Alexander the Great at nearly twenty. If a young king had had the necessary training – and we shall see shortly how that training was arranged – and was a man of ability, he could act with a freshness of mind, an energy of leadership and a vigour of body in battle which are not to be found in a man of advanced age. Thirdly, the greatest merit in the eyes of the Macedonians was something which does not always occur to us: their religious belief that the favour of the gods rested with the descendants of Heracles and that this had been made manifest in the reigns of Alexander I, Perdiccas II, Archelaus and Amyntas III. When their elected king proved himself worthy of their expectations, they became united in his service and showed an extraordinary degree of loyalty to him in peace and war. To fight for king and country seemed to have a dimension of devotion which was lacking in the citizens of the contemporary city-states.

The entourage of the king and the Royal Pages

As head of state and enactor of policy the king needed assistants. Each king chose his own men, who were called his 'Companions' (*Hetairoi*). He consulted them, when he saw fit; he appointed them to senior posts; he led them as Companion Cavalrymen in battle. In a society which was always on a wartime footing, he made no distinction between civil and military appointments; his Companions had to be capable of holding either, even to an advanced age. The Companions of any one king were a corporate body, called 'the Companionate'. They joined with the king in the worship of Zeus Hetaireios, and they had a festival called the Hetairideia. They were not chosen for life, because each king appointed his own Companions.

They were promoted or demoted by the king. Those of the highest category were 'Friends of the king' and 'those around the king'. They alone had immediate access to the ruler. When the services of a Companion were outstanding, the king might bestow upon him an estate; it was hereditable, but only with the approval of each king. With this flexible system there was no noble class (in terms of birth) and no continuing family privilege in the Macedonian state. Indeed, the king could even appoint non-Macedonians as Companions. Thus Archelaus appointed the poet Euripides, and the 'Companionate of Archelaus' paid honours to Euripides after his death in Macedonia.

The adult men of the royal house were influential members of the Companionate. They were often appointed to high military commands and they led diplomatic missions; and this experience was of value if one of them became king. As princes they had a personal prestige which a commoner lacked. They held the leading positions among the Friends of the king, and they were inscribed first after the monarch in a treaty of state with a foreign power. The order in which the princes and the commoners were so named was not fixed by any standing rule but was decided by the king each time.

It was crucially important to train the princes for kingship, not in isolation but in association with the sons of leading Macedonians. To this end a School of Royal Pages was set up at court, and the pupils boarded there from the age of fourteen to eighteen. They were taught by distinguished Greek philosophers. Socrates was said to have declined an invitation; Euphraeus, who was trained by Plato, taught in the reign of Perdiccas III; and Philip II employed Aristotle. The king was headmaster. He alone punished with the cane. The boys waited on him at table, guarded him in relays at night, hunted on foot with him (the king and the princes were required by law to hunt on horseback), and fought close to him in battle. They were trained to be superb horsemen, riding bareback with neither saddle nor stirrup; and when they graduated at eighteen they served in the Companion Cavalry. The close friendships which developed in this school were valuable to a king, for he would often make his contemporaries Friends and entrust high posts to them. And he too benefited from sharing the rough and tumble of the school with commoners of the same age.

There were dangers in the system. The first surviving mention of the Pages was the killing of Archelaus by the javelin of a Page on a hunting expedition in 399; and five years later Amyntas II was assassinated by a Page. There was speculation about their motives. Aristotle gave alternatives for the first instance – resentment over a homosexual relationship with the king, or disappointment at not gaining the hand of a princess – and one for the second instance: anger at being ridiculed for his youthfulness by the king. Trials were certainly held at the time. In the first it seems that guilt was not proved; in the second it was. For an adult to be a lover of a boy was neither unusual nor reprehensible in the mores of the times, whether in

Greek or Macedonian society, and many adults had both homosexual affairs of this kind (not so much between men of the same age) and heterosexual relationships. It was thus not improbable that the king and other adult associates of the Pages became involved in love affairs with them. Rumour associated other Pages with the killing of Archelaus. One of them was said to have commented in public on the foul breath of Euripides and to have been caned for his impertinence. School is full of strange and laughable episodes!

The women of the royal family did not attend the state banquets. Their tasks were those of a commoner household; to mind the home, make clothes and provide meals. The Queen Mother was the leading lady and might be given ceremonial duties; and the mother of a king's preferred successor may have been given some precedence over other wives. The princesses were bestowed in marriage by the king on men of his choice, who might be foreign grandees (Amyntas giving a daughter to the Persian governor, and Perdiccas a sister to an Odrysian prince). The king arranged his own marriages, which were not necessarily with Macedonian women. The establishments of the Friends of the king were run on similar lines, and there was naturally a tendency for their families to intermarry.

The Assembly of Macedones

'Macedones' or 'the Macedones' denoted the Assembly which elected or deposed a king (the first recorded instance being the deposition of Amyntas III in 393), was addressed by the king and heard the king prosecute in a treason trial. For all these purposes they met under arms. When a man wished to address the king in the Assembly, he took off his helmet. The only logical conclusion is that the 'Macedones' were the king's soldiers and ex-soldiers. In Greek terminology these 'Macedones' were the fully qualified citizens of the Macedonian State; for they alone had the franchise. They were described just before and after the death of Alexander the Great as 'the citizens' (*politai*) and as 'citizen soldiers' (*politikoi stratiōtai*) in contrast to other troops, some of whom had been recruited within the kingdom. Such a limited franchise was far from unique. According to Aristotle, 'in some states the citizen body consists not only of those who are serving but also of those who have served as soldiers. They constituted the citizenship among the people of Malis, and the holders of office were elected from those on the active list.' In Macedonia this limitation was a legacy from the pastoral past, and such a limitation of franchise was still appropriate for a state which was continually at war or under threat of war.

Macedones and King made up the State. The Macedones elected him, and he was thereafter 'King of Macedones' (*basileus Makedonōn*). Foreign writers, such as Herodotus and Thucydides, referred to him as such. In the treaty with Athens *c*.415 the officials who represented Macedones were the

King by name, his adult male relations and his leading commoners. In a treaty concluded c.391 with the Chalcidian League, 'Amyntas' and 'Macedones' were both mentioned in the text. In later Greek writers 'King X and Macedones' or 'Macedones and King X' was the formal description of the Macedonian State; but in general parlance it was sufficient to name just one or the other.

As the field army of Macedonia in 358 BC numbered 10,600 men, and as we may raise the total of Macedones to 12,000 by including ex-soldiers, we can see that they were not a large proportion of the available adult men in the kingdom. We may gain some idea of population figures from the census of 1961. There were then just over 1 million people living in the area of the kingdom (Eordaea, 'coastal Macedonia', Amphaxitis, Crestonia and Mygdonia), and one would reckon the number of adult males as a quarter of the total. If we halve the number to allow for the weak economy of the kingdom c.360, our conclusion is that one man in ten was a 'Macedon'. Those who were not Macedones armed themselves and were trained to protect their cities and their flocks. They may be termed 'militiamen', who were sometimes called up to serve outside their home area in an emergency. They were citizens of their city or their canton, as we shall see later, but they were not Macedones and did not attend the Assembly. Thus the conduct of the Macedonian State was entirely and solely in the hands of the king and his chosen Macedones.

The qualities of the Macedonian Kingdom c.360

We have to draw a distinction between the Macedonian Kingdom and the Macedonian State. The king's rule over those who lived in the kingdom but were not Macedones was direct. He governed them as his personal subjects and as free men, but they had no say in the policy of the Macedonian State. There is no indication that his direct rule was resented within the kingdom of c.360. Those who were by race Macedonian had inherited a tradition of revering and obeying the Temenid kings over some three centuries. Those who were by race Paeonian, Thracian or Greek and had been added to the kingdom, mainly by Alexander I, were treated like those who were racially Macedonian, and were free to use their own language, laws and customs and to practise their own religion. We may draw a contrast with the situation in the Spartan State. There the 'Spartiatai' corresponded to the Macedones as full citizens, and the kings (there being two royal houses) ruled directly over the rest of the population within the kingdom; but the difference was that the bulk of that population was reduced to serfdom and deprived of most rights. The Macedonian kingdom was the stronger of the two in that respect; for the king and the Macedones could and did count on the loyalty of the population.

The Macedonian State was streamlined for wartime needs, because it had developed under stress from aggressive neighbours and had engaged itself in conquest. Those who had the full franchise – the king and the Macedones – were the military arm of the kingdom. They had abundant experience of war, a willingness to fight in person for king and country, and a desire for martial glory. They were content to choose a man to be king, remove any treasonable pretenders and obey their commander in action. As an electoral body, the Assembly of Macedones had the vitally important task of electing and deposing a king. It also appointed a guardian to a king who was a minor and allocated powers to that guardian or to some other person. It elected some representatives in other states, and it dealt with some matters raised by other states. At the end of the fifth century Athens asked that the remains of Euripides, who was buried in Macedonia, should be sent to Athens. The Assembly decided 'with general agreement' to reject the request. It was probably responsible for decisions to go to war, because the king relied entirely upon the agreement of its members when it came to action.

There was no intermediate body such as a Council between the Assembly and the Executive, which was the king and his staff. Decisions were taken quickly, and they were put into effect immediately; for the king had all executive powers and all means for executive action in his own hands. He appointed his officers, provided finance from his own treasury, issued orders and checked achievement. The king was not burdened with a statutory body such as an Advisory Commission or a Cabinet; it was for him to choose advisers, and he would invite some of his Friends or his military staff officers to give advice, as the occasion demanded. In critical times a wise king addressed his Assembly frequently (as Philip did in 359/8), and consulted his advisers carefully; for he had to feel the pulse of public opinion and to carry with him the most influential leaders. The system was extremely simple but flexible. As it revolved round the king, he had the initiative in shaping policy and action.

The Macedonian State was designed to deal with the problems of its environment. Because Illyrian and Thracian raiders were quick movers and Athenian warships could land without warning to loot and kidnap for the slave market, speed of deployment was essential. For this purpose there were militiamen locally and the King's Forces (*basilikai dynameis*) on the ready for call-up and action. If a decision had to be taken – for instance in spring 358 to attack the formidable army of Bardylis – the king could convene the nearby Macedones and obtain a vote. Because the kingdom needed to be self-sufficient in foodstuffs, the great bulk of the population had to work on the land, and only a small proportion of men could be spared for weeks or months to become highly trained troops. Until late in the fifth century BC the military élite consisted of well-trained cavalrymen only, and not more than a few hundred of them. Yet usually they were enough to cope with invaders, whether from Upper Macedonia or from barbarian regions, because there the cavalrymen were the small ruling class. Then Archelaus improved the mobility of his troops by building direct roads to strategic points (often through wooded country). Above all he equipped and trained the first regiments of regular infantry, which were needed to face the increasing power of the Chalcidian League and of the Dardanians. But any progress was lost during the chaotic period after his death.

The next move was made by Alexander II, the young king of 370 to 368/7. He experienced the invasion of his kingdom by an army of Greek hoplites, for which his infantrymen were no match, and he therefore took a most important decision. He extended the honorific title 'Companions' beyond the few hundred cavalrymen to include a much larger number of infantrymen, who were trained to fight in a phalanx formation with files ten men deep (a hoplite file being eight men deep) and were brigaded in companies (*lochoi*). His purpose was 'to make cavalrymen and infantrymen be continually most zealous in his service because they shared in the Companionship of the King'. It was these infantrymen, trained under Alexander, Aëropus and Perdiccas in the tactics of Greek hoplites, who were to be the backbone of Philip II's army. They were intensely proud of their title 'Infantry Companions' (*pezhetairoi*).

The Macedonian kingdom differed radically from a contemporary Greek city-state in various ways. Its political structure was totally divorced from that of a Greek democracy, and the enormous powers of the king were unparalleled and widely condemned by the average Greek. The capital resources of the Macedonian kingdom were almost entirely in the hands of the king; for he had a monopoly of precious minerals and of Macedonia's most valuable export, timber. In a Greek city-state capital resources were not state-controlled; they moved freely in private hands. The Macedonian way of life was agrarian without any basis of slavery, whereas the Greek way of life was increasingly urban, commercial and capitalistic, depending on very large numbers of slaves who worked in mines, handicrafts, agriculture and ranching. The population of the Macedonian kingdom, being composed almost entirely of free peasant cultivators, was unlike the population of a Greek city-state such as Athens, in which the gap between rich and poor citizens was very great and the plight of the poor citizen was aggravated by the presence of cheap slave labour. Macedonia thus had an inner social cohesion. The average city-state was divided by the violent form of social unrest which was called *stasis* and often led to open revolution. The Macedonian *polis* did not suffer from this defect.

V

Life and Art in the Period Before Philip II

Upper Macedonia

One way of life, transhumant pastoralism, which we described earlier (see p. 2), was practised in many parts of Macedonia, and it was predominant in this period in Upper Macedonia, where there were very extensive areas of summer pasture at high altitudes (see Plate 4). The same way of life was practised on the western side of the Pindus range and of its northern extensions.

The best insight into this way of life has been provided by the report of Iulia Vokotopoulou on her excavations at Vitsa on the west side of the watershed (in ancient Molossis and modern Zagori). The site, 1030 metres above sea-level, consists of a settlement with a meeting-house, a dozen or so little houses, and an immediately adjacent cemetery of graves, laid above one another to a depth of up to seven layers in a confined area, which testifies to the very close-knit nature of the community. The site was in continuous use by this community from c.900 to c.325, when the houses were burnt and abandoned. Occupation was in the six summer months, when the herds of goats, sheep and cattle were on the high country. One piece of defensive wall is all that remains of a circuit-wall, built probably to protect the animals as much as the houses. It is possible to calculate from the number of burials that the pastoral group (*parea*) fluctuated around 430 persons. The men were quite tall, many being 1.7–1.8 metres (5 feet 7 inches–5 feet 11 inches) and the women averaged 1.65 metres (5 feet 5 inches). Their clothing, in which the dead were buried, was of heavy wool, woven by the women, and a short woollen cloak (like the modern shepherd's *kāpa*) was secured by two pins or brooches (see Plate 2). The men were buried with many weapons, and the women with jewellery; much meat was eaten; and by ancient standards the level of life was not low. The herds were a form of capital wealth, and the group could afford to acquire fine bronze vessels by barter. Coinage was not in use, and it is doubtful if writing was practised. They were clearly of vigorous and physically tough stock.

The Vitsa group went south-west for their winter pastures. The groups on the east side of the watershed went mainly to the lowlands of Macedonia and Thessaly (e.g. with 6000 sheep from Mount Babuna in Pelagonia to Thessaly at the end of the last century), so that the Macedonian kingdom

45

was known to many of them. An interesting link between Vitsa, Spilion (high on the eastern side of the watershed) and Aegeae on the edge of the Emathian plain is seen in the burials of young women with very rich offerings and jewellery, and in particular with the distinctive Minoan-type headdress (see p. 12). It seems that the pastoral groups shared a worship of a goddess, perhaps guardian of animals, who was originally native to the Bottiaeans of Lower Macedonia in the ninth century.

Near Spilion, remains of a small settlement and probably of a shrine were found by A. K. Vavritsas with prehistoric, sub-Mycenaean, classical and Hellenistic pottery. At Perivoli, near which copper and lead were mined, pottery of the archaic and classical periods was collected, and a number of chance finds were reported: a fine bronze cauldron (*lebes*), iron spearheads and a sword of the same periods. Both sites were those of transhumant pastoralists in this very high country.

The cantons of Upper Macedonia had considerable areas of good arable land, many consisting of the alluvium of dried-up lakes, and these were used for growing cereals. But it is only in the north in Derriopus and in the south in Elimeotis that there is archaeological evidence of the development of small towns and a little imported Attic pottery. Thucydides referred probably to those in the north as 'the villages of Arrhabaeus' which Perdiccas II wished to attack in 423; his term *komai* expressed his view of their small size, but they may well have been called *poleis* locally. Excavations at Tsepicovo in Derriopus showed that the level of life was low and only an occasional coin was found which dated to before 359.

It was perhaps from these small towns and from others – as yet undiscovered – in Lyncus that the hoplites of the Lyncestae whom Thucydides mentioned were derived; for such must have been 'the cities [*poleis*]' – i.e. of Upper Macedonia – which Bardylis occupied in 359 according to Diodorus, following Ephorus. The lack of known sites today is due not to their absence but to our lack of exploration. Whatever these small towns were called, they were few and far between in the classical period. A team of scholars from Carleton College and the University of Minnesota conducted in 1987 and 1988 a survey of the Grevena region (mainly in Tymphaea) which found many sites of the Hellenistic period but hardly any of the classical period. The situation was the same in the Molossian territories west of the watershed; and there we have the evidence of ancient geographers that the people inland were living 'in villages' (*kata komas*) c.360.

We conclude, then, that in Lyncus, Orestis and Tymphaea the bulk of the population lived, like the people of Vitsa in Epirus, in tiny villages or on individual holdings, and had a diet mainly of pulses, nuts and game, and the milk and meat of any animals they raised (as they did in 1941–4). Men were buried with their spears and only occasionally with a helmet of the type called by archaeologists 'Illyrian' but probably made and exported from

46

Corinth and her colonies. The general impression is of isolation and stagnation c.460–360.

Although Eordaea was geographically part of Upper Macedonia, it had been settled by the Macedonians around the middle of the sixth century. The settlers were not organized at first in *poleis*, as in Lower Macedonia, but they had a cantonal system. Small towns developed earlier here than in most of Upper Macedonia – for instance, Boceria (Pharangi) and Cellis (near Petres), where a little imported Greek pottery of the classical period has been found. Eordaea was of great importance in that it held the easiest entry from the north into Lower Macedonia, first through the pass called Kirli Dirven and then over the Moharrem Khan Pass above Edessa.

To the south of Eordaea the canton of the Elimeotae was rich in pasture and agricultural land, and it had easy access to central Thessaly. Current excavations have shown that it was far in advance of the other cantons of Upper Macedonia. We have already noted the offerings in some pit-graves of the Persian period at Elimea (Aiane) (see p. 16). On the nearby hill, called Megale Rakhe, a large public building with well-cut ashlar walls and a stoa was dated by Attic pottery to c.450 BC, and its position on the hillside indicates that it lay within a fortified city of considerable size. Occupation of the site was continuous from the Late Bronze Age until late in the Hellenistic Age.

The most exciting discovery was a group of twelve monumental cist-tombs near the cemetery of pit-graves. The box-shaped chamber of the largest tomb measured 4 × 4 metres, and it formed the centre of a wide and deep rectangular platform, 10 × 10 metres, which was composed of finely cut, close-fitting rectangular blocks of stone. The chamber was roofed with long rectangular stone blocks, which were supported laterally by the platform and from below by a beam, probably of wood, and an unfluted stone pillar. The top of the roofing blocks was level with the top of the platform, which itself served as the stylobate for some form of shrine with Doric pillars. This combination of a cist-tomb and a shrine may be regarded as a forerunner of Tomb I and its adjacent shrine at Vergina (see p. 55). Of the other three large tombs, one had roofing blocks 3 metres long. There was no evidence of a shrine above these or the eight smaller tombs. Although they had been looted, the tombs of this group were dated to the fifth century BC by imported pottery, gold and silver-gilt jewellery, and pieces of archaic-style sculpture in local marble. One of the last was a male head wearing a diadem, presumably the portrait of a dead king, since it was found within a tomb. The wealthy kings of the Elimeotae, who lived and died here, were worthy rivals of the kings of the Macedones during the fifth century, and indeed in the following decades.

Lower Macedonia

The standard of life in Lower Macedonia was higher than it was generally in Upper Macedonia. Since the latter part of the sixth century men had lived in *poleis*; Xenophon and the ancient geographer Scymnus commented that there were many *poleis* c.360, of which Pella and Beroea were the most distinguished. The people of Lower Macedonia cultivated much larger areas of fertile land, both in the coastal plain and on the very well-watered hill-country between the plain and its ring of mountains (Olympus, Titarium, Bermium, Barnous, Orbelus and Dysoron). They were able to export timber and any surplus of cereals and animal products, even though the profits went mainly to Greek cities and Greek shipping. Yet little progress was made in the century from 460 to 360, because the pressures exerted by Athenian sea-power and by Illyrian and Thracian neighbours arrested development. When Sitalces invaded in 429, it seems that Eidomene and Europus were the only fortified cities in Amphaxitis. Excavations indicate that Aegeae and Pella may have been fortified in the reign of Archelaus: but Pella was then quite small, because on the site of the later Agora a cemetery was in use on both sides of 400 BC. During Sitalces' invasion, according to Thucydides, 'the Macedonians betook themselves to the strong places and to the fortifications that there were in the territory; and they were not many; but later Archelaus built those that there are now in the territory.'

Yugoslav excavations have shown that a Macedonian city was planted probably by Archelaus at Manastir, which lies at the northern entry of the Iron Gates of the Axius (Demir Kapu). Across the river from Manastir the top of the steep hill (pierced today by the tunnel of the main road) was fortified with a square tower and a circuit-wall 520 metres long. Fine Attic pottery of the late fifth century was found at Manastir; and the fort was judged by the excavators to have been contemporary with the foundation of the city. City and fort were well placed to block invasion from the north into Amphaxitis. Archelaus no doubt cut the road which ran through the rocky defile; it was used by wheeled vehicles, the ruts in the rock being 10 centimetres wide and 1.25 metres apart. A fortress of similar size crowned the top of Mount Cissus (modern Khortiatis), serving as the acropolis of the like-named city. The fortification wall was 2 metres wide, as on the hill above Demir Kapu. Imported pottery of 375–50, found inside the wall, suggests that it was built when there was danger of an Athenian landing and of invasion from Chalcidice in the 360s.

The royal cemetery and the settlement on the nearby Toumba at modern Sindos were both very prosperous during the Persian period, but there was a steady decline at the settlement through the rest of the fifth century and a lower level still in 400–360. This decline was probably typical of Lower Macedonia; for Sindos, as a port of exchange, provides an index of trade. There are relatively few examples of fine jewellery in graves in the region of

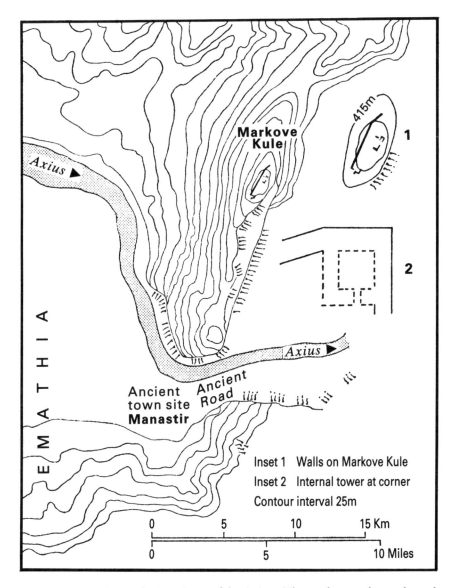

Fig 4 Ancient sites at the Iron Gates of the Axius. (The modern road runs through
a tunnel under Markove Kule.)

Therme and Thessaloniki in 400–360. Even at the old capital, Aegeae, only a little imported pottery of the fifth century BC has been found. That is after all what we should expect from the course of events c.460–360; for Macedonia and Athens were hostile to one another during most of that period, and Macedonian exports were controlled and sometimes blocked by Athenian fleets. Lower Macedonia was fortunate in having ample internal resources to feed its population, so that it did not depend on the favour of Athens for survival.

The king's coinage

The royal family and the members of the court certainly enjoyed a much higher standard of living than the commoners of the kingdom. Since the king owned all deposits of precious metal, the only coinage of the realm was 'the king's coin' (to basileion nomisma); his name in abbreviated form or in full in the genitive case was inscribed upon each coin. Alexander I, the first king to issue coinage, produced large denominations in silver (octadrachms and tetradrachms), but none of his successors rivalled him until Philip II. The largest coins of Archelaus, Aëropus, Amyntas II, Pausanias, Amyntas III and Perdiccas III were didrachms. The chief reason was that Alexander I held the Bisaltic silver-mine for most of the years between 478 (when he started coining) and 452, whereas his successors rarely controlled that mine for any length of time. It is probable too that the successors of Alexander had less access to Asia, where large silver coins were in demand, and that they were less able to engage in bulk trading. We may compare some of their neighbours. Amphipolis, as an independent city-state after 424, coined in tetradrachms, Damastium showed ingots on its tetradrachms, and the Chalcidian League had particularly fine issues of tetradrachms. A Thracian king, Sparadocus, issued tetradrachms c.445–25. The successor of Sitalces, Seuthes, had a revenue in gold and silver which amounted to 400 talents of silver a year, not far short of the revenue Athens drew from her empire. The Odrysian kingdom was reunited by Cotys I, who ruled c.384–59, issued a fine coinage in silver and bronze, and employed Greek specialists, such as the Athenian mercenary general Iphicrates. During Cotys' reign the lowest levels of coining were reached by Perdiccas II, who usually issued silver tetrobols as his highest denomination, and by Alexander II, who coined only in bronze.

Within the kingdom the beginnings of a monetary economy were marked by coinage in bronze, introduced by Archelaus and continued by all his successors. The need of the kingdom to trade through the independent city-states on the coast is reflected in the use of the same symbols on the bronze coins of the kings and the city-states: an eagle striking a snake on coins of Amyntas III, Pydna and Aphytis; a lion biting a spear on coins of Amyntas III, Perdiccas III and Methone; and a butting bull on coins of Perdiccas III, Dicaea and Aenea.

50

The interests of the kings were illustrated on their coins. Alexander showed himself setting off to hunt on a large horse (probably bred from the Nesaean stock of the Persian kings); he wears hat, diadem and short cloak, has two hunting spears with blades of different size, and sits well forward on his horse, beneath which runs a dog (see Plate 7a:v). Some other kings followed suit. Amyntas III and Perdiccas III had a lion teasing a spear, and Amyntas showed a horseman (certainly himself) about to strike a lion, which was on the other side of the didrachm. Love of horses inspired a favourite motif – the unattended horse in a position of dressage or at the gallop (see Plate 7b: i, ii, iv).

Religious emblems were very prominent: the goat, vine leaf and ivy leaf for the cult of Dionysus; the man walking with two horses for the cult of Rhesus; the crested helmet for the goddess of war, Athena Alcidemus; the crescent moon for Artemis; and the caduceus (wand) for Hermes. These were in use from Alexander I onwards. Archelaus added the eagle, and Alexander II the thunderbolt, both as emblems of Zeus; Amyntas II introduced Pan; and the wolf which appeared on coins of Archelaus and Amyntas II may have been in honour of a wolf-god, such as Apollo Lykeios. The ancestor of the royal house, Heracles, with his bow and club and one of his prize victims, the boar, was introduced by Perdiccas II when he entered into alliance with Argos, the homeland of Heracles and of the royal house; and Heracles' themes were emphasized by Archelaus and by Amyntas III especially on their coins. The artistic level of the coins is uniformly high, and it is clear that the kings employed the best die-cutters available, whether indigenous or of nearby Greek cities.

When Alexander I captured the prolific silver-mine of the Bisaltae, he took over from them and continued to use their religious emblems – the Rhesus motif, and the goat of Dionysus worship (see Plate 7a:i, ii,iv). It seems that he did this in order to emphasize the community of worship and thus to ease the incorporation of the Bisaltae into the kingdom. For Amyntas and Alexander were the kings who changed from the policy of expelling to that of incorporating the conquered peoples. We may attribute to them the Macedonian practice of not erecting a *tropaion* (trophy) to commemorate for all time the 'rout' of an enemy, which was the common practice of the Greek city-states and engendered nothing but bitterness.

The court as a cultural centre

Whether the fortunes of the kingdom were high or low, the king himself was far wealthier than any contemporary Greek statesman. Because he owned the conquered land, he could offer sanctuary to exiled communities and individuals alike. Alexander I planted within Macedonia the people of Mycenae in 468, and Perdiccas II the refugees from Histiaea (Oreus) in 445, and there may have been other cases unknown to us. These and other Greek communities within the kingdom maintained their traditional way of life, and they contributed to the force of 3000 hoplites which Perdiccas and Brasidas commanded in 424. The kings were in touch with Peisistratus and his descendants, with the Persian branch of their family in Asia, with the aristocratic Aleuadae of Larissa in Thessaly, with the city-states of Boeotia, and the leaders of the Greeks in 480–79. Alexander entertained lyric writers – in particular Pindar and Bacchylides – at his court; and he was certainly well known to Herodotus, who collected some Macedonian traditional stories. One of the family won an athletic event at Argos *c.*450. The famous doctor, Hippocrates of Cos, and a dithyrambic poet, Melanippides, were visitors at the court of Perdiccas II. Archelaus was most hospitable. Musicians such as Timotheus of Miletus, writers of epic such as Choerilus, and historians such as Thucydides and Hellanicus visited him.

When Euripides encountered hostility at Athens, he was received in Macedonia and became a Companion of Archelaus, who was said to have given him a gold cup at a banquet. In Macedonia, Euripides composed and produced two plays: *Archelaus* in 408/407, when he foisted into the Temenid genealogy in Macedonia an ancestor called Caranus and an early king, Archelaus; and *Bacchae*, probably in 407, which may have been inspired by the more primitive form of the Dionysiac cult which prevailed in Macedonia and Thrace. The Chorus of initiated women sang of Dionysus waving his sacred wand:

> In the deeply-wooded glens of Olympus, where Orpheus used once to draw after him the trees and the wild beasts with his music, as he played the lyre. O blessed Pieria, the god of the Bacchic cry reveres you. He will come to dance with his Bacchic revellers, and he will bring his whirling Maenads with him as he crosses the swift-flowing Axius and father Lydias, the blissful giver of prosperity to men, whose most lovely waters, I have heard, enrich the land of fine horses [*Bacchae* 560–75].

Euripides paid this tribute to his adopted country, which he had come to love. It is likely that he produced these two plays in the theatre below the palace at Aegeae, from which the spectators looked out over the plain irrigated by the Lydias and the Axius. The *cavea* (auditorium) of the theatre was formed by earth slopes (as at Eretria), on which wooden benches were set, much as when it was excavated by Professor Andronicos in 1981 (see Plate 8). Euripides chose to go to Macedonia probably because he knew that music and drama flourished there.

The leading tragedian after Euripides, Agathon, also left Athens for the court of Archelaus and died there *c.*401. No doubt he too produced plays in the theatre at Aegeae and also at Dium, where the Festival of the Muses was instituted by Archelaus. Hellanicus of Lesbos, a leading writer of regional and local history, stayed at the court and introduced Aeolus as the father of Macedon, the eponymous ancestor of the Macedonians. Another eminent Athenian, Thucydides, wrote with dry humour of Perdiccas II and expressed admiration for Archelaus; as he spent some of his exile in the Strymon basin, where he had property, it is likely that he knew both kings personally. A visitor who had very great influence was Zeuxis, who painted frescoes in the palace of Archelaus, probably at Pella, late in the fifth century. He was famous for subtle gradations of colour, the use of highlights and shading, and a combination of emotional power and realistic detail. Archelaus, like Alexander I, was well known in Greece; for his team won victories at Delphi and Olympia in the four-horse chariot-race, the most prestigious event of the Games.

Macedonia saw more than it wanted of generals and soldiers from Sparta, the Peloponnese and Boeotia in the period 399–59. Hostages were taken to Thebes in Boeotia, where they were held for three years or more. The leading Greek powers contended with one another for influence in Thessaly and Macedonia, and the rise of Jason, who united the Thessalian city-states under his leadership, led to closer relations with Macedonia. Amyntas was restored to his throne in 391 by the Thessalians; he entered into alliance with Jason in the 370s; and he acted as arbitrator between a city of Perrhaebia and the king of Elimeotis in a frontier dispute. In 371 Amyntas sent a deputy to a conference of Greek city-states, which Athens and her Allies had convened, and the deputy voted in favour of establishing a general peace, of which Persia and Athens and her Allies would be guarantors, and of helping Athens to regain Amphipolis. The presence of Amyntas' deputy at the conference was a measure of Amyntas' weakness in relation to Athens rather than any acceptance of Macedonia as a member of the Greek world. Alexander II entered the political arena in Thessaly, where he restored the Aleuadae to power in Larissa and placed Macedonian garrisons in some other cities; but the result was the intervention of the Boeotian League and the invasion of Macedonia by Pelopidas.

Employment for capable Greeks was available at the court of Amyntas and his sons. The father of Aristotle was hired as a state doctor. A philosopher of Plato's school, Euphraeus, taught the Royal Pages and advised Perdiccas III on matters of state; but his lectures were said to have cast a chill over the Companionate of the king. A statesman exiled from Athens, Callistratus, revised the collection of the harbour-dues in Macedonia, which were put up at auction to contractors, in 361/60. He increased the number of bidders by reducing the deposit, and this raised the royal revenue they brought in from 20 to 40 talents – not a large sum, even so.

Tombs of the kings and the well-to-do

In recent years we have learnt much from the excavation of tombs about the standard of architecture and art at court and among the well-to-do. The stone which was used by the architects was *pōros* stone (a form of tufa), which was easily worked. In the early fourth century the rich were buried in unusually large cist-tombs, of which the interior walls sometimes carried painted decoration (e.g. at Nea Mikhaniona near ancient Aenea). Such a tomb, 5.2 × 4.2 metres, was found at Katerini north of Dium. It contained two chambers, separated from one another by a crosswall, in which there was a double-leafed marble door. In the inner chamber, which was slightly less high, there was a low couch. The flat roof of the tomb had been made of stone beams and wooden beams laid across the width of the tomb and resting on the side-walls. The tomb was covered by a considerable tumulus of soil, which put undue weight upon the roof. Where some of the soil had fallen within the tomb, a coin of Amyntas III of the period 381–370 was found. This coin dates the tomb probably within the 370s.

The next development was a vaulted roof, which was capable of carrying the weight. A description of such a vaulted tomb was given by Plato, who thought it suitable for the burial of his senior statesmen in the ideal state of his dialogue *Laws*:

> Their tomb shall be constructed underground, vaulted, oblong and of *pōros* stone as long-lasting as possible, and fitted with couches set side by side; in this when they have laid him who is gone to his rest, they shall make a mound in a circle round it and plant thereon a grove of trees, save only at one extremity, so that at that point the tomb may admit of enlargement for ever without need of a (further) mound for those who are being buried [*Laws* 947 D].

Because such a form of burial was unknown in the Greek states, it is evident that Plato, writing *c*.350, learnt of the Macedonian practice from Euphraeus, who saw it in the 360s when he was at the court. Plato also provided for a parade of cavalry and infantry in full equipment for the funeral, as was the practice in Macedonia but not in Athens. We infer then that the vault had come into use by the late 360s in Macedonia, and this inference is supported by Professor Andronicos' discovery of an extremely large vaulted tomb (10 metres long) at Aegeae, which is dated by pottery to *c*.340 (see p. 98) but is as yet not fully described.

All the tombs we have mentioned were plundered. The first unplundered tomb was that of Philip II, who died in 336. It resembles the Katerini tomb in that it has two chambers and a connecting two-leafed marble door in the crosswall. It is now clear that a line of development within Macedonia can be traced from the large cist-tomb (at Aiane and at Nea Mikhaniona) to the two-chamber cist-tomb, and then, in order to carry the weight of earth, to the vaulted two-chamber tomb. We shall see further developments in a later chapter.

Mention should be made also of the foundations of the large shrine, 9.6 × 8 metres, which was adjacent to the tomb of Amyntas III but at a higher level, being on the original ground level. Fragments of marble – a rare material at Aegeae – belonged to an entablature, and there were two places nearby where burnt sacrifices had been made. It was then an 'Amyntaion', at which worship was paid to Amyntas; and it happens that an Amyntaion was mentioned as existing at Pydna.

The internal walls of the cist-tombs were plastered and painted, sometimes with a floral decoration, as at Nea Mikhaniona. In the two-chambered tomb at Katerini (as also in its neighbour, a large cist-tomb) the lower part of the walls was painted a deep red and the upper part white; and round shields were depicted on the walls, one of them carrying an emblem, a black dog. Thus the interests of the dead man were shown as warfare and hunting. The tomb of Amyntas III, who died in 370, was a large cist, 3.05 × 2.09 × 3 metres high, roofed with wooden beams and then stone beams across its width, at Aegeae. It was similar to other large cist-tombs of earlier dates and its inside walls were plastered and painted red below and white above (as at Katerini). Three of the walls carried painted frescoes of amazing beauty (see Plates 11a and b). The subjects are the Rape of Persephone by Pluto, whose two-horsed chariot is preceded by Hermes, while an attendant of Persephone raises her arm in horror; Demeter, wrapped in her cloak, seated in mourning on a rock; and the three Fates as spectators. The blue band below the frescoes is decorated with pairs of griffins, each facing the other with a flower in between. These frescoes have shown us that Zeuxis was followed by other leading painters at the Macedonian court; that Amyntas III had developed a school of painting which led the world; and that this school set a fashion which was followed in the Hellenistic Age and in Roman art at Pompeii and Herculaneum.

Indications of exceptionally fine workmanship in metals were found in fifth-century burials at Aiane and, from 425 onwards, in the region of Thessaloniki: for instance, gold-plated bronze vessels, gold plaques portraying a lion about to spring and a lion-head facing, a double-shanked gold pin, and gold lotus-leaves on a gold wire at Stavroupolis, and a silver hydria from Gephyra by the Axius crossing. More evidence has come from the two-chambered tomb at Katerini, which had been plundered, though not totally: a sword-blade of gilded iron, a gold ring from a sword-handle, a double-shanked gold pin, silver-gilt fittings for a leather cuirass, small gold plaques portraying a lion-head and a head of Heracles, two gold plaques shaped as a round shield, and ivory fittings for furniture. There was a long tradition of metalworking in Macedonia and Chalcidice, where gold, silver, iron and copper were available, and it is becoming clear that Macedonia led the way in the production of fine armour, the combination of two metals, and some kinds of jewellery.

Macedonian tomb-architecture, fresco-painting, and metalwork in armour and in jewellery were not derived from anything which has yet been found in the Greek city-states, where archaeologists have worked for very much longer. They had more in common with other regions of the Balkan area, where similar kings of tribal states had fine tombs and were the recipients of sacrifices after death. Thracian kings, such as Cotys I, had gold and silver vessels in abundance; and sacrifices were made for some decades to the dead Paeonians – probably kings and other royals – who were buried at Karaorman near Štip in the fifth century BC. The coins of the Odrysian kings have a startling resemblance to those of Alexander I and his successors.

Most Greeks regarded the Macedonians and their kings as barbarians, similar to their barbarian neighbours. Thus a political pamphleteer, addressing the men of Larissa, exclaimed 'Shall we who are Greeks be slaves of the savage, Archelaus?' Plato described Archelaus as an arch-villain who rose from his servile birth to win the throne by a series of murders. To Athenian democrats the Macedonian monarchy was a barbaric institution, in which scandalous affairs were the order of the day. Eurydice, the daughter of a king of the Lyncestae, the wife of Amyntas III, and the mother of Alexander II, Perdiccas III and Philip II, was a favourite butt for journalistic writers. She was reported to be 'Illyrian, thrice-barbarous, illiterate until old age', to have committed adultery with Ptolemy, plotted to murder Amyntas and succeeded in murdering Alexander II and Perdiccas III. These calumnies were paralleled by contemporary Greek writers, who portrayed Cotys as a self-indulgent drunkard, a brutal sadist and a sacrilegious criminal. Although the Athenian democracy had conferred its citizenship on Cotys, the people voted honorary citizenship and golden crowns to his two assassins as benefactors of Athens. It was certainly very rare for any Greek writer to express for anything Macedonian the admiration which Thucydides accorded to Archelaus.

VI

The Creation of the Greater Macedonian Kingdom

The enlargement of the kingdom in the north-west

Leading religious sanctuaries of the Greek mainland kept in touch with Greek-speaking communities by sending sacred envoys (*theōroi*) to them to deliver reports and requests, and the names of those who received them – called *theōrodokoi* – were listed at the sanctuaries. Such a list has survived at Epidaurus. It names hosts of the late 360s for the following places in our area: Pydna, Methone, Aenea, Dicaea, Potidaea, Olynthus, Calindoea, Apollonia, Arethusa, Argilus, Amphipolis, Berge, Traïlus, and Macedonia. The host for Macedonia was 'Perdiccas', who evidently acted on behalf of cities in his realm. All the cities in the list were independent of Macedonia. The first five, facing the Thermaic Gulf, were in the power of Athens; indeed Potidaea was occupied by Athenian settlers in 362. Olynthus stood for the cities of the Chalcidian League, of which it was the leader. Calindoea, a city of the Bottiaeans in Chalcidice, lay south of Lake Bolbe; its host was Pausanias, who was a pretender to the Macedonian throne and had the support of Cotys, the powerful Odrysian king. The cities east of Calindoea were independent of the Bisaltae; they were probably allied with Amphipolis to resist the aggression of Athens.

One of Perdiccas' last acts before the Illyrian invasion was to send Macedonian troops into Amphipolis, which Athens tried but failed once again to capture in 360; he was anxious to prevent any further growth of Athenian power. The Bottiaeans showed hostility to Perdiccas in supporting Pausanias. Of the tribal states of Upper Macedonia, the Pelagones and the Lyncestae were mentioned by an ancient geographer as independent at this time; and the Orestae were defined as Molossian in an inscription found at Dodona, which can probably be dated to the late 360s. We do not know what the status of the Elimeotae was; but being stronger than the other states of Upper Macedonia, they were probably independent.

It was this diminished and impoverished Macedonian kingdom which was attacked early in 359 by the Illyrian army of Bardylis, the greatest military power in the Balkan area. He had expelled Amyntas III from his kingdom twice and made him pay tribute (see p. 29). In a set battle, Perdiccas and more than 4000 soldiers were killed. Most of the Illyrians went home with the loot; but others stayed in occupation of the cities of

Upper Macedonia, which would be bases for the next campaigning season. The prospect for the Macedonians was appalling. Diodorus (using the contemporary historian, Ephorus) wrote as follows:

> The surviving soldiers were terrified and had no heart for continuing the war, the Paeonians in scorn of the Macedonians were ravaging the country, the Illyrians were collecting large forces in preparation for the invasion of the Macedonian kingdom, Pausanias was set on gaining the throne through the help of the king of the Thracians, and the Athenians intended to put Argaeus on the throne.

As the vultures gathered round the kingdom, it must have seemed that only a miracle could save it.

That miracle was provided by the genius of Philip II and the spirit of the Macedonians. As a hostage at the age of twelve in the court of Bardylis, and as a soldier in the defeat of 359, Philip had considerable knowledge of the army of Bardylis. For three years, from the age of fourteen to sixteen, he had been a hostage at Thebes and had studied the equipment and tactics of the triumphant Boeotian army and its crack corps, the Sacred Band of 300 Thebans. On becoming eighteen in 364 or soon afterwards, Philip had been given a force of Macedonians to command and an area, probably Amphaxitis, to control and defend against the Paeonians. Thus Philip knew the Macedones as soldiers and they knew him, when they elected him not king (that office having been given to Amyntas IV, the infant son of Perdiccas) but guardian and deputy of the king as commander-in-chief.

His first acts were to recall the troops from Amphipolis, since he had need of them; to buy peace with Paeonia by gifts and promises; to make gifts to Cotys' successor, Berisades, in exchange for the elimination of Pausanias; and to arrange the assassination of another pretender to Amyntas' throne, Archelaus, his own half-brother. Thus he was free to deal with the next crisis – a landing at Methone. For to continue with Diodorus' account, 'The Athenians had sent Mantias with 3000 [citizen] hoplites and a considerable naval force and were intending to put Argaeus on the throne . . . in their desire to recover possession of Amphipolis.' Argaeus and the émigrés with him had their own mercenaries. The expeditionary force was comparable to that which had operated against Perdiccas in 432. Handled properly, it might well overpower the demoralized Macedonian army and substitute Argaeus for Amyntas IV.

Mantias had the advantage of surprise; for the fleet came unheralded. He chose Methone as the friendly port nearest to the old capital, Aegeae, and presumably made his landfall at dawn. He sent the émigrés, their mercenaries and some Athenian observers on their way to Aegeae; but he kept his own forces at Methone, presumably waiting to see if Argaeus would be elected king. He was not. The Macedonians in the fortified town were not overawed by the mercenaries, and Argaeus had no option but to retreat to Methone, some 30 kilometres distant. On the way he was intercepted by Philip, who had been alerted, presumably, by smoke signal and marched post-haste, perhaps from Pella (about 40 kilometres from Aegeae). Philip's force killed many mercenaries at the first attack. The rest withdrew to a hill. Philip offered terms: return without ransom to Methone, restoration of anything the Athenian citizens had lost, and a request for alliance with Athens, all in exchange for the surrender to him of the émigrés. The Athenians and the mercenaries accepted. The émigrés were no doubt tried on a charge of treason and executed. Mantias had lost his chance of using the 3000 Athenian hoplites effectively. He sailed back to Athens, carrying the letter asking for 'alliance and friendship'. Philip's envoys followed. The Athenian Assembly granted peace and probably alliance, on the understanding that Philip recognized Athens' claim to Amphipolis and made no claim himself.

The intermission which Philip obtained by bribery on a generous scale and by astute diplomacy was essential for the reconstruction of the field army before the next campaigning season. He put his faith in a new weapon, his own invention: a 16-foot pike (*sarissa*) with a sharp blade and a cornel-wood shaft, so counterweighted at its spiked butt-end that it balanced with 12 feet of its length in front of the holder. It was held with both hands and was thrust with the full weight of the body (see Fig. 5). Cornel-wood was used because it was light and strong. Even so, the pike was relatively heavy.

Otherwise the pikeman carried relatively light gear: dagger, leather jerkin, bronze greaves and bronze shield some 2 feet in diameter, which was suspended from his neck and hung over his left shoulder. The pikemen fought in a phalanx – an extended rectangular formation, in which each file consisted at first of ten men. Each man in line needed 1½ feet of space, since his shield was at an inclined angle, so that a very close formation could be achieved if it were desirable.

The pikeman-phalanx was designed to fight against the hoplite-phalanx, invented by the Greek city-states and adopted by some Balkan tribes. The hoplite took his name from his circular bronze shield, 3 feet in diameter, which he carried on his left forearm, and he wore a bronze helmet, bronze greaves and a bronze cuirass. He fought with a 7-foot spear, which he wielded with one hand, and with a sword. The first line of the hoplite-phalanx, which was normally eight men deep, engaged the first line of the opposing phalanx, and on some occasions the phalanx, closing up from rear to front, used its weight to push the opposing phalanx back or over. Thus at Coronea in 394 the hoplites of the Theban phalanx, having adopted a deeper formation, 'pushed, fought, killed and were killed.' Philip's phalanx compensated initially for its lack of weight in armament by being ten men deep.

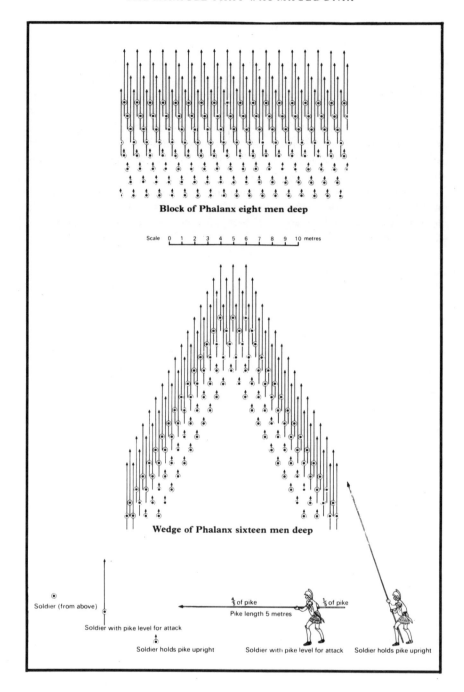

Fig. 5 The Macedonian phalanx in action.

One advantage of the pikemen-phalanx was that each man of its front line was protected by four pike-points and had a reach of 12 feet with his own pike-point (see Plate 10b), whereas each hoplite was protected only by his own spear and had a reach of 4 feet. The pikeman struck a heavier blow, because he used both arms and could put his full weight behind his pike. In addition, the hoplite needed a space of 3 feet in order to present his shield full-face to his opponent, whereas two pikemen occupied that space, when their formation was in close order. Thus a hoplite might find himself facing eight pike-points, of which the holders were beyond the reach of his own spear.

The superiority of such a pikemen-phalanx was obvious enough in theory if it maintained its formation and if its flanks were guarded. But if the formation should collapse and the hoplites should get among the pikemen, disaster would follow; for the pikeman's pike was then of no use, his dagger was outreached by the hoplite's spear and sword, and his little shield and his lack of a bronze cuirass left him almost defenceless. The pikeman therefore required exceptional courage himself and full confidence in his general. To this end 'Philip convened the Macedones in a series of Assemblies, urged them in brilliant speeches to be courageous, filled them with confidence, was accessible in conversation, and promoted the fullest loyalty in all ranks by his rewards and his promises.' Because it was essential to maintain the formation in close order and in extended order, in advancing and in retreating, and in inclining to right or left, rigorous drill was necessary and physical fitness was a high priority. 'Philip held continuous manoeuvres under arms and training exercises under combat conditions. He made them march often thirty-five miles carrying helmet, small shield [pelta], greaves and pike, and in addition flour for thirty days on their backs and other gear for day-to-day existence . . . and he allowed only one batman to carry grinders and ropes for each ten infantrymen.'

Because the king owned all minerals and fine timber, it was possible for Philip to re-equip his infantrymen with the new weapons and the small shield without delay, and to make good the Macedonian losses by recruiting, training and equipping 4000 more men. As we have seen (p. 44), these infantrymen were 'Companions of the king' and were therefore called pezhetairoi. 'Philip selected the largest and strongest of them to serve as the Royal Guards with the title Pezhetairoi', thus encouraging a competitive spirit. All the pezhetairoi were of Macedonian racial descent. They, the Companion cavalrymen, and the ex-soldiers were the full citizens and they alone sat in the Assembly. Each man took the oath of loyalty to the king (see p. 33). For their survival in 359–8 they depended on their own solidarity of spirit and uniformity in action, and on the genius of Philip as their commander.

Early in 358 Philip attacked the Paeonians, whose king had just died, defeated them in a set battle, and 'made them obedient to the Macedones'.

'Without delay he convened an Assembly, raised the war-spirit in his men by suitable words, and led them into the territory held by the Illyrians, his army numbering not less than 10,000 infantry and 600 cavalry'. Bardylis had not yet mustered the huge forces he had intended to lead into Lower Macedonia. He therefore offered peace on the basis of the status quo. Philip replied that peace was acceptable only if Bardylis would evacuate his troops 'from all the Macedonian cities' (i.e. those of Upper Macedonia). This Bardylis was not prepared to do. Confident in the marvellous record and the numerous victories of his élite Illyrian troops, numbering 10,000 infantry and 500 cavalry, he advanced to engage in the open plain of Lyncus. The battle-cries of 20,000 voices resounded from the hills.

Whether there was a preliminary cavalry engagement or not, Bardylis realized that he was outclassed in cavalry. In order to protect the flank and rear of his spearmen-phalanx from attacks by the enemy cavalry, he made his infantry form a hollow rectangle, of which the front facing the enemy was held by his best men and the other sides by less skilled troops, all facing outwards. The disadvantage of this formation was its immobility. The initiative lay now with Philip, who saw at once the merit of an attack on the enemy's leftmost front and left-hand side. He marched his phalanx forward at an oblique angle to the enemy's front, his right being advanced and his left retarded, and he massed his cavalry on his right. The king and the Royal Guardsmen were the leading infantrymen of the Macedonian right. As they approached the stationary Illyrians, they charged the enemy's left front with their massed pikes lowered (pikes never before seen by the Illyrians), smashed the corner of the square completely and let the cavalry in to attack the disrupted formation in flank and rear. The Illyrians broke and fled. The pursuit by the cavalry over the plain caused huge casualties: 7000 out of 10,500. Bardylis sent envoys to sue for peace. Philip buried his dead on the battlefield in accordance with Macedonian custom, and made terms of peace, which included not only the recovery 'of all the Macedonian cities' but also the cession of territory up to the north-east shore of Lake Lychnitis. The peace with Bardylis was cemented by the marriage of Philip to an Illyrian princess, Audata.

The honours of the battle went to the cavalry and the Royal Guards, and to Philip as a heroic fighter and as a general. The victory proved the efficacy of the pikemen-phalanx. The terrifying ascendancy of the Illyrian raiders, which had lasted for a generation, was completely overthrown. But Philip knew that Bardylis had huge reserves of manpower, that there were many other enemies, and that Macedonia would never be safe with an army of only 10,000 men. He was now able to persuade the liberated tribal states of Upper Macedonia to enter his kingdom completely, depose their own kings and enlarge his field army; for it was in their interest too that the Illyrians should be kept at bay. Those members of the royal houses who were willing were received into Philip's court and given honourable positions, and Philip himself married Phila, sister of Derdas, hitherto king of the Elimeotae. Others escaped to join Macedonia's enemies.

A remarkable programme of integration was based on the Macedonian city. Philip transplanted entire city populations from Lower Macedonia to suitable sites in Upper Macedonia (one such was probably Heraclea Lyncestis), and he also moved people from Upper Macedonia into cities in Lower Macedonia. Those who were transplanted to Lyncus, for instance, became Lyncestae; and this was true of members of the royal house who were moved there (for example, Alexander Lyncestes). Those who were moved to Lower Macedonia took on a city citizenship. Each tribal state retained its name and its administrative organization, which was thenceforth concerned with local affairs. It was subject to the decrees of the Macedonian State, with which contact was maintained through delegates of the king. One object in planting cities in Upper Macedonia was to develop agriculture and commerce at the expense of transhumant pastoralism: another was to recruit from the cities suitable men for the field army and make them Macedones.

Such a radical redistribution of populations was inconceivable in a Greek city-state (as it would be in a modern democratic state), and Greek and Roman historians later wrote of the king's despotic power and of the misery of the displaced persons. But the Macedonians had a tradition of being moved at the king's order; and the people of Upper Macedonia, being mainly transhumant pastoralists, were accustomed to moving their habitat. The introduction of Upper Macedonians into the army was perhaps more difficult to achieve. The existing Macedones must have been reluctant to admit into their élite citizen ranks men who were not Macedonian by race and who spoke a different dialect of Greek. To some extent the distinction between the old and the new citizens lived on in the field army. The infantrymen brigades of the old kingdom were called *pezhetairoi*, as before, and those of Upper Macedonia were called *asthetairoi*, which meant 'Townsmen Companions' (recruited from the towns, *astea* evidently being the local term). The Royal Guard continued to be selected only from the *pezhetairoi* brigades, and it came to be called 'The Guard of Macedones', that is the original Macedones. It was this Guard and these brigades which liked to speak the Macedonian dialect. The brigades of *asthetairoi* were named by territory – for example, 'from Lyncus'. The cavalry was also organized on a territorial basis, mainly by cities in Lower Macedonia, and as 'the Squadrons of Upper Macedonia'.

Philip must have started the process of integration immediately after his victory, for within six years the overall number of his Companion Cavalry and his Companion Infantry had doubled, and by the end of his reign it had almost trebled. The building of new towns and of new roads was done in part by his army and in part by the local population on the king's orders. Philip must have inspired his people with something of his own youthful enthusiasm and energy. In the westernmost part of his enlarged kingdom there were Illyrians whom he made his 'subjects' (*hypekooi*); they were subject to his direct rule and paid taxes to him, but they were left to speak their own language, practise their own religion and manage their own affairs.

In advancing to the east shore of Lake Lychnitis, Philip went far beyond the frontiers of the Greek-speaking tribal states (these were formed by the high mountain ranges of Peristeri (2601 metres) and Plakenska). He crossed the next parallel range, that of Petrina (1734 metres), and then descended into the lakeland area, where he annexed Lake Prespa and Lake Little Prespa (see Plate 4). Strategically he was able to enfilade any army moving along the western side of the corridor of the lakes (now the Albanian border). Moreover, he included in his kingdom the main route from Illyria into Macedonia, which was later used by the Via Egnatia, and a second route through the toe of Lake Little Prespa. His control of these areas safeguarded the Orestae, who discarded their tie with the Molossians and became part of the Macedonian kingdom. As the king owned all mineral resources, he took over at least one of the mines which supplied silver and lead to Damastium (see p. 28). The borders of Lyncus were extended westwards to take in the new territory north of Lake Prespa, and a separate canton south of that lake was called Eordaea. Towns were planted and fortifications were built to provide strongpoints in this frontier area; one of the latter was a castle at St Erasmus, suitable for a garrison.

The achievement of Philip in this area was to be long-lasting. By incorporating the Greek-speaking tribal states and by opening the élite citizenship to suitable Upper Macedonians, he created a reservoir of tough highlanders from which the military power of the Macedonian State was to be derived for two centuries to come. The western frontier which he formed and fortified was penetrated only once in that time by an army coming from the west. The economic changes which he initiated in Upper Macedonia soon increased the prosperity and the population of the region, which was able to produce half of the Companion Infantry brigades by the end of Philip's reign.

The enlargement of the kingdom in other directions

Philip's next acquisitions were to the east. His first operation was conducted to acquire control of the Bottiaean base of the pretender Pausanias and of the independent cities Apollonia, Arethusa and Argilus, which gave him access to the Strymon basin. At the same time he probably forced the Bisaltae to enter the kingdom, and he took over the Bisaltic silver-mine. It was these advances (not recorded in our sources) which alarmed Amphipolis and the Chalcidians. Some incident occurred which Philip claimed was a justification for an attack on Amphipolis. Before he did attack, envoys from Amphipolis reached Athens and offered their city to the Athenians; but Athenian forces were already engaged in operations in Euboea and in the Chersonese (Gallipoli peninsula), and Athens let the opportunity slip. Philip attacked with a large army and an effective siege-train. The city had very strong fortifications, which Athens had repeatedly failed to overcome, and some months passed before continual assaults and a breach made by rams, operated under moveable penthouses, led to the collapse of the defence. During those months the Chalcidians made an alliance with an Illyrian king, Grabus, probably in the hope that he would invade Upper Macedonia and force Philip to raise the siege of Amphipolis. Philip sent envoys to Athens, no doubt trying to calm Athenian fears; and he was exceedingly fortunate in that a group of Athens' allies revolted and her fleet sailed to the east Aegean. The Chalcidians too approached Athens. They offered alliance, but Athens had her hands full with the war at sea. Philip sent envoys again, offering to give Amphipolis (if he should take it) to Athens in exchange for Pydna, then an ally of Athens. Some secret agreement was made between Philip and Athens, but its details are not known.

On capturing Amphipolis Philip declared the city independent. The Assembly there banished the pro-Athenian leaders. Philip laid siege at once to Pydna, which was betrayed from within. Athens declared war; the danger was that she and the powerful Chalcidian League, which had 1000 cavalry and 10,000 hoplite infantry, might combine against him. He therefore offered an attractive bait to the Chalcidians: the territory Anthemus and Potidaea, if he and they should capture it. A fragment of the resulting treaty of alliance survives: 'The god [Apollo of Delphi] declared that it is better and fitter for the Chalcidians and Philip to become friends and allies on the agreed terms'; and one of the terms was that both should war against Athens and neither should make a separate peace with her. Thereafter Athens negotiated an alliance with three kings in the Balkans: 'Grabus the Illyrian, Lyppeus the Paeonian, and Cetriporis the Thracian and his brothers.' This was expressly against Philip, with whom no separate peace was to be made by any of the parties. Without doubt, Philip came off best in these diplomatic manoeuvres.

The diplomatic negotiations extended from late in 357 to summer 356, Athens being hard pressed in the Aegean. Meanwhile Philip was not idle. In spring 356 he and the Chalcidians laid siege to Potidaea. Athens decided to send help, but she was too late. The natives of Potidaea were sold into slavery, the Athenians were sent home without ransom, and the city and its properties were handed over to the Chalcidians. With them so friendly, Philip was able safely to advance beyond Amphipolis to Crenides, a colony of Thasos, which was asking for help against the neighbouring Thracians. Victorious there, he enlarged the city with additional territory and settlers, changed its name to Philippi, and treated it as an independent Greek city. Later in 356, he advanced to the river Nestus, defeated the forces of Cetriporis and probably made him a client-king.

In the region between the Axius and the Nestus rivers, which we may call henceforth east Macedonia, Philip's treatment of Greek-speaking cities varied in accordance with their compliance or resistance. His opponents in the wealthy city of Apollonia – which had previously issued a bronze coinage with a marsh-bird and a fish as emblems of its control of Lake Bolbe – lost their lands to Macedonian settlers, who were given estates by the king; one squadron of Companion Cavalry was recruited from Apollonia later in Philip's reign. At Amphipolis, too, the estates of Philip's opponents were given to Macedonians, who provided a squadron of Companion Cavalry. Because Philip declared Amphipolis independent, the city contin- ued for some years to issue tetradrachms in its own name. Thereafter its mint produced only the coins of Philip.

Philippi, which Philip had entered as an invited ally, did not yield any estates or provide any Companion Cavalry; indeed there is no record of a 'Macedon of Philippi'. The city issued gold coinage in its own name till the end of Philip's reign, and silver coinage until at least 346. But there are indications that Philip's representatives had a say in the issue of the coinage at Philippi and at Damastium, which likewise continued to coin; for the good Macedonian name 'Heracleides' and two other names in abbreviation appeared as mint-masters on issues of both cities, which were some 200 kilometres apart.

At Philippi, Philip took a large part of the gold and silver in bulk; for 'by installing equipment he so increased the hitherto utterly scanty and inglorious output of the local gold-mines that they could yield him a revenue of more than one thousand talents'. Some of the gold was used in Philip's own coinage with some of the emblems of Philippi's coins. We learn from a later inscription (see p. 109) that Philip gave additional territory to Philippi and let the defeated Thracians cultivate other land for a rent. In each case Philip was dealing with 'spear-won land', the king's own property. Thus, in practice, the king fixed the frontiers of each city, whatever its nominal status, and his foreign policy had to be accepted.

Philip planted some 'cities of Macedones' in east Macedonia. One, named Philippoupolis, was in the Kumli valley, probably near the Bisaltic silver- mine. To the east of the Strymon, Philip destroyed Galepsus and Apollonia in Thracian Pieria for unknown reasons. In the same area, Oesyme, a colonial city of Thasos, became 'a city of Macedones, named after Macesse and Emathia', and was thereafter called Emathia. Philip thus transplanted a city population from Lower Macedonia (possibly from a city there called Emathia), gave them good land, and renamed the place. The Oesymaeans may have stayed on with lesser rights (see p. 109 for an example). The foundation of other 'cities of Macedones' in eastern Macedonia is probable enough, but evidence is very patchy.

In the latter part of 356, Philip and his general defeated the coalition of kings, before they could combine their forces, and 'compelled them to associate themselves [*prosthesthai*] with the Macedones'. We have already mentioned that Cetriporis became a client-king. The same was probably the fate of Grabus and his like-named tribe, the Grabaei. But Lyppeus, king of the Paeones, seems to have enjoyed a different status. He issued silver tetradrachms, drachms and tetrobols in his own name and with his own portrait into the reign of Alexander, from the rich deposits of gold and silver in his kingdom; and he provided cavalry to fight under Philip's command. The implication is certainly that Lyppeus maintained his own army. The higher degree of autonomy and the closer relationship of Lyppeus and Philip suggests that Paeonia was included – like the Bisaltae, for example – within the Macedonian kingdom. The reason for this favoured treatment is clear. Paeonia was a buffer-state between Lower Macedonia and the dreaded Dardanians. It was vital that it would have the will and the ability to defend itself, and thereby to defend the heart of the Macedonian kingdom.

The capture of Pydna was followed in spring or summer 354 by the capture of Methone after a siege, in the course of which Philip was struck by a catapult bolt and lost his right eye. The city surrendered on terms, before help could arrive from her ally, Athens, and the citizens were allowed to depart with one garment each. 'Philip then razed the city and distributed its lands among the Macedonians.' As he already held the fortified city and harbour of Pydna, he had no need of Methone for himself and he wished to eliminate the base which Athens had used against him in 359. The new occupiers of what were probably smallholdings became citizens of nearby Pydna. Methone ceased to exist. The western coast of the Thermaic Gulf was entirely in Philip's hands, as was the coast of the Strymon basin. Since he had abundant timber in both areas, he built triremes and smaller warships, such as triaconters ('thirty oarers'), and his daring Macedonians raided Athenian bases on Lemnos, Imbros and Scyros, intercepted corn-ships off Euboea and even landed troops at Marathon.

In 349 Philip ordered his ally, the Chalcidian League, to surrender his two half-brothers, who were pretenders to his throne. The Chalcidians refused and asked Athens for help, thereby breaking the undertaking in their treaty with Philip not to make a separate peace with Athens. A war against the Chalcidian city-states, some Bottiaean city-states and the Athenians, who sent two forces of mercenaries and 150 Athenian cavalry, culminated in the isolation of Olynthus. When the Olynthian cavalry deserted to Philip, the city was invested. It fell before a third Athenian force, delayed by northerly summer winds (the Etesian winds), could reach the city. On Philip's order Olynthus was razed, its contents looted, and the population sold into slavery as treacherous allies and breakers of solemn oaths. By way of comparison it may be noted that Philip and the Chalcidians had sold the native people of Potidaea into slavery in 357, and Athens had massacred the adult males and sold the rest of the population of Sestus in 353/2. Two other cities – one being Stagirus, Aristotle's birthplace – are known to have been destroyed. An inscription of Alexander's time shows that Philip regulated the frontiers within a group of Bottiaean city-states in Chalcidice, granting additional territory to one which had evidently earned such a reward. Two known grants of estates to Macedonians by Philip were within Bottiaean territory, called Bottice. Other grants were made in territory previously owned by Potidaea. Thus Philip was making arrangements in spear-won lands at his own discretion, exercising direct rule over subjects. We can assume that he acted similarly in dealing with the Chalcidian city-states and with the territory of Olynthus.

In the two frontier areas Philip acquired territory. In 352 he took the northern parts of Magnesia and Perrhaebia into his kingdom, so that he controlled the approaches from the south to the important passes leading into the old kingdom (Tempe, Petra and Volustana). The arrangements he made in Perrhaebia were supervised by an appointed 'manager' (*epimeletes*). A later inscription shows that Elimeotis was extended to include Pythium (*en route* to the Petra Pass); and the population of Balla, a Macedonian city in Pieria, was transplanted to Pythium probably at this time rather than in the third century BC. Other additions were Tymphaea and Parauaea, both at the expense of the Molossians *c*.343. Tymphaea included passes leading into Elimeotis, and Parauaea passes leading into Orestis (via Ephtakhori and Khrisi). Each was the territory of a tribal state, rich in summer pastures and fine timber, and its people were hardy mountaineers, hitherto engaged mainly in transhumant pastoralism. Philip incorporated them as he had incorporated the tribal states of Upper Macedonia; and the Tymphaei contributed at least one brigade of Companion Infantry, which was commanded by a member of their deposed royal house in Alexander's army.

The only frontier of the kingdom which we have not considered was that defended by the Paeonians. It extended northwards to two passes in the watershed range between Macedonia and the Danube valley (Kačanik and Preševo), and north-east to the watershed with the Strymon valley. The Paeonians held also the Strumitsa valley, within which two cities of Macedonians (Astraea and Doberus) were planted, probably by Philip. In the whole immensely strong frontier system there was only one salient. To the west of the Kačanik Pass there is an easier entry from Dardania into the headwaters of the Axius river, where it turns south-west. From this fertile area (modern Polog) the Dardanians were able to enfilade Paeonia and threaten Pelagonia.

The military and economic base of the kingdom

In the enlarged kingdom, the 'cities of Macedones' played an important role. It was primarily from them that Philip and his successors recruited young men, already trained as militiamen, into the ranks of the King's Army (*basilikai dynameis*) and thereby made them Macedones. The close and continuous relationship between the king and the Macedones in the Assembly and in the Army created a strong bond, which extended also into the 'cities of Macedones', where the citizens of the Macedonian State held a privileged position. Thus the words of encouragement with which Philip addressed the frequent meetings of the Assembly in 359/8 were conveyed by small groups of Macedones to their own cities and raised the morale of the citizens of each. This was particularly important because each city had a trained militia for local defence. When Philip moved the population of a Macedonian city to a new site in spear-won land, it is probable that he associated with it some of the native population, who lived sometimes in the city and sometimes in its subsidiary villages (see p. 109). Thus common interests developed between the two populations and some merging took place in shared activities. In the areas where the city was not the only unit of local administration but was incorporated in a cantonal administration – probably called, for instance, 'the community of the Lyncestae' (*to koinon tōn Lynkestōn*) – it is probable that the representatives of the 'cities of Macedones' took the lead but were associated on an equal footing with leading non-Macedones of the canton. The activity of a leading Macedon as a member of the King's Army, of a 'city of Macedones', and of a cantonal system, is seen in nomenclature such as *Philarchus Macedōn Eleimiōtes ek Pytheiou* (Philarchus a Macedonian citizen of Elimiotis from [the city] Pythium).

We probably owe to Theopompus, a contemporary Greek historian, an illuminating comment on Philip's policy and its effects, which were already apparent *c.*346:

> As shepherds move their flocks now to winter, now to summer pastures, so he transplanted populations and cities at his own discretion, wherever he thought that places should be replenished or abandoned . . . Some populations he placed on the very frontiers opposite his enemies; others he settled in the furthest parts of the kingdom; and some peoples whom he had captured in war were divided up and sent to supplement the populations of the cities. And so it was that he created out of many tribes and races one kingdom and one people [*unum regnum populumque constituit*].

The responsibility for defending the kingdom and conquering its enemies on foreign soil was squarely placed on those who were selected for service in the King's Army as Companion Infantrymen. They were recruited only from the Macedonians of the old kingdom, from the Macedonians transplanted to new cities, and from the men of Upper Macedonia – all speaking Greek as their native language, but of two different dialects, although a bridge between dialects was being formed by the spread of standard Greek (*koine*) in this century. Although Perdiccas II had included in his army 'the Greeks living in Macedonia' as hoplites, and although the Chalcidians had fielded 1000 cavalry and 10,000 hoplites, Philip did not include any of them in the King's Army; and the same may be said of the warlike Illyrian, Paeonian and Thracian infantrymen who lived within the frontiers of the kingdom.

The numbers of Companion Cavalrymen in the King's Army were somewhat increased by the ability of Philip to recruit able foreigners (especially Greeks) and draft them into the Companionate of the king. Some squadrons of auxiliary cavalry were recruited from the peoples within the kingdom who were not racially Macedones, but in relatively small numbers.

The king in person 'led' three select units, called *agemata*. The King's Own Squadron of Companion Cavalry numbered 300. The Infantry Guard of Macedones protected the king's person in peace as well as in war. In the latter part of his reign, when he had the financial resources, Philip maintained a force of 3000 Companion Infantrymen, who were called Hypaspists. From these he formed a King's Own Infantry Guard of 1000 men, who were permanently under arms and provided garrison troops for the palace. There was keen rivalry between the select units and also between the *pezhetairoi* brigades and the *asthetairoi* brigades of the infantry phalanx; and between one brigade and another. At the end of his reign Philip commanded the services of 2800 Companion Cavalrymen, 1400 auxiliary cavalrymen, and 24,000 Companion Infantrymen.

Philip often employed Greek mercenary troops – cavalry, infantry and specialists of all kinds – rather than deploy men of the King's Army or recruit men within the kingdom. He used them particularly for service abroad and for garrison duty. The engineers who developed his excellent siege-train were professionals. They were led by a Thessalian called Polyidus, and the transition from the mechanically strung catapult which fired stones and bolts to the torsion catapult of greater power and range was probably thanks to him. Supporting services were provided from within the kingdom as occasion demanded – pioneers, grooms, attendants, labourers on roads, etc.

The function of the indigenous populations, whether they were racially Macedonian or not, was to develop the economy of the kingdom so that it could maintain the King's Army with its auxiliary troops and services. We have seen that the change from large-scale transhumant pastoralism to settled agriculture was all-important in the early history of the Macedonians.

The same change was made in the cantons of Upper Macedonia. Alexander the Great made this point clearly in a speech to the King's Army in 324:

> When Philip took you over, you were resourceless nomads, most of you were clad in skins, feeding your few sheep in the mountains, and you fought unsuccessfully against Illyrians, Triballians and the neighbouring Thracians. He gave you cloaks instead of skins to wear, brought you down from the mountains to the plains, made you worthy opponents of the barbarians on your borders, so that you trusted for your survival not any more in natural strongholds but in your own prowess in arms. He made you inhabitants of cities, and he gave you an orderly existence with good laws and customs. He made you leaders instead of slaves and subjects of the very barbarians who used to pillage and carry off your persons and your property . . . By taking for himself the best harbours and stretches of the coast he laid commerce open to the whole country and rendered the working of the mines free from fear [of raids etc.]

The description of these internal changes rings true to anyone who has seen the change in Albania since 1944 from dominant pastoralism and subsistence agriculture to improved farming, developing towns, a ban on vendetta, and working of mineral resources. In both instances it was primarily the towns which encouraged peasants to rise above subsistence level by providing a market, and which brought them into contact with more capable farmers, in Macedonia's case transferred from Lower Macedonia.

When the plains of Macedonia were used primarily for pasture, the flooding of the rivers twice a year and the deposits of alluvium were beneficial in encouraging the growth of grass and providing swampy ground. Cultivation of cereals on the plains was possible only when rivers were controlled, swamps were drained and shrubs removed. 'Philip enlarged Pella from being a small city'; it was probably due to him that a controllable branch of the Axius was led into Pella Lake and that a waterway from the lake went to the coast. This required skilful engineering, because the floods of the Axius were formidable. The result was an all-weather, riverine harbour, protected from enemy shipping. A similar harbour was made at Dium. In the plain of Philippi, which was forested and waterlogged when the Thracians possessed it, we learn from a contemporary botanist, Theophrastus, that 'the water was drained off, the land mostly dried out, and the whole territory brought into cultivation'. An inscription of 335 referred to 'the fallow land' near Philippi, evidently recovered for cultivation in this way. If such methods were practised throughout the kingdom, the increase in production must have been very great indeed.

In order to maintain a fairly active army, cultivate large tracts of reclaimed land, and fill gaps due to the transplantation of populations from Lower Macedonia, a considerable increase of people on the land was desirable. We hear twice of Philip bringing captives back to Macedonia: 'more than 10,000' Illyrian men, and presumably their families also, from Sarnous c.345, and 20,000 women and boys from Scythia in 339. Nor were these the only instances, since we are told with reference to 346 that 'he divided up some peoples whom he had captured and sent them to supplement the populations of the cities' – i.e. as groups of workers on the land.

Coinage gives some indication of prosperity. There were no coins of Amyntas IV. In 356, a year after he was elected king, Philip began to coin with precious metal mainly from Damastium, from the Bisaltic mine, and from Philippi (see Plate 9a). His gold coins – the first issued by a Macedonian king – had the same emblems as those of Philippi, namely the head of Heracles wearing the lion-skin cap and on the reverse Heracles' club, bow or tankard; but his largest denomination was a half-stater, whereas Philippi issued staters. The stater was the standard large coin, comparable to the gold sovereign in the period of real-value currency. His silver didrachms had the head of Heracles, as on the gold coins, and on the reverse a jockey on Philip's racehorse, which won at the Olympic Games of 356. At this time and until 348 the Chalcidian League was issuing a finer coinage and in larger denominations than Philip. With the dissolution of the League in 348 Philip acquired the deposits of gold, silver, lead, copper and iron in Chalcidice. He now issued his famous gold staters, called *Philippeioi*, which showed the same Apollo as the Chalcidian coins and on the reverse a two-horse chariot at the gallop, commemorating a victory in that event at Olympia in 348; and silver tetradrachms with the head of Zeus and on the obverse a bearded horseman, wearing hat and cloak, and raising one hand in salutation. The horseman was certainly Philip; for the ribbon ends of a diadem hang down behind his head. The coinage of Philip from 348 until his death was the most prolific, had the widest distribution in the Balkans, and was current also in Central Europe.

Bronze coinage was used for local trade, as excavations at Olynthus and its port, Mecyberna, have shown; of Philip's coins 105 bronze pieces were found but only one silver. Whereas the most popular head on gold and silver coins was that of Heracles, the head on the bronze coins was of a young man, wearing a diadem without ribbon ends (see Plate 7b: iii). This was probably Caranus, the supposed founder in Macedonia of the Temenid dynasty. It is clear from the quantity of bronze coins issued by Philip that a monetary economy was thoroughly well established in the kingdom. One stimulus to the circulation of coinage was the payment in cash to the soldiers of the King's Army when they were on active service, which it is probable that Philip made, at least after 348, even as Alexander was to do. Thus Macedonia was modernized in one aspect of the capitalism which was so highly developed in the Greek city-states, but with the very important differences that the concentration of capital was in the hands of the king and not, as at Athens, in those of an extremely wealthy class of individual entrepreneurs, and that the owners of considerable estates were not successful businessmen, but the recipients of the king's generosity for their services to the state.

VII

Philip's Other Achievements

The Balkan Empire

In 1985 a hoard of 165 silver vessels was found in a field at Rogozen in
north-west Bulgaria. Thirteen pieces carried the name of Cotys; two had
the name of Satocus; and one the name of Cersebleptes. The names were
dotted or cut in rather poor Greek lettering, and they were usually in the
genitive case. With most of these names there was a note of origin from a
named place, either in full, such as *ex argiskes* (twice thus, and twice *ex
ergiskes*), or perhaps in abbreviated form, such as *ek beo*. It seems then that
these vessels at least were presented to these Odrysian kings or royals by a
city or by a tribe (*ek geiston* on two vessels, differently spelt). We shall
discuss the artistic quality of these vessels later (see p. 100). The point of
interest here is that the Macedonian kings also had great numbers of silver
vessels of similar design, though not inscribed in this way, and it may be
that they too were presented with silver goblets by their cities. For a
Macedonian writer of this period wrote as follows: 'Whenever the king
enters the city, someone carrying a vessel full of wine goes to meet him. He
takes it and pours a libation'.

Thracian kings resembled Macedonian kings in many ways. They had
absolute powers of command in the field. The adult males of the royal
house were sometimes associated with the king in making a treaty. The
funeral of a king was an occasion for mourning, feasting, games and single
combats of warriors. The king entertained lavishly. He and his guests drank
deeply of wine, and the last drinker of a loving-cup poured the residue of
wine over his neighbour. The Thracian king had a monopoly of coinage,
and the devices on the coins were startlingly like those of the Macedonian
kings. Their aristocratic cavalrymen were portrayed with short cloak and
one or two spears; and it is clear that they enjoyed great prestige. The kings
employed Greek specialists in generalship and warfare. Thracian armies
differed in some respects. Both horse and rider were armoured. Because the
cavalry ranked so high, some infantrymen were trained to fight alongside
and among the cavalrymen. The infantrymen of the line were called peltasts
by the Greeks, because they had a light shield (*pelta*) and a longer spear than
the hoplite spearman; they were feared as mercenaries and as committers of
atrocities. In Thrace, but not in Macedonia, the peasant on the land was
despised (see p. 22) and there was a lively traffic in peasant families captured
and enslaved or sold as slaves.

Thracians and Macedonians had much in common in their religious beliefs. They had lived as neighbours in Pieria, and they had then been much influenced by the beliefs of the Phrygians. They both worshipped Dionysus, Orpheus and the Muses, Ares, a goddess of war (Cotys among the Edones and Athena among the Macedonians), and a goddess of animals (Bendis in Thrace and Artemis Tauropolos in Macedonia). The cults were orgiastic in both countries, and the inclusion of so many Thracians in the enlarged kingdom of Philip led to a further sharing of cult titles such as Sabazius and Gazorius. Royal houses traced their ancestry back to a divine progenitor, such as a wind-god equated with Hermes and the war-goddess Cotys in Thrace, and Zeus in Macedonia. Both peoples had great faith in oracles, the most famous being that of Dionysus in the Rila mountains of Thrace, where trees and vegetation are extraordinarily luxuriant. The silver vessels of Rogozen were adorned with cult scenes, showing a close relationship with Macedonian cults but a more primitive form of belief. The closeness of Thracian worship to the natural world has recently been illustrated by the discovery of observatories from which the movement of the sun was noted, and of rock-graffiti recording phases of the moon's orb.

'Because I have my horses and my soldiers I live now by plundering the land my father once held': this was the frank statement of Seuthes, a dispossessed prince, to Xenophon who entered his employment. The ravaging, looting, burning of villages and taking of hostages – so reminiscent of 'reprisals' in occupied Greece – were typical of the Thracian way of life. Xenophon received a share of the proceeds: a talent, 600 oxen, 4000 sheep and 120 slaves. The last were some of the villagers who failed to escape or were forced by snow to come down from mountain refuges. Under such unstable conditions there were no towns. Xenophon wrote only of castles occupied by grandees and of open villages (*komai*).

The Illyrians and the Macedonians of Lower Macedonia had less in common, as far as one can judge from the very limited evidence that exists about the Illyrians. Their chief worships were probably of a sun-god, a snake-deity and a goddess of animals (Thana). They had faith in amulets worn to guard against evil, and human sacrifice was made to win divine favour and avert defeat. Their way of life was like that of the tribal states of Upper Macedonia, because transhumant pastoralism was very widely practised in the regions west and north-west of Macedonia, and there were in consequence very few towns (some *polismata*, lesser forms of city, were developed by Bardylis near and north of Lake Lychnitis). The Illyrian tribal states (see p. 28) were led by kings or by men whom the Greeks called 'dynasts' – a very small group of rulers. Illyrian aristocratic cavalry and an infantry trained in the tactics of the hoplite-phalanx were the most formidable of all Balkan fighters in the first half of the fourth century. To most Greek writers they were just 'Illyrians'; even in the official treaty with Athens, Grabus was just 'the Illyrian', as Cetriporis was just 'the Thracian'.

The Illyrian neighbours of the greater Macedonian kingdom extended from the region of Lake Lychnitis to the sources of the Morava. They were, from south to north-east, Parthini, Encheleae, Atintani, Penestae and Dardanii, and they were probably all in the cluster of tribes which made up the power of Bardylis, himself the king of much the strongest tribe, the Dardanii (in modern Metohija and Kosovo).

The earliest campaigns of Philip against the Thracians and the Illyrians were undertaken both to discourage raiding of Macedonia and to reap the benefits of conquest: in 356, as we have seen (p. 67), against Grabus and against Cetriporis and Cersebleptes; and in 353 against Amadocus (in south-western Thrace). From then onwards Philip's aim was conquest: in 353, 346 and 345 against Cersebleptes in south-east Thrace; c.345 against the Dardanii and other Illyrian neighbours; c.345 against Pleuratus, king of the Ardiaei (extending from Scodra to Kotor and beyond); in 342–40 against Cersebleptes and in central Thrace; in 339 against Atheas, a Scythian king in north-east Thrace; and c.337 against Pleurias, king probably of the Autariatae. He clashed too with the Triballi of the lower Morava valley, who carried their raids as far as Abdera on the Aegean coast.

The strategy which Philip and his generals pursued was a set battle and then a relentless pursuit with a view to breaking the will of the enemy cavalry, which was the ruling group. By 356 he had extended the use of a long weapon from the Infantry to his Companion Cavalry. What was then called a *sarissa*, and we may call a lance, was 9 feet long, with a blade at each end (the heavier being aft), and some 5 feet of it were in front of the rider, who held it with one hand at the point of balance. Thus the lancer could strike an opponent wielding a 6-foot spear but holding it at the middle, before the opponent was within striking distance. The cornel-wood shaft of the lance was most likely then to break, whereupon he used the aft part, attached by a loop to his wrist, as a spear. The Companion Cavalryman wore helmet and cuirass, both of metal (see Plate 15), and carried a sword high on his side; but his horse was not armoured. Philip trained them in squadrons (200 strong, except for the Royal Squadron which was 300) to move in wedge formation, the commander at the point of the wedge being able to exercise command and indicate changes of direction. He also recruited light cavalry, of which the 'Scouts' were armed with the lance.

The cavalry's aim was to charge, disperse the enemy cavalry and harass the infantry when in disorder or flight; for they could not charge an infantry force which kept formation and presented a hedge of spears. That was left to the pikemen-phalanx. The combination of these Macedonian forces with some specialized mercenary units enabled Philip to win numerous set battles and other engagements in the Balkans. Each victory was exploited by a long cavalry pursuit. In such a pursuit of Pleuratus' army c.345, one Companion Cavalryman was killed and 150, including Philip, were wounded. We are not told what the Illyrian casualties were. In the campaigns of 342–40

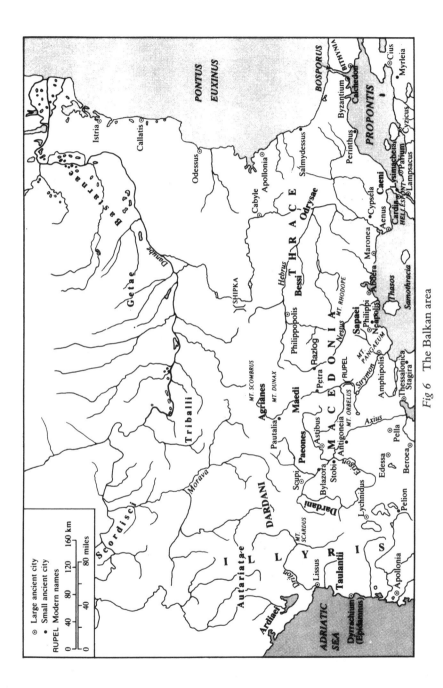

Fig 6 The Balkan area

operations continued throughout the hard Thracian winter – a season which Greek troops avoided. Philip's strategy was fitted to a country in which there were few, if any, large urban centres.

Philip's actions in the Balkans were in two phases. In the first he fought against the tribal states near to the coast and sought the alliance of the Greek city-states on the coast: in Illyris south of the Drin, in Thrace south of Mount Rhodope and east of Mount Rhodope as far as the Thracian Bosporus. After 346 his range was very much greater. He established what may be called a Balkan Empire, of which the northern provinces were southern Montenegro, Metohija, Kosovo, Blagoevgrad, the south face of the Haemus range, and the Dobruja by the mouth of the Danube. Beyond those frontiers he defeated Ardiaei, Autariatae, Triballi, Getae and Scythians in some engagements. His policy evidently was to ally himself with independent powers outside the empire. He married Meda, daughter of the Getic king Cothelas, and his intention was to become the successor of a Scythian king, Atheas, who offered to adopt him by making him his son-in-law. When Atheas went back on his word, Philip defeated him, probably took his daughter in marriage, and set up a statue of Heracles at the mouth of the Danube. He was expressing his own rivalry with Heracles, who had set up pillars at the Straits of Gibraltar, the limit of his adventures.

Within the empire all the native tribes, whether republican (*autonomoi*) or governed by kings, were subject to the orders of Philip, who might demand troops, supplies and services. One-tenth of all produce from the spear-won land which they were allowed to cultivate was paid as annual tribute 'to the Macedones'. Thus they were the subjects of the Macedonian State. Some peoples had suffered severely. For instance, the Dardanians' territory was ravaged, small towns stormed, and much booty removed before they were subjugated. Others lost the cultivation of lands which became royal estates or were awarded by the king to deserving Companions. On the other hand, the peoples were in general left free to cultivate the same lands as before the conquest, to practise their religion, use their laws and speak their own language; for Philip and his Macedonians wished them to govern themselves in their traditional way and to retain their self-respect. One great change was that, with the weakening of the aristocratic cavalry, the peasants earned respect as cultivators of the soil.

In Thrace 'he founded important cities in strategic areas and put an end to the outrageous conduct of the Thracians' – i.e. to their raiding of one another and of the Greek city-states. Philip allocated tracts of spear-won land to the new cities, and they were peopled by 'mixed populations' – by Macedonians, Greeks and Thracians (in one case 2000 Greeks, which suggests a city of some 10,000 adult males at the start). The cities were designed to be factors in promoting peace and prosperity as features of the Macedonian Empire; for the Macedonians, like the Greeks, were experienced in agriculture, land reclamation and trade, and it was to be expected that native cities would soon come into existence. The most fertile areas in Thrace were in the great central plain, where Philippoupolis (Plovdiv) and Cabyle were founded by Philip.

Less is known about the Macedonian Empire in the Illyrian area. Philip certainly controlled access to the rich coastal plain of central Albania (see Plate 32). He was probably in alliance with the Greek city-states Apollonia and Epidamnus (Dyrrachium). The extension of trade which resulted from Macedonia's control of her own coastline and the northwards extension of her empire was indicated by the coinages of Damastium and those of Daparria, Pelagiteis and Tenestini, which were linked to Damastium by some emblems and the same standard. The whole group had affinities with the coinage of the Paeonian king, who used the same standard. The distribution of these coinages was northwards and north-westwards. A hoard at Risan (Rhizon), of the period 360–30, consisted two-thirds of tetradrachms of the Damastium group and one-third of coins of Corinth and her colonies. Thus Macedonia inherited and extended the northern sphere of trade which Bardylis had developed in the Balkans. Macedonia probably stimulated the development of mines in Metohija, Polog and Kosovo (in Dardanian territory), as she had done at Philippi. The establishment of peace within the conquered area gave the peasants security and did more than anything else to encourage production.

The Macedonian Empire is of interest as the first land empire in the history of Europe. It is notable for the absence of such features as the Athenian maritime empire's imposition on its subjects of an Athens-favoured constitution, Athenian jurisdiction in certain cases, Athenian weights and measures, garrisons, inspectors (*episkopoi*) and cleruchies (citizen-colonies). Macedonia's founding of mixed cities was a forward-looking policy, which was expected to develop the resources of the native peoples and spread the use of the Greek language. Macedonia relied not on garrisons but on a swift-moving army, which would reach centres of trouble rapidly, using all-weather roads such as the paved track for cavalry which has been discovered by Albanian archaeologists on the line of the later Via Egnatia. Macedonian methods were more enlightened than those of other Balkan peoples; for the Illyrian Ardiaei had as many as 300,000 serfs, and the Thracians enslaved the populations they overran or else sold them on the slave market. The one-tenth of the produce which was levied as tribute may be compared with Sparta's treatment of the conquered Messenians, 'toiling like donkeys under great burdens and rendering half of the ploughlands' produce to their masters'. Macedonian imperialism was relatively liberal. Philip imposed conditions of peace and planned for economic development, and the foundation of the mixed cities looked forward to some degree of integration.

Philip's relations with the Greek states

The Greek world was in a sorry condition politically when Philip appeared on the scene. In most city-states the tension between the richer citizens and the poorer citizens led to violent party-strife and often to seizure of power, now by a dictator or a junta, now by an extreme democracy. Money was the dominant consideration. The rich in power were often corrupt and repressive, the poor in power extravagant in welfare and aggressive in policy. Even at Athens in this period the dictum 'You leave the Assembly after dividing the surplus like shareholders' was only too true of their slave-based society, in which the citizen body which alone attended the Assembly scorned manual employment, even if it was available. 'The best state', said Aristotle, 'will not make any citizen a manual worker, because the bulk of the labour force today is slave or foreign.'

One party or the other was always ready to invoke intervention by an outside power. In this unstable world it was easy for a large state with a particular ideology to win adherents in other states and to build up a coalition which might become an empire. Competition between large states which aimed at such 'hegemony' resulted in an almost unbroken sequence of internecine wars from 460 to 346. The two major wars in Philip's earlier years were the Social War of 357–5, in which Athens was forced to relinquish her imperial grip on many states in the Aegean basin, and the Sacred War of 356–46, which was concerned with the secular control of the Temple of Apollo at Delphi and involved almost all mainland states. This second war was fought mainly by mercenaries, hired by Phocian politicians who melted down the gold and silver offertories of centuries in the Temple, and by the citizen armies of Boeotia, Thessaly and Macedonia, which claimed to be fighting in the cause of Apollo. Tens of thousands of professional mercenaries were readily available; for, as political refugees proliferated, 'it was easier to raise a bigger and better force from the floating population than from the citizen population'. The citizen soldiers of Boeotia set the tone of the Sacred War from the start by executing all prisoners-of-war as sacrilegious criminals. The mercenaries responded by killing their prisoners.

Greek perceptions of Macedonia varied. To the masses, the Macedonians were backward barbarians who needed a monarchy to keep them from falling apart, and the Macedonian king was no better and no worse than a Thracian king such as Cotys, whom a contemporary writer of Attic comedy presented as drunken, sacrilegious and vulgar. Theopompus wrote of Philip and his Companions as a set of drunken, spendthrift sodomites, 'more brutish and bestial than the Centaurs'; and Demosthenes told the Athenian Assembly in 349 that Philip's court was the scene of daily drunkenness and lewd dancing, and that the power of Philip, being based on greed, perjury and deceit, would collapse at the first reverse. On the other hand, Philip was known to many capable Greeks as a generous employer, a genial host and a patron of the arts; and Isocrates, a political thinker at Athens, believed that Philip was a king of culture and intelligence, and that he alone in 346 might be able to unite the Greek city-states and lead them in a war against Persia.

Philip had a personal entrée into Greek politics as a Greek of the most distinguished ancestry, being descended from Heracles. He enjoyed special favour with the ruling group at Larissa in Thessaly, the Aleuadae, who claimed the same descent, and he fought a series of wars with their support as the champion of democracy against tyranny, of federalism against separatism, and of Apollo against temple-robbers. His opponents were the tyrants of Pherae in central Thessaly and the Phocians' armies of mercenaries. In 353 Philip and his Thessalian allies suffered two defeats, the second a serious one. The Phocian commander concealed sets of stone-throwing catapults on the wings of a crescent-shaped hill, and his phalanx of mercenaries, making a feigned retreat, drew the Macedonian phalanx into the space between the two wings, whereupon the catapults pelted the dense phalanx (see Plate 10b) with showers of large stones. The mercenaries turned about and attacked the disrupted formation. The pikemen-phalanx withdrew with considerable loss and shattered morale; for in previous engagements the pikemen had suffered minimal casualties, protected as they were by the hedge of pike-points. During the withdrawal Philip, fighting alongside his men, remarked, 'I withdraw like a ram, to butt the harder.'

In 352 Philip's army of Macedonians and Thessalians, wearing laurel wreaths as soldiers of Apollo, and totalling 3000 cavalry and more than 20,000 infantry, intercepted the Phocian army of 500 cavalry and 20,000 experienced mercenaries in 'The Crocus Field', an open plain on the coast south of Pherae. While the pikemen-phalanx made a frontal attack, the cavalry rode in on the flank and the rear. The routed army fled to the coast, where an allied Athenian fleet lay offshore to pick up survivors; but 6000 mercenaries lay dead and 3000 were captured. Their fate as temple-robbers, in accordance with Greek and (probably) Macedonian practice, was to be bound and drowned in the sea. After this defeat Pherae surrendered on terms of a safe conduct for the tyrants and their 2000 mercenaries. Its strongly fortified harbour town, Pagasae, was captured before a relief force from Athens could arrive; it was then held by a Macedonian garrison.

Three or four inland city-states which had sided with Pherae and the Phocians suffered destruction or loss of territory, and pro-Macedonian settlers occupied two of them, Tricca and Pelinna. Gomphi, in south-west Thessaly, changed its name to Philippopolis, probably receiving Macedonians as settlers. Philip had married a lady of Larissa, Philinna, in 358/7, and now he married a niece of Jason of Pherae, Nicesipolis. His popularity was at a high point. The Thessalians, united in victory, put themselves under his command for the prosecution of the Sacred War. The combined forces advanced to the pass of Thermopylae, which was held by Phocis' mercenaries and Phocis' allies (Sparta, Achaea, Athens and the ex-tyrants of Pherae). Philip withdrew. His policy had always been to avoid confrontation and embitterment with Athens, and he did not relish the association of Thermopylae with the defence of Greek freedom.

During Philip's war with the Chalcidian League (see p. 67) Athens sent some help to her ally, but she was distracted by a revolt of her Allies in Euboea, who were aided by some of Philip's mercenaries. She lost Euboea, her last relief force failed to reach Olynthus in time, and her appeal to the Greek states to join her against Macedonia went unanswered in the winter of 348/7. She was isolated. The protagonists in the Sacred War were nearing exhaustion – the Phocians running short of Apollo's gold and Boeotia short of men. The Macedonians and the Thessalians might join the Boeotians, finish off the Phocians and attack Athens, the only ally of Phocis north of the Isthmus. Instead, Philip offered peace and alliance to Athens, and, after a false step by Athens and then prolonged negotiations, an alliance was concluded in July 346 with Athens and her Allies. Philip twice invited Athens to send troops to join in ending the Sacred War, but Athens declined on the advice of Demosthenes and Hegesippus. Before the month was ended, 8000 mercenaries received a free pass to the Peloponnese, and the defenceless Phocians surrendered unconditionally to Philip. The Temple at Delphi was restored to Apollo with no loss of life – a remarkable finale, orchestrated by Philip, who was said to pride himself more on his diplomacy than on his prowess in battle.

Philip referred the decision about the fate of the Phocians to the Council of the Amphictyonic League, which had made the declaration of the Sacred War. The members of the Council were the delegates of the twelve tribes of north and central Greece, each with two votes, except that one vote of the Ionians was held by Athens and one vote of the Dorians by Sparta. The Council stripped the Phocians of their votes and conferred them on the Macedonians, whose delegates were appointed at once by Philip. A clear majority of votes was held thereafter by Macedonia, her allies and her friends. At the meeting of the Council the delegates of the Oetaeans proposed the massacre of all male Phocians and the sale of the rest as slaves. Such an act of genocide was carried out by the Boeotians against two of their own cities (Orchomenus and Coronea) which had been forced into the camp of the Phocians. A less brutal decision was taken by the Amphictyons, at the prompting of Philip: the disarming of all Phocians, the splitting of towns into village communities, and the repayment annually of debts to Apollo's Temple. The Council elected Philip president of the Pythian Games and associated the Thessalian and Boeotian delegates with him. It arranged the management of Apollo's Temple, and announced a programme 'for proper religious observance and for general peace and concord among the Greeks'. The voice behind that announcement was known to be that of

Philip. He was suggesting some form of union, which would lead to reconciliation and end the period of internecine wars.

Reconciliation was difficult to achieve. Athens and Sparta had sided with the Phocians. Priority in consulting the Oracle at Delphi, which the Phocians had accorded to Athens, was transferred to Philip, and the military 'hegemony' in central Greece was exercised not, as from time to time in the past, by Athens, Sparta or Thebes, but by Macedonia. Athens refused at first to recognize Philip's presidency of the Pythian Games, but when the alternative was war, an apology was made on the proposal of Demosthenes. Philip accepted it. He was honouring the alliance he had made with Athens; for he had hoped that the Athenians would join him in leading the Greeks towards a general peace.

But the decision in Athens and in the other Greek states was now a matter of party politics, in which the shift of the well-to-do citizens was towards trust in Philip's stated intentions and that of the less well-to-do towards distrust. The former party could point to Philip's dealings with the Thessalians, who proceeded to elect Philip president (*archon*) for life of the Thessalian League, entrust him with the revenues, and give him command of their troops; indeed, Isocrates wrote *c*.344 to congratulate Philip on the benefits he had conferred on the Thessalians. The latter cited the examples of Greek cities destroyed by Philip (Potidaea, Methone, Olynthus, Oesyme and others) and they claimed that he would subjugate the Greeks and destroy any opponent, Athens included.

Despite various offers by Philip the pendulum of opinion swung towards the latter's views in the years from 346 to 340. Demosthenes and Hegesippus, the leading orators in the Athenian Assembly, obtained alliances with Byzantium, Abydus, Chios and Rhodes, which were alarmed by Philip's conquest of south-east Thrace, and money was sent by Persia to an Athenian commander in the Chersonese (the Gallipoli peninsula), who was attacking Philip's allies. On the mainland Athens had obtained as allies Euboea (which had broken away from Philip), Megara, Corinth and some of her colonies, Acarnania and Achaea. Their forces were scattered and not strong in relation to Macedonia. In March 340 a conference of Athens and her allies was held at Athens to plan war against Macedonia, and Demosthenes was awarded a gold wreath for his services to the Athenian people.

Between 346 and 340 Philip had created the Balkan Empire which would secure his rear if he should fight a war in Greece or against Persia. He had also brought Epirus firmly into his sphere of influence by deposing the Molossian king and placing on the throne his brother-in-law, Alexander, the brother of Olympias, the Molossian princess whom he had married in 357. He enlarged the scope of the Molossian state by forcing three Greek cities in the peninsula of Cassopaea to be subject to the Molossian king. He then threatened to attack Ambracia, but he desisted when its foundress, Corinth, and Athens were prepared to help it. However, he made an alliance with the Aetolian League, thus extending his influence to the shore of the Gulf of Corinth in 342. When the chance of winning Athens by diplomacy ended in March 340, Philip took advantage of the current peace and alliance with Athens to pass his fleet through the Hellespont under the noses of the Athenian settlers on the European side, landing his siege-train at Perinthus, where his army was ready to attack. For Perinthus and Byzantium had broken the terms of their alliance with Philip, and he hoped through conquering them to control the passage through the Bosporus of Athenian corn-ships, on which Athens depended for her food supply. Philip then notified the Athenians that he was about to retaliate for their breaches of the treaty of peace and alliance. His fleet seized a large convoy of corn-ships. On the proposal of Demosthenes, Athens went to war. Persia as well as Athens and her Allies sent help to the beleaguered cities; and, despite his army of 30,000 men and siege-towers 120 feet high, Philip was foiled. During negotiations for peace with the two cities he let a (false) report of a rising in Thrace fall into the hands of the Athenians, and while their fleet went to investigate he brought his own fleet out through the Hellespont.

Because Philip went from the Bosporus to attack the Scythian king Atheas, he did not return to Pella until late summer 339. Meanwhile, another Sacred War had been declared. The command against the miscreants – the Locrians of Amphissa – was offered by the Council of the Amphictyonic League to Philip. He accepted. His army avoided the Pass of Thermopylae, which the Boeotians had occupied while a dispute with the Macedonians was under discussion. The army ascended the mountain pass to Cytinium in Doris; but instead of heading for Amphissa it marched through Phocis to Elatea. It encamped there, close to the border of Boeotia, which was in alliance with Macedonia. Philip sent envoys to address the Boeotian Assembly, which was in session at Thebes. He invited the Boeotians to join him against Athens or at least to give him free passage to Attica.

The news that a Macedonian army was at Elatea caused consternation at Athens. Demosthenes was the man of the moment. He led a group of envoys to Thebes, where the Boeotians had not yet come to a decision. Athens asked for alliance against Macedonia, offering to pay two-thirds of the cost of the war and to give Boeotia overall command by land. A majority of the Boeotian Assembly voted in favour of alliance. It was a courageous decision, taken in the name of liberty; but it was one which broke the oaths of alliance with Macedonia and exposed the Boeotians to the possibility of suffering as Olynthus had suffered. Each side fortified its position. During the winter Philip offered conditions of peace to Boeotia and Athens; and through his influence the Phocian state was reconstituted by the Council of the Amphictyonic League as an example of reconciliation. Philip's offers were rejected, Athens' existing allies committed themselves to the war, and Demosthenes was awarded a golden crown at the Festival of Drama at Athens in March 338. A peaceful solution seemed impossible, and if there was further delay Persia, already at war with Macedonia, might give Athens more than financial aid.

The Greeks made the mistake of dividing their superior forces into two detachments, some two days' march apart. The smaller, consisting of 10,000 mercenaries, was deceived by a (false) message of a rising in Thrace and by a daytime withdrawal of the Macedonians. It relaxed its guard. Philip came back during the night, destroyed perhaps half of the mercenaries and captured Amphissa. He then offered terms of peace to Boeotia and Athens. They were rejected. On 2 August 338 the decisive battle was fought at Chaeronea. The Greeks held a strong defensive position in the plain between the fortified acropolis of the town and the riverbank of the Cephissus. Some 5000 light-armed infantry held the slopes below the acropolis, and the hoplite infantry, some 30,000 in number, was drawn up in a continuous phalanx of spearmen, eight men deep and some 3 kilometres long. The 10,000 Athenians held the left part of the line, the 12,000 Boeotians the right part, and the allies and 5000 mercenaries the centre. The Greek cavalry was in reserve. Philip commanded a smaller but much more experienced army of 2000 superb cavalry – part Macedonian and part Thessalian – 24,000 Macedonian pikemen, and some 6000 light-armed infantry.

The initiative lay with Philip. His problem was to create a gap in the continuous line of hoplites, so that his cavalry, commanded by his son Alexander, could ride through the gap and take the line in flanks and rear. He achieved this by a daring parade-ground manoeuvre. He advanced leading his finest pikemen on the right wing of the phalanx line, which was in oblique order in relation to the Greek line, while the left wing was retarded, Alexander riding beside it with ten cavalry squadrons. Philip's men marched in close order. When they approached the extreme left of the Greek line, still facing the enemy they retreated to their right rear, 'step by step, Philip keeping the phalanx contracted and the men protected inside their weapons'. The rest of the Macedonian line was still not engaging the enemy. The Athenians pursued impetuously to their left front, thereby causing the rest of the Greek line to move to its left in order to keep formation. But the right-hand Boeotians did not dare to leave the protective riverbank and stood still, so that a gap opened up and widened in the phalanx line. Into the gap rode the Cavalry of Alexander and fanned out to attack the enemy in flanks and rear. At the same time, Philip ordered his men and the rest of the pikemen-phalanx to charge their opponents. The Greek line broke in disorder and a general flight ensued, except on the extreme right, where the Theban Sacred Band fell fighting to the last man. Philip halted his troops as soon as victory was won. There was no cavalry pursuit.

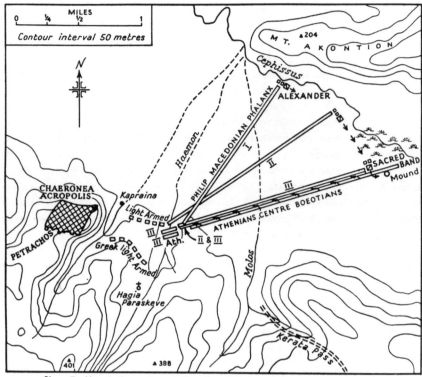

Phase I   Macedonians advance; Greeks stationary
Phase II   Philip retreats, his centre and left advancing; Athenians, Centre and
           Boeotians advance to left front, but the Sacred Band stands firm
Phase III Alexander charges, the centres engage, and Philip drives the
           Athenian wing up the Haemon valley

Fig 7   The Battle of Chaeronea

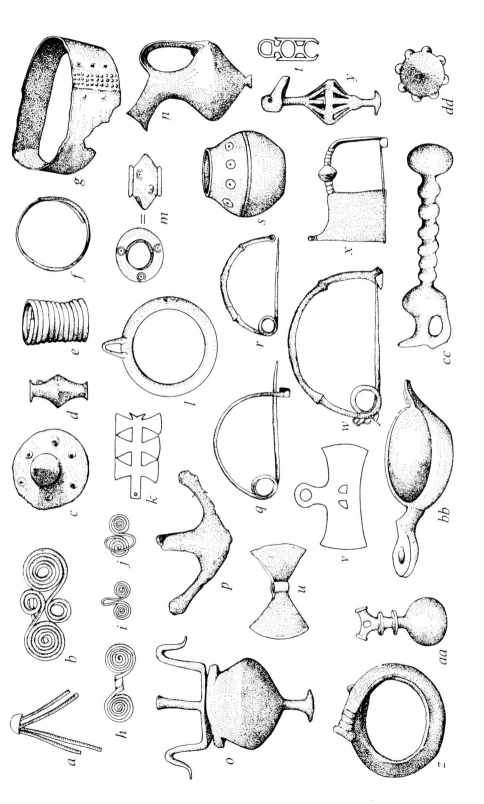

1. Bronze Ornaments

2. Shepherds and sheep

(b) Kresna defile

3.(a) Mount Olympus

4. West Macedonia, seen from the satellite. The lakes from west to east are: Ochrid, Large Prespa, Little Presp
and Ostrovo, and further south Kastoria and Ioannina. (Photo NASA)

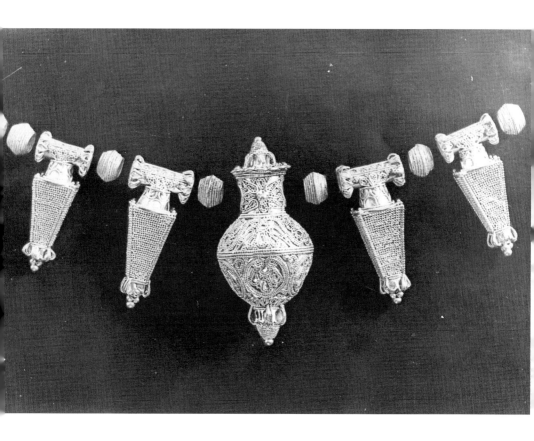

a) *Above*: Gold Necklace (centrepiece 5.7 cm high)
b) *Below*: Gold Pins (21 cm long)

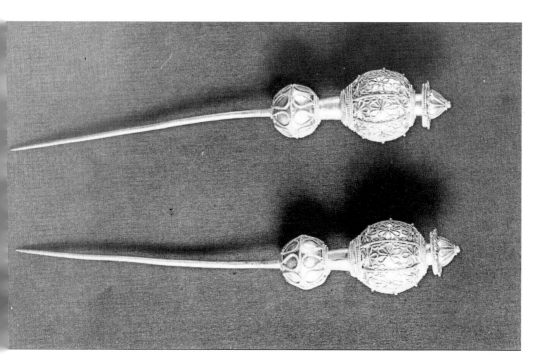

6.(a) *Above*: Gold Mask (helmet 22 cm high)
   (b) *Below*: Gold Mouthpiece (12.2 cm long)

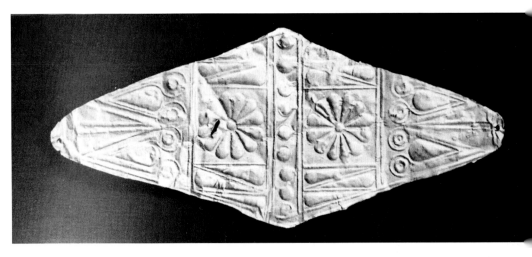

a, i   a, ii

a, iv   a, v

Above: Coins c. 550–450

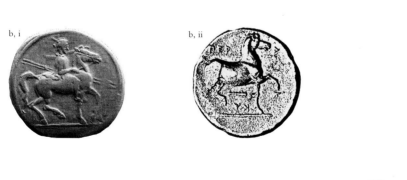

b, i   b, ii

b) Coins c. 450–360

b, iii   b, iv

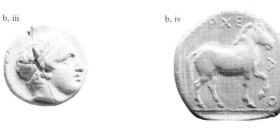

b, v   b, vi

8. Theatre at Aegeae

a, i a, ii a, iii a, iv a, v a, vi a,vii

9. *Above*: Coins of Philip II

(b) *Below*: Medallion of Philip (diameter 6.5cm). This gold medallion was found in a hoard, which had been buried c. 230 AD near Tarsus. The diademed head facing left is identified with Philip II. His cuirass is decorated on the shoulders with a Victory holding a trophy and below the neck with an eagle carrying off Ganymede. On the reverse a winged Victory, holding a palm-frond, is driving a four-horsed chariot, to celebrate the triumph of Alexander. The maker of the Medallion c. 200 AD copied early Hellenistic figures

10.(a) *Above*: Relief from Aeane

(b) *Below*: Phalanx of Pikemen

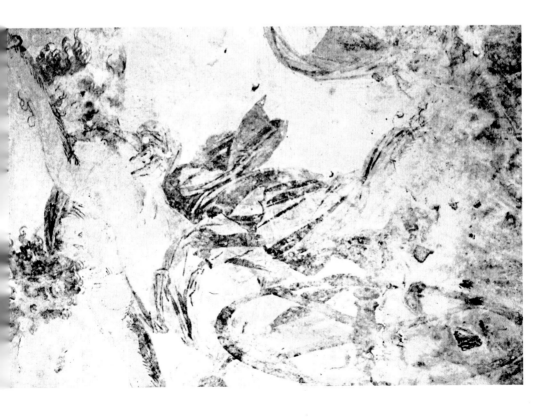

11.(a) *Left*: Rape of Persephone
(b) *Above*: Demeter mourning

12.(a) *Above*: Tomb of
Eurydice (4.485 m
wide)

(b) *Left*: Eurydice's Thro
(1.18 m wide)

omb of Philip II (fresco 5.56 m long)

14.(a) *Above*: Heads of Philip and Alexander (each 3 cm high)

(b) *Below*: Five ivory heads (each 3 cm high)

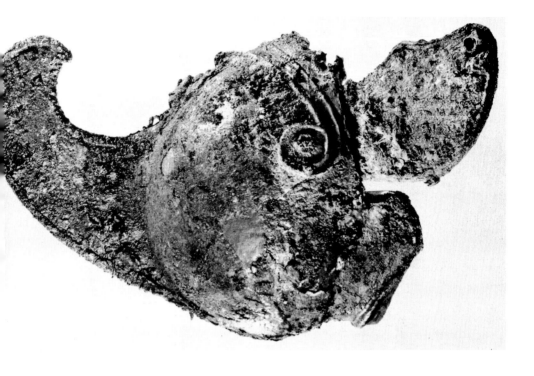

15.(a) *Above:* Cuirass and (*right*) (b) Helmet

16.(a) *Above*: Gold Larnax (37.7 cm long)
  (b) *Below*: Queen's Gold Diadem (central part)
  (c) *Right*: Silvergilt Diadem and Head of Silenus
      (diadem's diameter 21 cm)

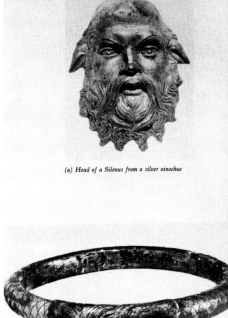

(a) Head of a Silenus from a silver oinochoe

When it became clear that Philip intended not to 'destroy', as Demosthenes was asserting, but to implement his policy of reconciliation, the plans of Athens and other states for further resistance collapsed, and Philip entered into agreements with individual city-states. He treated Thebes as guilty of sacrilege in breaking the treaty of alliance with Macedonia. Theban corpses on the battlefield had to be bought by their relatives, except for the members of the Sacred Band, who were accorded honourable burial as brave men. Theban captives were to be ransomed or else sold as slaves. Theban exiles were restored, an oligarchy of 300 was established (it executed or banished the previous leaders), and a Macedonian garrison was placed in the Cadmea (Thebes' citadel). There were plenty of precedents for such treatment of a treacherous ally in Greek history, and Philip no doubt intended it to be a warning to any would-be defector. At the same time, Thebes suffered less than Olynthus in 348. The Boeotians were compelled to restore the three cities which they had destroyed and to let survivors return to occupy them (Plataea, Thespiae and Orchomenus).

In the case of Athens, 2000 Athenian prisoners were restored without ransom, and the ashes of the cremated dead (1000 in number) were escorted to Athens by Alexander, Antipater and Alcimachus – a gesture of respect which no modern state has shown in victory. Philip undertook not to enter Attica, added to Athens a frontier town which was in dispute with Thebes, and made an alliance with Athens. The Athenian Alliance was disbanded; but Athens was to keep possession of five Aegean islands, including Delos and Samos. Philip did not ask for the extradition or penalizing of politicians who had opposed him, such as Demosthenes and Hegesippus. Even Demosthenes expressed surprise at his 'humanity' (*philanthrōpia*), though he chose 'not to dwell on it'. Towards other states Philip showed similar clemency. In particular he arranged through the Council of the Delphic Amphictyony to reduce the indemnity which the Phocians were paying and to pardon the Locrians of Amphissa. He rewarded his friends in the Peloponnese by awarding to them some frontier areas at the expense of Sparta, whose territory he invaded. He did not attack Sparta town.

The next step by the victor of the battle of Chaeronea was unprecedented. He presented to the Greek city-states the blueprint of a federal union for them to consider during the winter months. Isocrates, now ninety-eight years old, wrote a letter to Philip, urging him 'to end the madness and the imperialism with which the Greek states have treated one another, to bring them into concord, and to declare war on Persia'; he had a shrewd idea of what Philip intended, but he did not live to see it fulfilled. In spring 337 the blueprint was adopted by all Greek states of the mainland except Sparta and by many states of the Aegean islands at a meeting of their delegates in Corinth, at which Philip delivered an address. The federal union was adopted. Its members styled themselves 'the Greeks'. They undertook to observe a general peace among themselves; to take common action against any violator of the peace (our term being 'collective security'); to respect one another's existing constitution; each state to change its constitution only by legal process, to act within that constitution and not to engage in any revolutionary procedure contrary to current laws; and to suppress brigandage and piracy. One aim, like that of the European Union, was to call a halt to wars among its members. Another was to prevent revolutionary party-strife.

The government of the Community of the Greeks (*to koinon tōn Hellēnōn*) was vested in a Council of elected delegates from each state, the number of delegates and so of votes being determined in accordance with the military and naval strength of each state (thereby avoiding the risk of a lot of small states exploiting the principle of one state = one vote to outvote the large states, which alone could implement a policy). The decisions of the Council were binding on the member-states; and its powers included foreign policy, finance, jurisdiction and conscription in matters concerning the Community. The united states of Greece were not forced to make any internal changes. Some were tribal states; others democratic city-states; and others oligarchic city-states. Each was to enjoy liberty and autonomy within the limits set by the Community.

In summer 337 the Council itself met. It decreed the allocation of disputed territory to Megalopolis at the expense of Sparta, which perforce had to agree. It appointed officers called 'Defenders of the Common Peace'. But its most important acts were to enter into an offensive and defensive alliance with Macedonia for all time, and to appoint in the event of a joint war Philip himself as commander of the joint forces (*hegemon*).

It was probably at the autumn meeting that Philip addressed the Council on the subject of war against Persia. The Council voted to go to war, and Philip as *hegemon* 'arranged the size of contingents in accordance with the alliance' – that is, in relation to forces to be supplied by Macedonia. The placing of garrisons in Thebes and Ambracia as malcontents and in Corinth, the headquarters of the Community, was approved by the Council. In spring 336 a vanguard crossed to Asia, established control of the Hellespont and the Bosporus, and secured a bridgehead for the crossing of the main body, which was to follow in the autumn. Persia had been distracted by two years of dynastic confusion, and a new king, Darius Codomannus, ascended the throne in early summer 336. The avowed aim of the allies was 'to liberate the Greek states' in Asia and 'to exact retribution from Persia for her profanation of the temples' in the wars of 490–79. Philip, as commander-in-chief, asked Apollo of Delphi whether he would prevail over the Persian king. The answer of the Oracle was ambiguous: 'Garlanded is the bull, the end is come, the sacrificer is at hand.'

The skill with which Philip and his Macedonians advanced from being exposed to Athenian attack in 359 to become the leading military power in the Greek world in 338 is truly amazing. The chief casualties south of

Mount Olympus were incurred in 352 and in 338 on the Greek side by mercenaries who were feared by settled populations. Macedonian casualties were minimal. Philip tried to avoid embitterment of his Greek opponents, except for Thebes, which was punished for treachery. He succeeded to a considerable extent; for he was given Athenian citizenship by Athens, and various honours by Peloponnesian states. When the Community of the Greeks and Macedonia were at war with Persia, Athens and most of the other leading states sent envoys to confer gold crowns on Philip on the occasion of his daughter's wedding at Aegeae. It was a spontaneous form of congratulation.

The statesmanship which Philip showed in using his military victory to create a union of Greek states was without parallel. Coalitions had been formed by some Greek states for military ends, and the concept of a general peace had been exploited by Sparta and then Boeotia to bolster their own supremacy with Persian subsidies. But Philip brought about a practical form of union with a fully developed system of proportional representation and a complete apparatus of self-government. He was adviser and spectator in the opening stages. When the Council of the Union entered into alliance with Macedonia and gave Philip command of its own forces in the forthcoming campaign, a power block was created which was capable of guaranteeing peace throughout the Greek main-land, liberating Greek states in Asia and providing an outlet in Asia for the excess of population which contributed to the internal troubles of the Greek states. Hypercritical and censorious though Theopompus was, he appreciated the importance of Philip in his own Greek world when he wrote that 'Europe had never produced such a man all in all as Philip, son of Amyntas'.

The Macedonians and Philip

Because a king attracts attention, it is easy to overlook the Macedones who formed with him the Macedonian State. Philip alone was powerless. The Macedones took some basic decisions in the Assembly, and their agreement was essential to the policy which Philip put into effect. The demands made upon them were extraordinary. They and their families were cultivators of arable land, who had to sow and reap. They might be moved *en masse* to a new city on the frontier, where they had to build houses and fortifications. Their labour was needed for the development of cities, the making of roads and the construction of siege-engines on campaign; for there was no slave population in Macedonia, and the prisoners taken in war were probably settled on reclaimed lands. The Macedones played a leading part in the organization and administration of local affairs, whether in a city or a region.

Their primary function was military. Hardly a year passed in which a large proportion of them was not on active service, sometimes during the winter, and their form of warfare required constant training and physical fitness (see p. 61). Mutual trust and strict obedience were essential between soldier and soldier and between men and officers in a phalanx of pikemen. They had a justifiable pride in their own prowess and a love of the glory which victory brought them. But they were free men – free to criticize a commander or refuse their service. In 353, when Philip had led his army into the trap set by the Phocian commander, 'he himself was in the utmost danger and his despondent soldiers deserted him, until he put heart into the mass meeting and with difficulty made them obey orders.' Those orders included a ban on looting in the campaigns in Greece, and the silence of Demosthenes and other outspoken critics show that the order was obeyed. The courage and the steadiness of the pikemen who made a controlled retreat, the disciplined formations of the cavalry, and the co-ordination of infantry and cavalry in the breaking of what seemed to be an immensely strong position at Chaeronea marked a new era of Macedonian military expertise, which was to prove invincible in Asia.

The king depended also on the loyalty of the members of his own family and of the senior officers; for it was they who undertook military, diplomatic and civilian duties as his deputies. Philip saw to it that disloyal members of the royal house, such as Argaeus and Pausanias, were liquidated, with or without trial. On the other hand, he trusted and trained Amyntas, son of Perdiccas, after he was deposed; in 338 Amyntas led the diplomatic mission to Thebes, and shortly before Philip's death Amyntas was married to Cynna, a daughter of Philip. Of the sons who survived him (other sons died in action or of disease) Arrhidaeus was half-witted, while Alexander was so brilliant that Philip left him as his deputy in Macedonia in 340 and, as we have seen, placed him in command of the cavalry at Chaeronea in 338, when he was just eighteen.

Philip courted the loyalty of his senior officers by his lavish entertainment of them at banquets, which were remarkable not for the presence of courtesans and boys, as in sophisticated Athens, but for much drinking of unmixed wine, which the Athenians found extremely barbaric. The court was very much a man's world. The women of the royal household made their men's clothes and looked after the children, whereas at Athens a wealthy house had fifty household slaves to do the chores. Philip rewarded his leading Companions with generous gifts and sometimes estates, and he might admit their sons to the school of Royal Pages, where they waited on the king and performed other duties which in Athenian eyes were fit for slaves and not for free men. We do not hear of any plot or suspected plot by any Companions or Pages against the life of Philip in the years before his assassination.

Philip was twenty-three or twenty-four when he made his first marriage, but he lost no time in taking three more wives within the next year or so.

PHILIP II'S WIVES AND DESCENDANTS

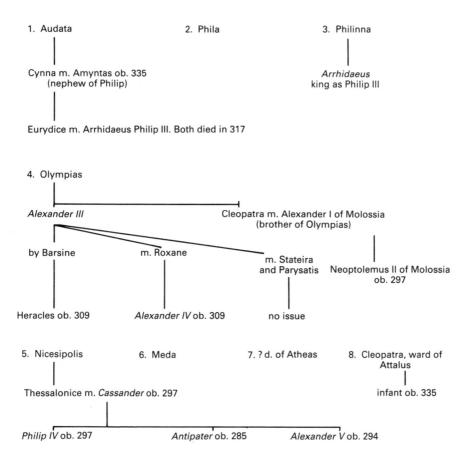

Note   Those who became king of Macedonia are in italics.

Fig 8   Philip II's wives and descendants

'He married always with war in mind', or, as we should say, with the
interest of a warring state in mind; for these marriages improved relations
with Elimeotis, Dardania, Larissa and Molossia. But it was even more
essential to beget heirs, and two of these wives bore the sons who were to
survive him – Arrhidaeus and Alexander. The marriage to Olympias was
also an affair of the heart; for they had met when they were being initiated in
the mysteries of the Cabiri on Samothrace, and he had fallen in love with
her. He married Nicesipolis, the niece of Jason, in 352; Meda, the daughter
of Cothelas, in 341; probably a daughter of the Scythian king Atheas in 340;
and Cleopatra, niece of a leading Companion, Attalus, in 337. He was said
to have fallen in love with the last of these, and that was probably true,
because in terms of state policy a marriage with a Macedonian commoner
brought no political advantage and it might lead to pretensions in that
commoner's family. As we have noted (see p. 35), all the wives were
queens, and all their children were legitimate members of the royal family.
When the royal women reached maturity, they were given in dynastic
marriages either to members of the royal house or to foreign kings and
princes. Thus Cynna was to marry the king of the Agrianes.

The sexual life of Philip interested Greek contemporaries and indeed
many since his time. Polygamy was normal for a Macedonian king for
reasons of state. The first clutch of wives, to which Nicesipolis was added,
must have seemed enough for the production of sons as possible heirs; but
by 341 it was clear that this was not so and that the first four wives were
almost too old to bear children. It was prudent in terms of state policy to
take two or three more young wives, and Cleopatra did bear him a child
before his death. Greek writers misunderstood or misrepresented the *mores*
of the Macedonian court, regarded Philip as licentious, and transformed his
wives into a legal wife and a number of chorus girls or prostitutes. They
then portrayed Arrhidaeus, when he became king, as a bastard; and they
suggested that when Philip married Cleopatra he was reducing his son
Alexander to the status of a bastard and Olympias to the status of a mistress
or a divorcee.

The most important woman in the household was the Queen Mother.
We see this in the case of Eurydice, the mother of three kings, who made a
dedication in her own name to the goddess Eukleia ('Fair Fame') at Aegeae.
It is probable that she was buried in the largest of all the built tombs at
Aegeae, which has recently been found by Professor Andronicos (see p.
98). Her position at the court attracted the attention of writers hostile to
Macedonia, as we have seen (p. 56). If the Queen Mother was dead, the
Queen-Mother-to-be ranked first in importance. By 337 Olympias, the
mother of Philip's choice as his successor, namely Alexander, was in this
position.

When Philip married Cleopatra, 'he dishonoured Olympias the mother of
Alexander and he made Alexander suspicious of himself'. The dishonour

92

was so serious that Olympias withdrew to the court in Molossia, where her brother was king, and her side was taken by Alexander, who was supported by five close friends of his own generation (Harpalus, Ptolemy, Nearchus, Erigyius and Laomedon). This was a major fracas, not just inside the palace but with repercussions in the state. Alexander withdrew with his mother and went on to stay with a client-king in Illyria, and his five friends were exiled (whether by fiat of the king or by some legal procedure we do not know). Alexander and Philip soon became reconciled, and Olympias was restored to honour as Queen-Mother-to-be; for the group of statues in ivory and gold which were commissioned in 337 by Philip to stand in his Philippeum at Olympia (see p. 95) represented Amyntas, Eurydice, Philip, Olympias and Alexander as the royal dynastic group. The wedding of Cleopatra, daughter of Philip and Olympias, to Olympias' brother Alexander, king of Molossia, and the presence of Alexander, son of Philip and Olympias, at Philip's side as his intended successor in 336 were public indications that the breach had been healed and that Olympias had precedence over Philip's latest wife. But Alexander's five supporters were still in exile at that time. We may conclude that Philip had made a very serious error in marrying a Macedonian commoner.

The other form of sexual relationship which interested Greek writers was paederasty, the mutual love of a man and a boy. That relationship was regarded as an important bond within a select military unit. Thus Xenophon wrote of a plan to form a battalion of such lovers; and when Philip saw that the Sacred Band of Theban 'lovers and beloved' had fought to the death, 'he wept and cursed any who supposed that anything dishonourable had been done by them or been suffered by them'. The association of the Royal Pages with the king and his entourage of leading Macedonians certainly led to paederastic liaisons and passionate jealousies (see p. 40–1). Aristotle is to be believed when he states that the assassin of Philip was motivated ultimately by a paederastic affair and a homosexual assault. Rumour had it that Philip was the beloved of Pammenes at Thebes and then the lover of Olympias' brother, Alexander, who lived as a boy at Philip's court; but such a rumour was to be expected, and the lack of other such stories suggests that Philip was primarily a heterosexual.

Because he expected to be absent on a campaign of months or years, Philip arranged in summer 336 the marriage of Cleopatra and Alexander, which would unite the Molossian and the Macedonian royal houses and present a united front within the royal families to the outside world. To this end he invited envoys from the states of the Greek Community, representatives from the Balkan Empire and leading Macedonians. The climax of the ceremony was held at dawn, when this company of guests was already seated in the theatre at Aegeae (see Plate 8). Philip was to enter with the two Alexanders. At the last moment he changed his mind. The Alexanders were sent ahead to take their seats of honour in the front row.

Philip, wearing a white cloak, came through the side-entry (*parodos*) into the theatre, while his Royal Guards and Bodyguards stood away from him so that he could be clearly seen. As the guests cheered, one of the Bodyguards ran forward and struck Philip dead. He was Pausanias, a senior officer. As he ran through the *parodos*, three of the Bodyguards went after him; but with the start he had he would have reached the horses which were waiting at the gate, had he not tripped over a vine-root and fallen. As he rose he was killed by the spears of the Bodyguards. (The court of inquiry into the crime belongs to the next chapter.)

Philip, at the age of forty-six, was at the height of his powers and his fortunes. There is every reason to think that he would have added victory over Persia to the laurels which he had already won as 'the greatest of the kings of his time in Europe'. The respect which was being shown him on the day of his death is notable. His entry into the theatre was preceded by a magnificent procession, which included statues of the twelve gods 'and with them a statue of Philip, fit for a god, since he was showing himself off as sharing his throne with the twelve gods'. The full meaning of these words is far from certain. Such a procession at Aegeae was possible only if the Macedonians had conferred 'divine honours' (which Alexander was to request for himself from the Macedonians without success) on their king in recognition that his achievement on their behalf was equivalent to that of a benefactor-god.

Philip's idea of 'sharing his throne' implied that the twelve Olympian gods had brought him to this pinnacle of success. In particular, Zeus had been associated with Philip's progress to attain 'divine honours'. The popular party at Eresus in Lesbos stressed the same association by erecting altars for the worship of 'Zeus Philippios', the Zeus who inspired Philip, probably in 340. And we should see nothing more than a similar compliment in the action of the popular party at Ephesus in 336, which placed a statue of him in their temple of Artemis; for there could be no question of a joint worship of Philip and Artemis, who were not compatible.

That Philip was worshipped as a god after his death is attested. In 317 the Macedonian soldiers and the Persians offered sacrifices at altars 'to the gods and to Philip and Alexander'. The citizens of Amphipolis 'sacrificed to Philip as a god', and there was a priest of Philip at Philippi, which implies a worship. The other worship of a Macedonian king was that of Amyntas III at Pydna, where there was a shrine, the Amyntaion. And if we compare the kingdom of 359 with that of 336, we shall conclude that no one deserved worship by Macedonians more than Philip, son of Amyntas.

We know from ancient writers that Alexander 'took every possible care for the burial of his father' at Aegeae. According to them, his remains were covered by a tumulus, at which the accomplices to the crime were executed; and the corpse of his assassin was exposed and later burnt 'above the remains'. The type of tomb under the tumulus could have been inferred from the description in Plato's *Laws* (see. p. 54). Then in 1977 Professor Andronicos discovered under such a tumulus the large, unplundered tomb, the shrine indicating worship of the dead king, the burnt swords of the two accomplices, the burnt trappings of the horses stationed for the escape of the assassin, the burnt spearhead used by the assassin, and the pyre of purification where the corpse of the assassin had hung above the cornice. What the ancient writers did not lead us to expect was the burial of a woman aged between twenty and twenty-six in the antechamber, with the offerings appropriate to a queen. Which queen? The most likely candidate is the Getic queen Meda, or the Scythian queen if Philip did marry the daughter of Atheas; for the particular offerings were appropriate to either, and they both belonged to peoples who killed a chosen wife and buried her together with the king.

The temptation to regard Philip as merely a cynical opportunist, who exploited the simple trust of the less capable, should be resisted. The evidence is very strong that he was typically Macedonian in holding strong religious beliefs. Heracles and Zeus were particularly important in his eyes. He had been brought up as a descendant of Heracles, son of Zeus, and from early in his life will have taken part in the worship of Heracles Patrous, his ancestor. His first coins carried the head of Heracles; his first city in Lyncus was called Heraclea; and he dedicated a statue of Heracles at the mouth of the Danube. In the earliest treaty of which we know the details, Philip and the Chalcidians were ordered by Apollo 'to sacrifice and do so with auspicious omens to Zeus the Accomplisher and the Highest'; and Philip in person swore to the treaty 'in the name of Zeus, Earth, Sun and Poseidon'. A copy of the treaty was to be set up in the temple of Zeus Olympius at Dium. His silver tetradrachms had the head of Zeus on one side and himself riding on the other side (see Plate 9a: vi, vii), the association suggesting that Zeus was the guardian of Philip.

Zeus had three aspects: supreme god of the Hellenes, father of Macedon, and progenitor of the reigning Temenid dynasty. All were relevant to the alliance of the Greeks and the Macedonians under the leadership of Philip after the battle of Chaeronea. It was in that period that a building was commissioned by Philip to be placed in the precinct of Zeus, not at Dium (where it would have commemorated a Macedonian victory) but at Olympia, the religious centre of the Greeks and the scene of Philip's victories with racehorses and chariot; such a location emphasized the Greek descent of the Temenidae and Philip's policy of integration with the Greeks. Gold-and-ivory statues of Amyntas, Eurydice, Philip, Olympias and Alexander were placed within the building, not as objects of worship but as dedicators of the building, which was thus a thanks-offering of the royal house to Zeus. (The name of the building, *Philippeion*, was not official; it meant 'Philip's building').

Apollo was also important in the eyes of Philip and of the Greeks. In the treaty with the Chalcidians, the approval of Apollo of Delphi was cited; the god was to be honoured with sacrifices of thanksgiving; and copies of the treaty were to be set up at Delphi. When the Olynthian leaders of the Chalcidian League broke their oath, they became exposed to the proviso in the treaty that 'many evils shall fall upon the perjurers'. As a worshipper of Apollo, Philip entered the Sacred War, drowned the impious temple-robbers, and placed the head of Apollo on his gold *Philippeioi*. He asked Apollo of Delphi in 336 whether he would prevail over the king of the Persians, and he was very happy in the answer, 'believing that the gods are fighting on his side, so that Asia will be subject to [the] Macedones'. It was a belief which Alexander was to inherit.

Most of the Athenian envoys in 346 found Philip charming and courteous; a generous host and a convivial drinker; brilliant in his power of memory and an excellent orator. In diplomatic negotiations he was a ready talker, affable and approachable; he was said to pride himself more on his diplomatic successes – such as his persuasion of the Greeks to form their Union – than on his military victories. In personal matters he was not vindictive; for though he had lost the sight of his right eye in the siege, he treated the people of Methone better than the people of Potidaea. He praised courage in his enemies, and he wept at the sight of the Theban Sacred Band, each man dead at his post. He and his Companions celebrated the victory at Chaeronea in a drunken party; but when he was rebuked by an Athenian prisoner (Demades) for behaving like Thersites, he came to his senses and set the prisoner free. He treated the Athenians thereafter with a humanity which, as we have noted, even Demosthenes acknowledged. On the other hand, he was relentless in punishing the perjury of his ally Thebes, and he ordered the drowning of the sacrilegious Phocian mercenaries after the Battle of the Crocus Field.

The key to Philip's personality is probably to be found in his religious faith, strengthened by the daily acts of worship which were customary for the king and confirmed by the favourable answers to his prayers. He showed extraordinary will-power and assurance from the start, dominated his commanders and his soldiers while living in close association with them, and fought in the forefront of battle throughout, though wounded seven times, lamed and blinded in one eye. His faith was that of his generation, polytheistic. One god he worshipped was Hermes, the god of trickery. His Balkan enemies claimed that he used verbal deceit, and in his early years he defeated the Athenians in their own game of double-dealing. 'Wealth' was a god in a play of Aristophanes. Where Macedonian gold could win a city, Philip preferred to spare his troops. He earned their love. In gratitude, his own people conferred on him 'divine honours', and his statue 'fit for a god' was carried after those of the twelve Olympian gods into the theatre in Aegeae. He had raised Macedonia from the depths of despair to a position of leadership by applying the principles of racial and religious tolerance. He had developed the hope of peace and prosperity on the same principles in the Balkan Empire. He had created the opportunity for the Greek states to govern themselves in unity and to co-operate with Macedonia in the invasion of Asia. His force of personality and his achievements were such that Theopompus, severe critic as we have noted that he was, declared that Europe had never produced so great a man as Philip, son of Amyntas.

Culture at the court of Philip

In 346 envoys from Athens, Sparta, Thebes, Phocis and Euboea competed for the favour of Philip. Pella had become the centre of power-politics in the Greek world, as in the Balkan world, and the web of diplomatic intrigue widened in the next ten years to include Greeks and barbarians of the Black Sea, the Propontis, the Aegean shores and islands, and some Persian satrapies. The power and wealth of Philip acted like a magnet in attracting to his court historians (Anaximenes of Lampsacus, Callisthenes of Olynthus, and Theopompus of Chios), philosophers (Euphraeus of Oreus, Speusippus of Athens, Aristotle of Stagirus, Theophrastus of Eresus), engineers (Polyidus of Thessaly, Aristobulus probably of Phocis), writers (Eumenes of Cardia, employed on *The Royal Journal*), and artists, as we shall see. Pella rivalled Athens as the leading cultural centre and foreshadowed the role of Alexandria. The interest of historians had already shifted away from the city-state to a wider canvas with the universal history of Ephorus, and now Anaximenes and Theopompus made Philip the central figure in their histories of their own time, the *Philippica*, even as Isocrates did in his *Philippus*.

The interest of Philip himself in the advancement of culture is undisputed. He chose Aristotle to teach Alexander in the school of Royal Pages, and when Alexander had graduated Aristotle stayed on during Philip's last two years. Philip planned the enlargement of Pella and the control of the rivers which gave Pella a riverine harbour. Although the excavations of the Acropolis are still under way, it seems likely that Philip first planned the complex of very large public buildings there and the swimming pool for the palace. He arranged the visit of Theophrastus as a botanist to report on the reclamation of land near Philippi. His patronage was enhanced by an open-handed generosity, which his enemies called bribery. The effect of these developments on leading Macedonians may be seen in the writings of Antipater on Macedonia's Illyrian wars, and in the substantial histories of Marsyas, Ptolemy and Nearchus, who went through the school of Royal Pages with Alexander and wrote later of Macedonian achievements.

A Letter of Philip, transmitted in the corpus of Demosthenic speeches, may well be the version which was sent to Athens in summer 340, stating his complaints against Athens and ending with the words 'since you are doing me as much damage as you can, I shall defend myself with justice on my side, and as I make the gods my witness I shall deal with the situation you have created'. It stopped short of a declaration of war; that was left to Athens. Philip's case was stated with clarity, directness and force. For instance, he contrasted Athens' condemnation of the tyrant Hippias for leading the Persians against the Greeks (in 490) and her appeal 'to me and all the other Greeks' to resist any Persian aggression (*c*.344) with her pursuit of a defensive alliance with Persia in 340. His criticism of 'the demotic speakers' at Athens is given not as his own observation but as the observation 'of those who have experience of your political system'. It is an impressive and measured letter. The mind behind it is certainly Philip's. The words may be his own, or those of his secretariate.

We have traced the development of tomb-architecture down to the description in Plato's *Laws* of a vaulted underground tomb, covered by a tumulus (see p. 54). In October 1987 Professor Andronicos discovered at Aegeae what was then the largest and the earliest such tomb. This vaulted tomb 5.8 metres high and consisting of two chambers – 5.51 × 4.485 metres and 2.5 × 4.485 metres – was set inside a parallelepiped of walls of *pōros* stone 10.6–10.7 metres long and 7.5–7.95 metres wide, which served in part to carry the weight of the soil. Within the tomb there was a dividing wall pierced by a two-leaved marble door. Another such door in the end wall faced outwards; but this wall had no architectural ornament on its outer face, which was close to the wall of the parallelepiped. However, the other end wall – that of the main chamber – was painted on the inside with a remarkable façade: a tall, central two-leaved door, four attached Ionic columns, a window-frame between each pair of columns, a frieze and a flat cornice. It is a delightful example of *trompe-l'œil*, creating the impression that one can enter a room beyond (see Plate 12a). The tomb had been robbed, but an inscribed Panathenaic amphora and other fragments provided a date *c*.344–40. It was probably that of a woman, and only one woman would have deserved so glorious a tomb; the Queen Mother Eurydice, as Andronicos has suggested. Other burials nearby were of women. Andronicos also discovered a tomb near that of Philip which seemed to mark a stage in the development of the built-tomb. In front of the rectangular foundations there were four free-standing Doric columns, fluted only on the outer face, because they had stood very close to the tomb's façade.

The tomb of Philip, 9.5 metres long externally, 4.46 metres wide and 5.3 metres high (both internally), consists of two vaulted chambers, connected by a two-leaved marble door, and a façade with a similar central door, an attached Doric column on either side of the door, two attached end-pillars, a frieze with a painting and a flat cornice on top (see Plate 13). The tomb of Alexander IV, built probably *c*.307, was of the same general design but lacked the two attached columns; and the painting, having been on leather and wood, has disappeared. Two circular shields in relief, one on each side of the door, carried signs of paint as decorative items. Two other built-tombs of the late fourth or early third century, excavated by L. Heuzey and K. Rhomaios respectively, had not a flat cornice on top but a pediment, which became a standard but not an inevitable feature of subsequent tombs. Each tomb at Aegeae had some individual features.

The strength of the vault and the function of the keystone were made known by Democritus in fifth-century Athens, and the vault was used then in an underground sewer. The credit for employing the vault in an artistic building must be given to Macedonian architects, who had to solve the problem of the weight of the soil of the tumulus pressing down on the building. The vault has aesthetic merits also. To anyone inside the building the impression of height and airiness is provided by the high vault in proportion to the width of the chamber. The Macedonian built-tomb was appreciated by Plato, who chose it as the most appropriate resting-place for his ideal statesman, and the principles of its architecture have been repeated in countless vaulted crypts and chapels over many centuries.

The façade was to be seen for a short time by the mourners – perhaps for the standard period of mourning – and then it was covered for ever by soil. It was not intended to represent a temple or a house. Rather, it was an architectural form in its own right, a holy place within which the spirit of the dead might live again, unseen by human eyes. It was to be a façade of beauty and dignity. To have had a vault-shaped façade corresponding to the vaulted chamber would have been neither beautiful nor dignified, and it would not have been suggestive of a holy place to contemporaries in the fourth century. The addition of a decorative façade to a building of a different shape has also had a long life (it has been a feature even of churches, banks, museums and railway stations), and it has not led the viewer to expect that the building itself would correspond with the façade.

It is the painting which creates the illusion, whether of depth or distance or movement. The *trompe l'œil* of the back-wall painting in the tomb of Eurydice is particularly delightful (see Plate 12a). The painted decoration of the façade of the tomb of Philip gives the illusion of depth to the epistyle, the triglyphs and the metopes (see Plate 13). The Rape of Persephone by Pluto, which inspired the marvellous fresco in the Tomb of Amyntas, is the subject of a painting on the flat back-rest of a huge marble throne, some 2 metres high and 80 centimetres wide, which had been left by the robbers of the tomb attributable to Eurydice (see Plate 12b). Pluto and Persephone stand upright, facing the viewer, in the chariot, and its four horses are springing into movement, two to one side and two to the other. The grasp of perspective is admirable. The publication of this painting is eagerly awaited.

Of Andronicos' discoveries, the masterpiece of painting is the fresco of the Royal Hunt, 5.56 metres long and 1.16 metres high, in seven colours of remarkable purity (see Plate 13). The three riders of the horses, which are in striking poses, are members of the royal house; for Macedonian law required them to be on horseback in this dangerous sport. The seven youths on foot are Royal Pages. The mature horseman with raised spear, who is about to strike the lion, which was reserved for the king to kill, is the dead king within the tomb, Philip. The central horseman, dominating the scene, is Alexander, laurel-wreathed, young and vigorous. The third horseman, wheeling his horse away from the viewer and so seen from the back, is probably Amyntas, son of Perdiccas, the royal next in precedence to Alexander. The composition excels in perspective, vigour of movement and detailed figures. Some points of resemblance with the Alexander-mosaic (see p. 134) have led Andronicos to suggest that the painter was Philoxenus of Eretria. In any case, it is clear that the finest painters of the period exhibited their work in Macedonia.

The offerings in the unplundered tombs show that Macedonia was also the home of the finest metalwork. Philip's weapons, helmet and cuirass were made of an iron which in its clean state had the shine of stainless steel, and they were decorated with engraving, gold fittings and gold miniatures (see Plate 15). The greaves were of bronze, one gilded pair in each of the three burials probably being for ceremonial wear. The queen in Philip's tomb was an archer; a pile of arrows and a quiver with a gold cover were placed beside her remains (see Plate 17a). An identical gold cover from the same mould was found in a Scythian royal burial of the same period. The very numerous silver vessels, often with miniature heads at the foot of the handle (see Plates 16c and 18b), were of the highest artistry, surpassing most of the vessels of the Rogozen treasure (see p. 74). They may have been a form of currency, comparable to the silver ingots shown on the coins of Damastium and related mints. The gold work is magnificent: a wreath of oak leaves and acorns for the kings (Philip and Alexander IV) and of myrtle leaves and flowers for the queen, the gold coffers in Philip's Tomb (see Plate 16a), the gilded silver diadem with the snakeskin pattern of the king (see Plate 16c) and the superb diadem with its bees and a tiny bird of the queen (see Plate 16b) and the gilded gorget (Andronicos' pectoral) of the queen (see Plate 17b).

Whereas the ore for the metalwork was mined within the kingdom, the ivory was imported. The workmanship of the ivory pieces in the tombs of Philip and Alexander IV is exquisite. The ivory heads, each an inch high, are most expressive portraits of real persons, probably Amyntas, Eurydice, Philip, Olympias and Alexander (see Plate 14b), of whom there were chryselephantine statues, made by the leading sculptor Leochares, in the Philippeum at Olympia. The ivory heads, hands and legs are all that survive of what had been five miniature chryselephantine statues. These and other ivory figures had been attached to a wooden couch. Other ivories in Philip's tomb and in that of Alexander IV represented religious scenes, especially of

Dionysus, Silenus, a Muse, Pan and two revellers – a jolly bearded man and a beautiful young girl (see Plate 18a). The portraits in ivory bear comparison with the portraits in marble by Lysippus of Sicyon, the greatest sculptor of this period, who made portraits of Alexander as a boy at the court of Philip.

In this collection of artistic treasures the guiding mind and the arbiter of selection was Philip, aided perhaps by his immediate entourage. There is a refined taste which is akin to Greek taste of the period, but it is combined with a display of wealth, a robust vigour, and an originality in architecture, which seem to be typical of Macedonia. The delight in plants and insects, in horses and chariots, in the hunt and the kill, in the realistic, lifelike portraits, and in fine arms and armour is characteristic perhaps of a relatively simple and unsophisticated society, at least as compared with contemporary Athens.

In Greece, too, Philip made his mark by erecting a building, unique in being within the sacred precinct of Zeus and Hera at Olympia (see p. 95). It was more grand than any of the Greek states' Treasuries. It was the first circular building (like the much earlier *tholos* at Delphi) and the first to have Ionic columns outside and attached Corinthian columns inside; for Olympia had hitherto been a centre of Dorian style. The use of gold and ivory for the statues of the Macedonian royals may have seemed ostentatious; for those materials had hitherto been used in Greece only for the statues of gods and goddesses. The site on the west side of the Altis was not far from the western metopes of the temple of Zeus, which portrayed the Twelve Labours of Heracles, the ancestor of Amyntas, Philip and Alexander.

The individual, whether as king or as an associate of the king, had far more importance in the Macedonian State than any individual or group of individuals in a socially democratic society. In consequence, realistic portraiture developed much earlier in Macedonia than in the Greek city-states. Thus the gold statues of Alexander I and his figure on his silver octadrachms were recognizably the king himself. It was probably from his reign, if not earlier, that a gilded statue of each king of Macedonia at his accession was dedicated at Dium, the earliest centre of the Macedonian State. The monumental tombs at Aiane yielded two striking portraits in local marble, one of a king wearing a diadem and the other of a distinguished commoner of the Elimeotae in archaic style (see p. 47), which may be dated within the first half of the fifth century BC. The silver didrachm of Amyntas III showed the king as a huntsman on horseback, and the Royal Hunt fresco on the tomb of Philip portrayed Philip and Alexander on horseback in a most realistic manner. Equally striking are the features of Philip, his closest relatives, and some associates in the ivory miniatures which were found in Philip's tomb. The Macedonian tradition of portraiture was to dominate the world of Alexander and his successors.

VIII

Alexander's Period of Conquest, 336–324

The establishing of Macedonia's authority

When a king or a president is assassinated, the fabric of the state and its foreign relations are shaken. Who is to succeed? Within Macedonia many were discontented with the demanding policies of Philip, and they suspected that his son Alexander, just twenty years old, would be no less ambitious. So 'they looked to Amyntas and the sons of Aëropus'. The son of Perdiccas III had been king as Amyntas IV, and Aëropus was a descendant through Aëropus II of an older branch of the royal house, starting from Perdiccas II. An Assembly of Macedones was quickly convened at Aegeae. Those who were entitled to attend were all soldiers and ex-soldiers of the King's Army (see p. 41); those who attended now came only from the vicinity of Aegeae. They chose Alexander, and the first leading Macedonian to accompany Alexander to the Palace was a son of Aëropus, also named Alexander. In the following days the oath of loyalty was taken by all the soldiers and ex-soldiers. Alexander chose his own Bodyguards, and he was provided with a Royal Infantry Guard.

The first need was to investigate the murder of his father. The fact that horses had been held ready for escape pointed not just to one assassin but to a plan for two or three accomplices, whose aim had probably been to kill Philip's like-minded son Alexander as well. Suspicion attached to the three Bodyguards who had killed Pausanias (see p. 94): Perdiccas and Leonnatus – both members of the royal house – and Attalus, uncle of Philip's youngest wife, Cleopatra; for they had prevented any interrogation of the assassin. Persons who would have been seated close to the king in the theatre were also suspected. When enquiries had been made, the Assembly of Macedones heard the charges of treason, the king prosecuting and the accused defending themselves (see p. 33–4). First, the corpse of the assassin was found guilty of treason: it was to be exposed for a time and then burnt. His three sons were to be executed, in accordance with the Macedonian law that a traitor's family had to be eliminated. Two sons of Aëropus were found guilty and condemned to death. The third son, Alexander, was acquitted; and he was exempted from the law concerning the relations of traitors, because the king interceded to save him. Other persons also were acquitted.

Because it was thought that there might have been yet other accomplices, investigations were put in train. Later in 336 some evidence was found which seemed to incriminate Attalus, then commanding part of the vanguard in Asia, and an officer was sent to arrest him or, if he resisted, to kill him; he did resist and was killed. His case was tried posthumously by the Assembly, who found him guilty of having been in treasonable correspondence with Macedonia's enemies, and his relations were condemned to death: among them Cleopatra and the baby she had borne recently to Philip. In the course of the winter Amyntas, son of Perdiccas III, was found guilty of having conspired to take the life of Alexander. He was condemned to death. The case was not yet closed; for Alexander suspected that Persia had had a hand in the conspiracy or conspiracies.

The first trial was held before the funeral. While the corpse of Philip was being guarded by his Friends, the chamber destined for his remains was being constructed. After the trial the corpse was cremated on a pyre. The sons of Pausanias, the two sons of Aëropus, and the horses which had been stationed for the conspirators were killed by or on the pyre. The burning ashes were doused with wine. The bones of the king were cleaned with alcohol, covered with fat, wrapped in purple cloth and placed in a gold coffer within the chamber, where the offerings were laid (see p. 98). The chamber was closed at once, although the internal plastering and the surface of the marble door were incomplete. The top surface of the vault was stuccoed, and a brick tray on the stucco received burnt objects from the pyre: a spearhead set upright (probably the assassin's weapon), two swords (of the sons of Aëropus), horse trappings, a bronze wine-pourer, and some gold acorns which had fallen from the king's wreath. The circumstances of the burial were very close to those of the burials of Patroclus and Hector in the *Iliad*, no doubt in accordance with the instructions of Alexander, who 'expended every possible care on the funeral of his father'.

As soon as the chamber was closed, Alexander set off 'at speed' (*citato gradu*); for there was news of trouble in Greece. During his absence the antechamber was completed and decorated, the façade constructed and the fresco of the Royal Hunt painted (see p. 99). The rotted corpse of the assassin had been set on a cross on the cornice of the façade; it was taken down and burnt. As we have seen, one of Philip's queens, aged between twenty and twenty-six had lain beside him on the pyre, and her cremated bones, treated with the same Homeric care, were placed in a gold coffer in the antechamber. It is uncertain whether she died a natural death, killed herself or was killed to accompany the king to the after-life (see p. 95). A circular tumulus of red soil was then constructed over the tomb of the king and queen.

The weeks which passed with the collection of evidence, the trial and the funeral were used by Alexander to impose his authority upon the leading Macedonians and the army by frequent exercises in weapon training and manoeuvres under combat conditions, in which much emphasis was laid on strict discipline. After the funeral of his father Alexander led his army south to the Pass of Tempe, which was held by dissident Thessalians. He and a group of mountaineers turned their position by cutting steps up a cliff, later known as 'Alexander's Ladder', and hastened to Larissa, where he relied on the support of the Aleuadae. Meetings were convened first of the Thessalian League and then of the Amphictyonic Council; at these Alexander was given the position and the powers his father had had. His army, reinforced probably by Thessalian cavalry, marched rapidly on Thebes, where a democratic party had seized power and voted to expel the Macedonian garrison from the Cadmea. The presence of Alexander and the army brought a change of heart in Thebes and an apology from Athens, which conferred honours on the young king.

The Council of the Greeks was convened at Corinth, to which the army advanced without encountering resistance, although Corinth's colony, Ambracia, had expelled its Macedonian garrison and Argos, Arcadia, Elis and Sparta had made some hostile moves. The Council elected Alexander to be *hegemon* (see p. 88), reaffirmed its alliance with Macedonia and its commitment to the joint war against Persia, and arranged to maintain its contribution to the naval and military forces already engaged in north-western Asia. In all these negotiations Alexander engaged in discourse with the Greek politicians and made 'seemly speeches'. He took no action against the dissidents, who lost support when he appeared. Alexander knew that there were pro-Macedonians and anti-Macedonians in every Greek state, and his hope was that the pro-Macedonians would prevail. He fortified that hope by exhibiting in Greece the power and the mobility of the Macedonian army during the autumn of 336.

Alexander had next to assert his authority in the Balkan Empire. He strengthened his defensive forces against the Illyrians, who were known to be planning a rebellion, and at the beginning of spring 335 he led the King's Army through the forested mountainous country of Pirin and Rila to the central plain of Thrace. By taking this route he cut any communications between the Odrysians of south-east Thrace and the Triballi, and he gave indirect support to the Macedonian and Greek troops holding the European approaches to the Hellespont. In two brilliant actions the Macedonians out-fought the 'republican Thracians' and the Triballians. They then joined a small Macedonian fleet on the Danube. Alexander felt an urge to cross the river and attack the Getae who held the far bank in force. During a June night, using local dug-out boats and making rafts, which were supported by tent-covers filled with straw as floats, 1500 cavalry and 4000 infantry made an unobserved landing. The amazed Getae were terrified by the sight of the massed cavalry squadrons in wedge formation and the bristling pikes of the phalanx, and they fled without fighting into the steppe country. This spectacular success caused the king of the Triballi and the republican Thracians to submit.

During the next three months Alexander enlisted some Thracian troops and arranged for the training of others who were to join in the invasion of

Asia. Reports of uprisings by the Illyrians drew him westwards to the court of the king of the Agrianians (near Sofia), a personal friend, who had already provided troops to Alexander and now undertook to attack another Illyrian group, the Autariatae. Alexander then marched at speed into Upper Macedonia and found just beyond his frontier a very large army of Dardanians. It was commanded by Cleitus, son of Bardylis, who had occupied a city of Dassaretis, called Pelium.

The Macedonians built a fortified camp as their base. The Dardanians sacrificed three boys, three girls and three black rams, delivered an attack and were defeated. They retired some to the walled city and most to the wooded heights overlooking the plain. Alexander intended to invest the city; but next day a large army of Taulantians, led by their king, Glaucias, joined the Dardanians. The Macedonian army of some 25,000 men and 5000 horses was now running short of supply. It soon became imperative for Alexander to withdraw to an area which had plenty of food and fodder. He did the unexpected. He put on a show of parade-ground drill by the phalanx of infantry, cleared his immediate flanks by sudden attacks, and at the head of his best cavalry captured a strongpoint (K2 on Fig. 9) which overlooked the route he intended his army to take through the middle of the enemy forces (via The Wolf's Pass). His catapult corps and his archers gave covering fire and his cavalry made a sudden attack, so that the enemy were driven back and the whole army went through the pass into the meadows around Lake Little Prespa. Not a man was lost. The Macedonians were now on home territory and obtained supplies from their own villages and towns. Three days later Alexander led an assault force through the pass at night, took the enemy by surprise and inflicted a decisive defeat, which was then exploited by his cavalry in a pursuit of nearly 100 kilometres. Later both kings made their submission and were left on their thrones as client-kings. Illyrian troops were to be provided for the invasion of Asia.

Alexander did not receive in person the submission of the kings, for news reached him that the Thebans were in revolt and had killed two Macedonian officers of the garrison. Setting off at once through the high country of North Pindus, where transhumant flocks of sheep were available for food and pack-horses could be replaced, the army marched in six days the 120 miles to Pelinna in north-west Thessaly. After a day of rest it covered the next 120 miles in six days to journey through the Pass of Thermopylae and encamp unheralded near Thebes. By this amazing march Alexander was just in time to isolate the rising. Athens had entered into alliance with Thebes, sent arms to the rebels and voted to despatch its citizen army to support Thebes. Demosthenes had received a large subsidy from Persia and envoys were on the way to the Persian court. Argos, Arcadia, Elis and Aetolia had allied themselves with Thebes, and Arcadian troops were approaching the Isthmus of Corinth. The Thebans and their allies had been

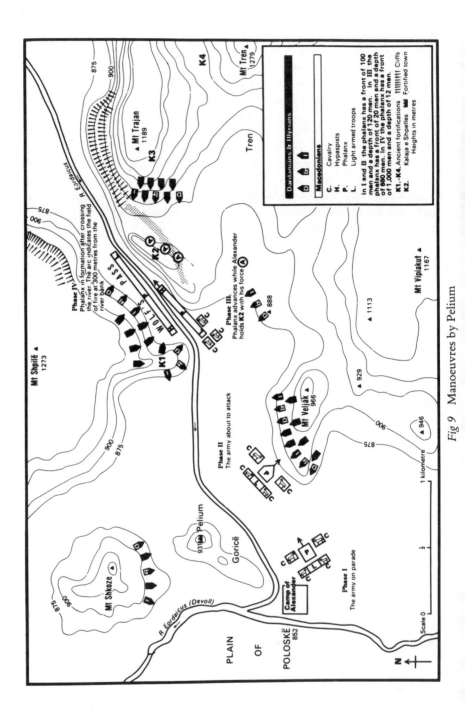

Fig 9 Manoeuvres by Pelium

encouraged by the report that Alexander had been killed and his army defeated in Illyria, a report fostered by Demosthenes.

If it had been true, the death of Alexander would have ended the oath of loyalty to him as *hegemon*. The Greeks could then have elected a Greek *hegemon*, maintained the Common Peace and rejected the alliance with Macedonia. If Alexander's successor as king should prove troublesome, the Greeks would be able to obtain subsidies and mercenaries from Persia, as Perinthus had done in 340. The news that Alexander was indeed alive, and his army at the gates of Thebes, caused consternation. The Arcadian troops turned back, expressing sympathy with the Thebans but saying that 'they were compelled by the times to give their personal service to Alexander'. They knew only too well what breaking their oath to the Common Peace and then being defeated might entail. The other allies made no move, not even Athens, though her army was within a few hours' march of Thebes.

Within the strongly fortified city the returned exiles who had seized power told the people that the Alexander in command of the Macedonian army was Alexander son of Aëropus, and making a sortie they killed some Macedonian soldiers. Alexander was careful to act not as a Macedonian commander but as *hegemon* of the Greeks. He therefore obtained troops from the nearby member-states of the Common Peace (Orchomenus, Thespiae and Plataea in Boeotia and the cities of Phocis), and he offered a pardon if Thebes would return to membership of the Common Peace and submit the rebel leaders to trial by the Council of the Common Peace. He was at pains to declare that the rebellion was against the Greeks and on the side of Persia. Inside the city some wished to negotiate, but the majority decided to fight, trusting in their walls, the help promised by their allies, and the hope of capturing the garrison in the Cadmea and using them as hostages.

On the third day after his arrival, Alexander was still waiting for a change of heart in the Theban people, his army being on the south side of the walls and within hailing distance of the beleaguered garrison. But his senior officers feared for the safety of the Macedonians in the Cadmea. Perdiccas, commanding a brigade of 1500 infantry, started an attack and he was joined by a second brigade-commander. Thereupon Alexander took charge. When the Thebans fled and left a gate undefended, the Macedonians and the Greeks joined hands with the garrison and gained the ascendancy in bitter street-fighting. Heavy casualties, estimated at 6000 were inflicted on the Thebans, particularly by the Greek troops who were repaying old scores. The prisoners numbered 30,000. The Macedonian losses were relatively small. Perdiccas, severely wounded, was later promoted for his gallantry to the rank of Bodyguard.

Alexander, still acting as *hegemon*, referred the decision about the fate of Thebes to the Council of the Common Peace. Not to have done so would have been tantamount to making the Charter of the Common Peace and the oaths he had taken to maintain the Charter null and void. The meeting of the Council was certainly attended by the delegates of the states hostile to Thebes, and perhaps not by the delegates of states which had made alliance with Thebes. In any case, the Council was guided by the Charter of the Common Peace, which prescribed the punishment of a defecting state, and by past treatment of states choosing to take the side of Persia. Some delegates proposed to kill all adult males and sell the rest of the population. In the end the Council decided to sell the 30,000 prisoners, outlaw Thebans who had escaped, raze the site except for the temples and – at Alexander's request – the house of Pindar, and rebuild two cities destroyed by Thebes (Orchomenus and Plataea). The sale realized 440 talents, which was no doubt used by the Council for the expenses of the war against Persia. Later, in October, the Council approved Alexander's request as *hegemon* for the provision of 2400 cavalry, 7000 infantry, and 160 warships with crews alone totalling 29,000 men for the spring offensive against Persia. Meanwhile, states which had allied with Thebes either executed those responsible for proposing the alliance, or changed their leaders, or made apologies. Athens even congratulated Alexander on his quelling of Thebes. He forgave everyone, excepting an Athenian mercenary general, Charidemus, whom the Athenian Assembly exiled.

The destruction of Thebes can be judged within its historical setting and also with long-distance hindsight. At the time both Alexander and the Council of the Common Peace had troops in Asia fighting against their common enemy, Persia, and their intention was to proceed with the campaign. The record of Thebes was bad. The people had voted to rise in rebellion in autumn 336. They had been pardoned then. Now they had actually rebelled. Should a second pardon by granted? It had to be borne in mind that even if pardoned now the Thebans would seek revenge, if possible with Persian subsidies, and that the example of a second pardon might encourage other malcontent states to rebel, with or without the leadership of Thebes and Sparta. On the other hand, the destruction of Thebes was likely to deter other states from rebellion. The long view is that reconciliation and then active co-operation between the Macedonians and the Greeks were more important even than the conquest of Persia, and that Thebes should therefore have been pardoned and given another chance to be loyal to the Charter of the Common Peace. On this view, blame for the destruction of Thebes attached both to the Council of the Common Peace and to Alexander himself.

On his return Alexander attended to religious affairs in Macedonia: a traditional sacrifice to Zeus of Olympus at Dium, a dramatic competition in honour of the Muses at Aegeae, and the distribution of animals for sacrifice to all ranks of the King's Army. He gave banquets at his Palace to his Friends, senior commanders and envoys sent from the Macedonian cities. Recently published inscriptions reveal that he transplanted the Bottiaeans of

Calindoea to another site and put Macedonians in their place; and in order to strengthen his new Macedonian Calindoea he attached to it the lands of three other Bottiaean cities and probably made the people of those cities live in dependent villages. During the winter he arranged for a survey of reclaimed lands near Philippi, which he allocated part to Philippi to possess, part to Philippi to cultivate at a rent, and part to Thracians to cultivate (no doubt on standard terms). The diction of the inscriptions shows that Alexander owned the spear-won land in both cases (Philip had defeated the Bottiaeans and the Thracians), and that he gave direct orders to the defeated peoples as his immediate subjects. On the other hand, he treated Philippi as an ally, owning its original territory, and he discussed with the envoys of Philippi the granting of further lands. When Alexander founded Macedonian Calindoea, 'he gave Calindoea to Macedones' – i.e. to the Macedones, who would decide in their Assembly which group or groups of Macedonians were to be sent there. One aim of Alexander in making these arrangements was to strengthen the Macedonian control of the route to Asia.

The campaigns of 335 had secured Alexander's base in Europe. During the winter 'he convened his senior officers and his leading Friends, and he consulted them about the crossing to Asia, for which he tabled his plan, the time of starting and the strategy of the war.' It was said that the most senior officers – Antipater and Parmenio – advised Alexander to beget an heir first; but that he refused (he was twenty-one at the time). In fact, the situation demanded an early crossing, because the bridgehead in Asia was under threat, and because the members of the Common Peace were already assembling ships and men. Alexander decided to cross to Asia and to attack the enemy in set battle as soon as possible. Because he intended to take to Asia his half-brother Arrhidaeus and three members of the royal house (Alexander, Perdiccas and Leonnatus), he appointed Antipater to be deputy-commander of the kingdom's military forces and deputy-*hegemon* in relation to the Greeks of the Common Peace. He entrusted his religious, ceremonial and financial duties to Olympias, the Queen Mother, who was highly respected and capable; she was to conduct state sacrifices, preside over festivals and handle the royal properties. He left in Macedonia 12,000 infantrymen of the King's Army, 1000 Companion Cavalry and 500 light cavalry; they were to defend the kingdom with the help of the local militias and to control the Balkan Empire. He selected for Asia 12,000 infantrymen of the King's Army, 1800 Companion Cavalry and 900 light cavalry. These troops 'having campaigned with Philip, were hardened in the hazards of war and almost undefeated in all their campaigns'; and they had weapons which the Asians and the Greeks in Persian service had not experienced – the pike and the lance.

In Asia during 336 the vanguard won control of the bridgehead and the west coast as far south as Ephesus, but in 335 it was driven back towards the bridgehead by superior forces of Greek mercenaries. During these operations the Greek cities killed or expelled the pro-Persian tyrants and juntas who were in power, and they set up democracies; but when the tide changed the pro-Persians took control again. The commander of the vanguard, Parmenio, tried to stem that tide by selling into slavery the Greek population of Gryneum, which had changed sides and been recaptured. Fortunately for the vanguard, the powerful Persian fleet had not been sent into the Aegean Sea, probably because Darius did not come to the throne until summer 336 and thereafter had troubles nearer home. Thus the Greeks and the Macedonians controlled the waters of the Hellespont.

In early spring 334 the main body crossed to Asia: the Macedonian part of the army including 1000 Agrianians and Archers and totalling 13,000 infantry and 2700 cavalry; the Greek allies being 7000 infantry and 2400 cavalry; the Balkan troops 7000 infantry (Thracians, Triballians and Illyrians); and 5000 Greek mercenaries, hired in Greece. The numbers of Macedonians and Greeks serving in the vanguard is not known, but we may estimate the total forces in Asia now as approaching 40,000 infantry and 6000 cavalry, a considerably larger army than Philip had commanded at Chaeronea or Alexander in the Balkans. The naval forces consisted of the Greek fleet of 160 triremes with crews totalling 29,000, and the Macedonian fleet of 22 triremes and 38 smaller warships, their crews numbering 7000. In terms of manpower, if we exclude the vanguard, the Greeks of the Common Peace supplied 38,000 men and the Macedonian kingdom 23,000 men. The size of the Greek contribution is the more remarkable when we recall that four years had not passed since the battle of Chaeronea.

Alexander needed to impose his will on the army. It consisted of several nationalities, each using its own language and its native weapons, and the Macedonians were in the minority. The various parts had never fought together. The Greeks had been allies only since 337, and the Balkan tribesmen had been subjugated only in 335. If the Macedonians should suffer defeat, the Greek and the Balkan troops might turn against them. For the set battle which Alexander wanted he could not combine the Macedonian phalanx with the Greek phalanx, which had different weapons and little training. He had to rely primarily on the Macedonians. They admired Alexander's ability, but they must have compared his experience at twenty-one with the long experience of Philip's finest general, Parmenio. Alexander acted with extraordinary boldness and, as it was to prove, judgement; and when the battle came, he himself commanded the Macedonians and placed Parmenio in command of the Greek cavalry.

As soon as the main body was encamped on the Asiatic shore, Alexander set out to find the enemy army. He took only the Macedonians, the Agrianians and the Archers, and the Thessalian cavalry – in all, 13,000 infantry and 5100 cavalry. After noon on the third day his scouts reported that the Persians were holding the far bank of the river Granicus. As Alexander continued to advance, he saw that the much superior number of

Persian cavalry held the level ground beyond the steep bank of the river, and that a very large force of Greek mercenary infantry held the ridge behind that level ground. The numbers were estimated at 20,000 cavalry and 20,000 mercenaries, all first-class troops; but the value of their superior numbers was largely lost through dispersal, in that Alexander could attack the cavalry first and then the infantry. He deployed his army at once into line of battle. The infantry phalanx formed the central part; the cavalry formed the wings but the Agrianians and the Archers were posted on the extreme right. The line was of the same length as the cavalry line of the enemy, some 3 kilometres; and because the phalanx would pin down the enemy cavalry in the centre, his cavalry on the wings would not be heavily outnumbered.

Alexander, wearing a white-plumed helmet, made himself deliberately conspicuous, so that the enemy commanders stationed themselves with massed cavalry on the opposite bank. To attack them he sent 1000 cavalry from his immediate left and from beyond them the Infantry Guard of 1000 Hypaspists into and across the riverbed. As soon as they were engaged in a desperate scramble up the bank, Alexander took all the right wing into the riverbed and extended it upstream against the current until his extreme right wing overlapped the enemy. The whole army now moved into action, Alexander leading the Cavalry Guard into the mêlée where both sides had suffered considerable casualties and the Persian commanders were posted. In fierce fighting Alexander unhorsed two commanders, was struck on the helmet by a scimitar and was saved from death only by Cleitus, son of Dropides. The long weapons, the strength and the experience of the infantry and the cavalry alike forced back the Persian cavalry, who fought with javelins and scimitar, and the Agrianians and the Archers wrought havoc from the flank. Finally the cavalry fled, leaving 1000 dead. The 20,000 Greek mercenaries outnumbered the Macedonian infantry. But their flanks and rear were exposed to the victorious cavalry and light-armed, while they themselves could make little headway with their spears against the massed pikes of the Macedonian phalanx. Only 2000 lived to surrender. Because they were Greeks fighting against the liberators of the Greek cities, they were sent to labour camps in Macedonia. Alexander lost some 85 cavalrymen and 30 infantrymen, the latter figure showing the effectiveness of the pike against the spear in phalanx fighting.

Alexander's authority was henceforth unquestioned. The report of his personal heroism and of his brilliant generalship won the loyalty of the soldiers of all nationalities under his command. The victory was in the cause of Greek liberty in Asia, and this aspect of the crusade was advertised at Athens by the dedication of Persian armour to Athena with the inscription 'Alexander, son of Philip, and the Greeks, Sparta excepted, gave these from the barbarians in Asia'.

The winning of naval supremacy by the Macedonians and the Greeks

In 394 a rising in Greece, encouraged by Persian gold, had forced Sparta to recall her liberating army from Asia, and the control of the sea had passed to Persia and her Greek allies. Would history be repeated? Alexander left his Macedonian fleet to protect the Hellespont, and he took to Miletus his Greek fleet of 160 triremes, provided mainly by small island-states. The Persian fleet of 400 triremes anchored off Cape Mycale and offered battle. Parmenio was said to have advised engaging; but Alexander disagreed, because his crews were untrained in comparison to the Phoenician, Cyprian and Egyptian crews, and because he was not prepared to lose Macedonians serving as marines. Moreover, he saw that a defeat at sea would counteract the victory of the army and might lead to a rising on the Greek mainland. Another factor, strange to us but important then, was the interpretation of a portent, an eagle (the bird of Zeus) standing on the beach astern of the Greek ships. Parmenio thought it favourable to action at sea; Alexander understood it to mean that victory over the Persian fleet would be won on land, by capturing the Phoenician and Egyptian bases on which the fleet relied for replacements of crews and gear. Having decided not to engage, Alexander disbanded the bulk of the Greek fleet, which 'was useless and involved great expense' at a time when 'he was short of money'. He kept a flotilla, which included the Athenian squadron of twenty triremes as their crews were the most experienced, and he used it mainly to transport his siege-train.

The Persian navy, concentrated under the command of Memnon, a Greek mercenary general, had four possible objectives: to hold a base on the coast from which to attack areas under Alexander's control; to win or capture the Aegean islands; to master the Hellespont; and to use Sparta as a base from which to instigate a rising on the mainland. Memnon started with the first and succeeded in holding two citadels at Halicarnassus (Bodrum), from which forays were made inland later. He moved to the second in 333, capturing Chios and Lesbos, except for Mytilene, which he stayed to besiege instead of pressing forward to the Hellespont. Alexander had time to send 500 talents to the Council of the Common Peace with instructions to reinforce the Macedonian fleet at the Hellespont, which was to take offensive action: and to send 600 talents to Antipater with orders to hold the western Aegean. Memnon died that summer. By then the Greeks had reassembled a fleet again of 160 triremes and the Macedonian fleet was reinforced. Memnon's successor, Pharnabazus, dissipated his forces by tackling three objectives: he reached Callipolis in the Hellespont, sent subsidies to Sparta and other states, and made a Persian salient from Halicarnassus inland. But the allied fleets halted him in the western Aegean and in the Hellespont.

In the autumn Pharnabazus' Greek mercenaries were recalled to join the army of Darius, but even so Pharnabazus advanced with 100 ships to

Siphnos, where he conferred with Agis, king of Sparta, about a rising in Greece. News then arrived of the utter defeat of Darius at Issus. Pharnabazus gave Agis ten ships and a meagre thirty talents, and he wintered at Chios, while Alexander began the siege of Tyre. In 332 the balance of naval power shifted. Cyprian and Phoenician ships, other than those of Tyre, deserted to Alexander, Rhodian ships joined him, and Antigonus defeated a Persian offensive inland of Halicarnassus; meanwhile the Greek fleet of 160 ships and the Macedonian fleet, both commanded by Macedonians, were regaining control of the Aegean islands, in which the people rose against pro-Persian tyrants, imposed by Pharnabazus.

When Alexander entered Egypt in December 332, the thalassocracy of the Eastern Mediterranean and of the Black Sea was won for Macedonia and the Greeks of the Common Peace. It had eluded the grasp of Athens in the fifth century, and it was to stay in the hands of Macedonians, commanding crews of various nationalities, until the intervention of Rome in Aegean waters. Its importance for the maritime trade and the general prosperity of the area were fully realized by Alexander. He encouraged the growth of the Greek cities and founded new cities on the Asiatic coast, and he built the chief port of exchange, Alexandria in Egypt. The Council of the Common Peace sent congratulations to him in Egypt for his services in their common cause. When Agis organized a rising in Greece in October 331, he had lost all contact with Persia and he was not joined by any maritime state. He was too late by two years.

Alexandria, being linked by the Nile and a Persian canal to the Red Sea, was a centre of exchange for goods from Africa and from Arabia. As Alexander campaigned eastwards, he crossed the great rivers of Meso-potamia and learned about the Persian Gulf, and later he sailed down the Indus into what he thought was probably the circumambient Ocean of Greek philosophical theory. With great daring he sent off a fleet of small warships, which proved this theory correct by sailing into the Persian Gulf in winter 324/5. Alexander built dockyards and a basin for 1000 ships at Babylon on the Euphrates, attracted crews and technicians from the eastern Mediterranean by high wages, and founded a city on the coast west of the Euphrates; for he intended Babylon to be a centre of exchange, similar to Alexandria, and he organized attempts to circum-navigate Arabia and link the Persian Gulf to the Red Sea, something which was achieved later. His understanding of waterborne traffic on the great rivers, his creation of large riverine harbours and his opening up of what was to be an intercontinental trade on the high seas were among his claims to greatness.

The winning of military supremacy by the Macedonians and the Greeks

Although the vanguard had been fighting for two years in Asia, Alexander marked his crossing of the Hellespont as the beginning of a new venture. He made sacrifice on both shores to deities and heroes of the Trojan War (Zeus and Achilles, his ancestor through Olympias; Athena of Troy, Poseidon and Priam), and he dedicated his own armour to Athena of Troy and took from her shrine a shield dating from the Trojan War, which was to be carried before him into battle. These acts gave meaning to the claim which he made as he leapt ashore from his flagship and drove his spear into Asian soil with the words 'from the gods I accept Asia, won by the spear' and with the prayer 'may these lands receive me as their king not unwillingly' (see Plate 21). From that moment he acted as 'King of Asia', owner of the land 'Asia' by divine favour and king in relation to the Asians. His army was forbidden to pillage (Agesilaus had collected 1000 talents of loot in one campaign in 395), honourable burial was given to the Persian commanders and their Greek mercenaries, and the peasants who came down from the hills after the battle at the Granicus river were told 'to return to their own things'. Moving southwards after the victory, he made dedications in thanksgiving to Athena of Troy.

When the Persian governor of Sardis surrendered the citadel and treasury, Alexander treated him as one of his Friends; and he declared the Lydians free (from Persian rule) and entitled to follow their traditional customs. In Lydia he made a start with the selection and training of Asian troops who were to serve the King of Asia: for 300 Lydian cavalry and 2600 Lydian infantry joined him in east Iran in 330. In Caria he accepted adoption by a dispossessed queen, Ada, and made her ruler, and thereby won the support of all the Carians, the envoys from their cities 'promising to co-operate in all things'.

At the same time Alexander was liberating the Greek cities from Persian rule through the surrender of Persian garrisons or by force of arms. 'He ordered the juntas everywhere to be overthrown, democracy to be established, the legal code to be obeyed, and tribute hitherto paid to Persia to be abolished.' In this last respect the Greek cities were favoured. Like Philippi, they owned their own territory. But the lands of the Asians were 'spear-won', and rent was therefore paid in the form of tribute to the owner, the King of Asia. The distinction between the Greek city and the native villages is seen in an inscription from Priene, in which Alexander said of the villagers' land 'I know that the land is mine'. He captured Miletus and the lower city of Halicarnassus by force of arms, the latter despite a powerful defence.

In a long winter campaign he overcame opposition in Lycia, won over the Greek cities in Pamphylia, and turned inland to meet at Gordium a detachment of the army, which had marched from Sardis through the central Anatolian plateau. His wheeled transport followed the excellent Persian roads, and in rough country his Thracian troops made new roads; and supplies were provided by his new subjects or captured in Persian depots. At Gordium in April 333 Alexander removed or cut the famous Gordian knot from the yoke-pole of the chariot of Gordius, a Phrygian king of long ago who had become King of Asia. The local story was that the untier of the knot would become King of Asia. That night there was thunder and lightning. Next morning 'Alexander sacrificed to the gods who showed the signs and the loosening of the knot'. His conquest-to-be of Asia was thus reaffirmed by the gods.

The next campaigns were into the area north-east of Ancyra (Ankara) and then into Cilicia, where he was delayed by illness at Tarsus. On his recovery he liberated the last Greek cities in Asia and followed the vanguard commanded by Parmenio to Issus, where he left his sick and wounded; for he expected to engage the army of Darius, which was reported to be in north Syria. But while Alexander marched south along the coast, Darius marched north on the inland side of Mount Amanus, and descending to the head of the Gulf mutilated and killed the sick and wounded at Issus. He then adopted a very strong defensive position on the river Pinarus (Payas). If that position should hold, Alexander's army would starve, since it was cut off from its base of supply. For the decisive battle Alexander had maintained the strength of his élite troops by receiving at Gordium 300 Macedonian cavalry, 3000 Macedonian infantry and 350 Greek allied cavalry; but his army was certainly much smaller than that of Darius, which was said to have huge numbers of cavalry, 30,000 Greek mercenary infantry, 60,000 Persians armed as hoplites, and 20,000 light infantry.

Because Darius stayed on the defensive, Alexander had the initiative. As he descended from the pass to the plain, his right wing drove back the enemy force on its right flank (F-F on Fig. 10) and he used some dead ground to alter his dispositions without being observed by the enemy. When he reached his intended position, each wing of his 4-kilometre line was composed of cavalry and light-armed infantry. The ground on the left of the line was level and the riverbanks on his side were no obstacle; the ground facing the right wing was sloping, the banks low and the riverbed strewn with boulders. The infantry in the centre of the line faced steep banks of conglomerate rock, except on its extreme right where the banks were low. Here Alexander posted himself at the head of the Royal Infantry Guard. Across the river he saw the Persian infantry armed as hoplites and the Persian archers, famous for their skill. Once within bow-shot, Alexander and his men rushed into the riverbed, ran through the boulders, formed up and charged with their bristling pikes into and through the Persian infantry. The Companion Cavalry followed through the gap and overcame the inferior number of Persian cavalry, while the light-armed infantry and cavalry on his right routed their opponents.

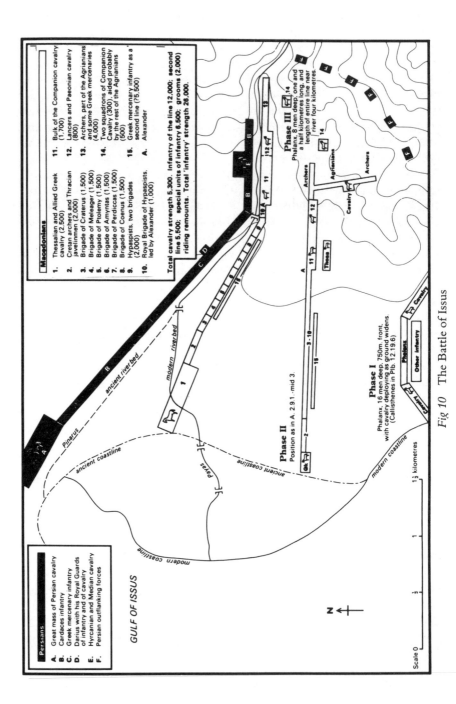

Persians

A. Great mass of Persian cavalry
B. Cardaces infantry
C. Greek mercenary infantry
D. Darius with his Royal Guards of infantry and of cavalry
E. Hyrcanian and Median cavalry
F. Persian outflanking forces

GULF OF ISSUS

Macedonians

1. Thessalian and Allied Greek cavalry (2,500)
2. Cretan archers and Thracian javelinmen (2,000)
3. Brigade of Craterus (1,500)
4. Brigade of Meleager (1,500)
5. Brigade of Ptolemy (1,500)
6. Brigade of Amyntas (1,500)
7. Brigade of Perdiccas (1,500)
8. Brigade of Coenus (1,500)
9. Hypaspists, two brigades (2,000)
10. Royal Brigade of Hypaspists, led by Alexander (1,000)
11. Bulk of the Companion cavalry (1,700)
12. Lancers and Paeonian cavalry (800)
13. Archers, part of the Agrianians and some Greek mercenaries (4,000)
14. Two squadrons of Companion Cavalry (300), aided probably by the rest of the Agrianians (500)
15. Greek mercenary infantry as a second line (75,500)
A. Alexander

Total cavalry strength 5,300. Infantry of the line 12,000; second line 5,500; special units of infantry 6,500; grooms (2,000) riding remounts. Total 'infantry' strength 26,000.

Phase I
Phalanx, 16 men deep, 750m. front, with cavalry deploying as ground widens (Callisthenes in Plb. 12.19.6)

Phase II
Position as in A. 2.9.1.-mid 3.

Phase III
Phalanx, 8 men deep, one and a half kilometres long, and length of entire line near river four kilometres

Fig 10 The Battle of Issus

116

The force that passed through the initial gap swung left, Alexander now mounted and leading the Royal Cavalry Guard towards Darius. Meanwhile the Persian cavalry had crossed the river and attacked the Greek cavalry on Alexander's left wing. Fierce fighting ensued and the excellent Thessalian cavalry, keeping in formation and charging squadron by squadron, more than held their own. The main infantry phalanx was now in the riverbed, trying to force its way up the cliffy bank. The right-hand brigades were helped by Alexander's attack from the flank, but the four brigades on the left were suffering losses; for whenever any group reached the top of the bank the Greek mercenaries charged in deep formation. But by now Alexander and his Companions, followed by the Royal Infantry Guard, were attacking the Royal Cavalry Guardsmen of Darius, who, standing in his chariot, turned to flight rather than risk being killed or captured (see Plate 22). Even the successful Greek mercenaries were now taken in the flank and rear, and flight became general as the news spread that Darius was on the run. The Macedonian and the Greek cavalry, pursuing for 37 kilometres, inflicted very heavy losses on the panic-stricken Persian cavalry, which crashed into and rode over one another at the narrow crossings of the gulleys.

In this battle, because he was to be a leading combatant, Alexander had issued detailed orders to all brigade and squadron commanders in advance. He had foreseen actual and possible developments; for instance, he had a second infantry line, which was to face about if the Persian cavalry were to break through on the left and attack from the rear. In the event 'it turned out as Alexander supposed'. Everything depended on his charge with his best infantry. The cavalry had no chance of crossing the riverbed there success-fully; the Persian archers would have made havoc of the unprotected horses picking their way through the boulders, and the cavalry would not have been able to charge an unbroken infantry line on the other bank. Alexander used the only possible way of breaching the enemy's defensive position, which was well chosen except that it did not give much play to Darius' far superior numbers.

It was a victory also of morale. Alexander had paid the greatest possible honour to those who had fallen at the Granicus river: ceremonial burial of the men and their weapons, bronze statues of the twenty-five Companions, and remission of taxes for parents and children. He had visited the wounded and heard each man's story. On this occasion, as the army was advancing slowly, Alexander rode along the line naming those of all ranks who were distin-guished for acts of courage. The men shouted to him: 'Do not delay but charge at them.' The phalanx was given a virtually impossible task. Yet 'the Macedonians were determined not to fall short of Alexander in action and not to dim the glorious record of their phalanx, famed as invincible up to that day.'

Alexander could have advanced eastwards, but he had still to defeat the Persian fleet on land. So he marched south, receiving the submission of the

Phoenician cities until Tyre, built on a fortified island half a mile offshore, refused to admit him within its walls. For Tyre, especially favoured by Persia, was the leading naval state and hoped for help from her powerful colony, Carthage. The siege lasted for seven months. Both the defence and the attack were heroic. The balance changed with the desertion of squadrons from the Persian fleet and the blocking of Tyre's harbours. When they forced their way into the city, 'the Macedonians went to all lengths in their rage, embittered by their own sufferings and by the Tyrians having killed Macedonian prisoners in the sight of the army, hurling them from the 150-foot wall into the sea'. Tyre suffered the fate of Thebes. Honours were paid to some 400 Macedonian dead with full-dress parades and athletic contests. The wounded were more numerous, and Alexander was one of them, a catapult bolt having penetrated shield and cuirass into his shoulder.

The last stronghold to resist was Gaza, defended by Arab mercenaries to the last man. The women and children were sold into slavery, and the stronghold was repeopled with local tribesmen and garrisoned. The army, supplied by the fleet, marched the 140 miles through the Sinai desert in seven days and was greeted by cheering crowds of Egyptians and the surrender of Egypt by the Persian governor. Alexander occupied the richest country of the Mediterranean without the loss of a single life, and he made a treaty of friendship and alliance with the Greek city-state Cyrene. He personally engaged in the founding of Alexandria on the western branch of the Nile delta, linked to river and sea, like the harbour of Pella. The circuit of its walls was to be 15 kilometres long, and its status was to be that of a Macedonian city, subject to the king's edicts but otherwise self-governing. He had already founded or was soon to found seven cities on the coasts of the Gulf of Issus (one of them an Alexandria, now called Iskenderun) and of Syria and in Jordan and Israel; and he refounded Tyre and held a dramatic and an athletic festival there. These acts show his confidence that he would prevail and win Asia. That confidence had been strengthened by the declarations or indications of Oracles at Didyma and Erythrae that he was 'born of Zeus', and he now took an army over 300 kilometres to the Oracle of Zeus Ammon in an oasis of the Libyan desert. There he consulted the god. The answers were to his liking, but secret. The fact that thereafter he showed a special reverance for Zeus Ammon means that his belief in his future was confirmed.

Darius assembled another huge army and adopted a position in the level plain of Gaugamela, where he had prepared runways for his new weapon, horse-drawn chariots with scythes protruding from the wheels, sides and front. Their task was to charge into and break the ranks of the Macedonian phalanx. Some of his extremely numerous and excellent cavalry had been equipped with lances and swords in the Macedonian style, but the majority had javelins and other missiles as their weapons. The infantry did not have any standard equipment or formation, and the best units – 1000 Guardsmen

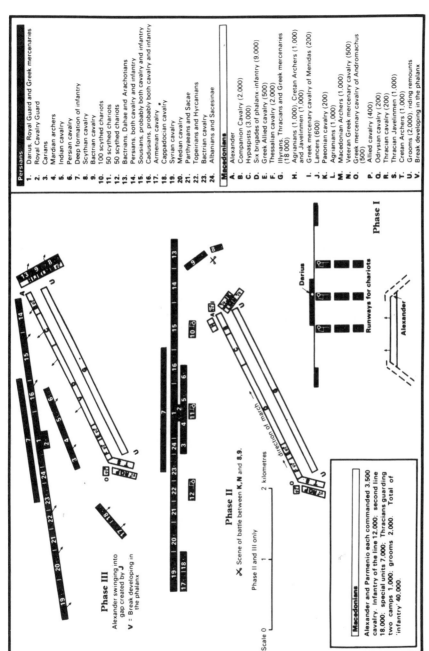

Persians

1. Darius, Royal Guard and Greek mercenaries
2. Royal Cavalry Guard
3. Carians
4. Mardian archers
5. Indian cavalry
6. Persian cavalry
7. Deep formation of infantry
8. Scythian cavalry
9. Bactrian cavalry
10. 100 scythed chariots
11. 50 scythed chariots
12. 50 scythed chariots
13. Bactrians, Dahae and Arachotians
14. Persians, both cavalry and infantry
15. Sousians, probably both cavalry and infantry
16. Cadusians, probably both cavalry and infantry
17. Armenian cavalry
18. Cappadocian cavalry
19. Syrian cavalry
20. Median cavalry
21. Parthyaeans and Sacae
22. Toperians and Hyrcanians
23. Bactrian cavalry
24. Albanians and Sacesinae

Macedonians

A. Alexander
B. Companion Cavalry (2,000)
C. Hypaspists (3,000)
D. Six brigades of phalanx-infantry (9,000)
E. Greek Allied cavalry (500)
F. Thessalian cavalry (2,000)
G. Illyrians, Thracians and Greek mercenaries (18,000)
H. Agrianians (1,000), Cretan Archers (1,000) and Javelinmen (1,000)
I. Greek mercenary cavalry of Menidas (200)
J. Lancers (600)
K. Paeonian cavalry (200)
L. Agrianians (1,000)
M. Macedonian Archers (1,000)
N. Veteran Greek mercenary cavalry (500)
O. Greek mercenary cavalry of Andromachus (500)
P. Allied cavalry (400)
Q. Odrysian cavalry (200)
R. Thracian cavalry (200)
S. Thracian Javelinmen (1,000)
T. Cretan Archers (1,000)
U. Grooms (2,000), riding remounts
V. Break developing in the phalanx

Phase III

Alexander swinging into gap created by **J**

V = Break developing in the phalanx.

Phase II

✕ Scene of battle between **K,N** and **8,9**.

✕ Scene of battle
Phase II and III only

Scale 0   1   2 kilometres

direction of march

Phase I

Darius

Runways for chariots

Alexander

Fig 11   The Battle of Gaugamela

Macedonians

Alexander and Parmenio each commanded 3,500 cavalry. Infantry of the line 12,000; second line 18,000; special units 7,000. Thracians guarding two camps 1,000; grooms 2,000. Total of infantry 40,000.

119

and 6000 Greek mercenaries – together with the 'Kinsmen Cavalry', were stationed with Darius in the centre of his 5-kilometre line (see Phase II in Fig. 11). If Alexander should aim his attack frontally at Darius, the scythed chariots would shatter the phalanx and swarms of cavalry would outflank, surround and annihilate the enemy. Would Alexander walk into the well-laid trap?

Alexander started as if he would do so. His 40,000 infantry were in a double phalanx, the rear phalanx of Balkan and Greek infantry having orders to face about if attacked from the rear. The Greek cavalry formed the left-hand part of the front phalanx, the Macedonian infantry the central part, and Alexander with the Companion Cavalry the right-hand part. Each wing was covered by units of light infantry and cavalry, which had orders to form the sides of a rectangular formation, should the rear phalanx have to face about. His army was drawn up parallel to the enemy line and facing its centre; but as he advanced, he inclined half right and marched smartly, with parade-ground precision, towards the left-hand end of Darius' line. Alexander's line was now oblique in relation to Darius' line, his right wing leading, his left retarded.

Darius tried to halt this movement by sending cavalry units to attack from the flank. Alexander countered by sending his flank-guard units successively into action, and while they arrested the outflanking cavalry Alexander continued his advance. He was already partly off the runways when the scythed chariots charged down them. They had little effect, because the phalanx opened ranks in accordance with earlier orders, let them through and reformed ranks. When the last flank-guard unit charged, Alexander was close enough to form a great wedge, infantry being on its left half and cavalry on its right half, break irresistibly through the enemy line, and swing left for the outflanking and encircling tactic.

Meanwhile, the charge of the chariots had been followed by a general advance of the Persians, their cavalry galloping ahead to outflank and encircle Alexander's left wing. The left-hand brigades of infantry were brought to a halt, a gap opened between them and the advancing brigades, and this gap was exploited by enemy cavalry, who rode on to sack the overnight Macedonian camp. The left-hand part now adopted the rectangular formation. Parmenio, commanding the left, sent a message to Alexander that he was in difficulties. Before the messenger arrived, Alexander's forces bore down upon Darius, who, seeing his left-centre crumbling, fled, his imperial banner high above his chariot. Alexander had broken opposition in the centre when the messenger arrived. He responded at once. 'Still abstaining from pursuit', he fought his way through the retiring enemy cavalry to find that Parmenio's superb Thessalian cavalry had made a successful counterattack. The cavalry pursuit, continued into the next day, covered 120 kilometres and broke all cavalry resistance. The Persian losses were in tens of thousands. Those of Alexander were in hundreds, because the pikes and the lances of men keeping phalanx or wedge formation protected those behind the front-line troops.

On going into action, Alexander raised his right hand towards the heavens and cried: 'Guard and strengthen the Greeks, if I am really from Zeus [Diothen].' His prayer was answered. The Persian Empire was broken, Alexander was acclaimed King of Asia by his Macedonians, and he inscribed on dedications to Athena of Lindus in Rhodes these words: 'King Alexander, having mastered Darius in battle and having become Lord of Asia, made sacrifice to Athena in accordance with an oracle.' Babylon welcomed the victor. Hard fighting ensued in Susiana and Persis before he captured Persepolis, the seat of Darius and Xerxes. By order of Alexander their palace went up in flames, a symbol of the vengeance taken by the Macedonians and the Greeks and of the ending of Persian rule. The army rested there for the early months of 330 and then advanced to Ecbatana (Hamadan), the last of the capital cities. There Alexander dismissed his Greek troops on the completion of their joint mission, paying their wages in full and giving generous bounties, especially to the Thessalian cavalry, who received a talent each.

The Greek part in the crusade had been as vital as the Macedonian. The Greek fleet of 160 triremes had made possible the initial advance to Miletus, and then it had prevented the fleet of Pharnabazus from capturing the Hellespont or landing troops in the Peloponnese. The Greek infantry, maintained probably at 7000, carried out minor operations, served as garrison troops and held positions in the second line of infantry at Issus and Gaugamela, which prevented any encirclement of the Macedonian phalanx in the latter battle. The Thessalian and other Greek cavalry contributed as much as the Macedonian cavalry to victory, except for the initial charges at the Granicus and at Gaugamela. The Greek troops richly deserved their bounty. It was the joint and harmonious effort of the Macedonians and the Greeks of the Common Peace which established supremacy by sea and by land over a huge area.

The conquest of east 'Asia' by the Macedonians

The Greeks had achieved their declared aims, liberation and revenge; but they had not acquired territory and serfs, as Isocrates for instance had advised, saying 'compel the barbarians to be serfs to the Greeks', nor loot and treasure. Alexander had established his own political and financial monopoly by declaring himself King of Asia at the start, and after his dismissal of their forces the Greeks of the Common Peace had no *locus standi* in the 'kingdom of Asia'. Nor did the Macedonian kingdom add any territory to its Empire, which remained limited to the Balkans; for Alexander was creating for himself a separate, self-standing Kingdom of

Asia. As the link between the two kingdoms, Alexander could and did transfer men and money from one to the other, and he made decisions which affected both. Those decisions were sometimes complicated by his dual role in Asia; for he was constitutional king of the Macedones in Asia and direct ruler of the Asians. Thus a decision taken by the king and the Macedones at Ecbatana, for instance, was a decision of the Macedonian State, valid for Macedones wherever they were. But he ruled the Asians by his personal decree. The reason for Alexander's choice is obvious. The forces of Macedonia and Greece were incapable of imposing and maintaining an imperial rule on 'Asia'. He needed the co-operation of the Asians with him as their king.

A vital question was the limit of Macedonian advance. Darius tried twice to check that advance by the cession, in the second offer, of all territory west of the Euphrates. Parmenio, it was said, advised acceptance, and Alexander commented: 'Were I Parmenio, I should do so.' In fact Alexander always claimed all Asia as his by divine gift, and he said so in his replies to Darius: 'You must come to me since I am Lord of all Asia' – i.e. come as a subject. But he also offered to Darius a role within Asia, as 'king ruling over other kings', which was the title of the king of the Medes and Persians. Thus he wanted Darius to be a client-king. It was for this reason that when Alexander captured the Queen Mother, Sisigambis, the Queen, the daughters and the son of Darius after the battle of Issus, he treated them as royalty, gave a royal funeral to the Queen, and left the Queen Mother and the eight-year-old son in royal state at Susa. Again, he drove himself and his men to the utmost limit in an attempt to capture Darius alive (unsuccessfully, because Darius died of wounds inflicted by rebels); for he wanted him to continue as king. On finding him dead Alexander laid his own cloak over Darius, and he sent the corpse to be buried royally in the cemetery of the kings at Persepolis. The son and heir was being brought up in state, in order presumably to succeed at the age of eighteen to the throne as a client-king.

Alexander knew that he could advance only as far as the Macedones were willing to go. Their acclamation of him as King of Asia after the victory at Gaugamela was all-important. He persuaded them in an Assembly after the death of Darius 'to serve for the rest of the campaign', and they kept their word for the next four years. What actuated them was loyalty to their king and love of glory, as well as pay, bounty and occasionally loot. But some of his Friends and Companions were opposed to his policy, because they foresaw some of its complications.

The first complication was the need for Asian troops to fill the gap left by the withdrawal of the Greek troops. Alexander had foreseen the need at the outset. He met it in two ways. From the battle of the Granicus onwards, he took into his army any Persian officers and some Asian soldiers who were willing. In autumn 330 he formed a Royal Cavalry Guard, the 'Euacae', of Persian officers, which was equal in status to the Macedonian Royal

Cavalry Guard, and in 329 he drafted Persian and Median cavalrymen into his Companion Cavalry hipparchies and he added to his army Bactrian and Sogdian self-standing cavalry units. The second method was the creation of an entirely new army of Asians. He started the process in Lydia in 334; continued it in Lycia and Syria in 333/2; and ordered the training of '6000 King's Boys (*basileioi paides*) in warfare' in Egypt in 331. The first Asians to complete their training reached Alexander in autumn 330–300 Lydian cavalry and 2600 Lydian infantry; the next were 1000 cavalry and 8000 infantry, Lycians and Syrians, in 329. The course of training had evidently been four years long, and the name *paides* implies a beginning at the age of fourteen, as in the School of Pages. Thus the method was not to retrain defeated Asian infantrymen but to educate Asian boys (Egypt being included in 'Asia') to become the Asian component of the King of Asia's Royal Forces (*basilikai dynameis*).

In autumn 330 Alexander went further. 'He selected 30,000 boys [*paides*] of one and the same age, utterly young [fourteen years old]' in his 'newly founded cities and the rest of the spear-won territory', and he appointed 'many supervisors [*epistatai*] and teachers [*didaskaloi*]', who were to teach the boys 'to become literate in the Greek language' and 'competent in the use of Macedonian weaponry'. The course was presumably for four years. Early in 325 the first year-class graduated, but Alexander was far away in the Indus valley. They stayed under the command of the satraps until 324, when as 'adult men already' they were brought by the satraps to Susa. There the drill of the pikemen-phalanx (they were all pikemen) was admired by the king. They were approved as 'the new generation [*Epigonoi*]' of soldiers, honoured members of the King's Army.

It stands to reason that this system of education was set up not for one year-class only but as a continuous process, a form of state education for selected Asian boys at the expense of the king, who appointed his education officers and teachers and paid them. The boys who graduated as soldiers in 324 and 323 stayed in the cities and served there as militiamen. The analogy with the Macedonian kingdom is clear; for the cities there trained their militiamen, and it was from the cities that the king selected the infantrymen of the King's Army. The same process continued in Lydia and Caria, from which 'armies' were brought by their satraps to Alexander in 323.

The need for such Asian troops was accentuated by the rising of Agis of Sparta, who hired 10,000 mercenaries with Persian gold, gained some adherents in the Peloponnese, and sat down to besiege Megalopolis in Arcadia. Antipater had to deal first with a revolt by the Macedonian commander in Thrace and then to raise large contingents of subjects and Greek allies. Almost six months passed before Antipater at the head of some 40,000 men crushed Sparta, which capitulated in May 330. He referred the fate of the dissidents to the Council of the Common Peace, which asked Alexander as *hegemon* to decide. He required Sparta to join the Common

Peace, fined the dissidents and gave the fines to Megalopolis. It had been a period of great danger; for if Sparta had been joined by the states of central Greece, Antipater might have been utterly defeated and Macedonia would have been in danger of invasion. It was clear to Alexander that he could not draw any reinforcements from Macedonia from 330 onwards, until he should return to the Eastern Mediterranean.

The next complication was the need to foster loyalty in the Asians. Alexander had succeeded generally in western Asia, Egypt and Babylonia by his policy of liberation and tolerance and even by participating in local religious practices – in Egypt sacrificing as Pharaoh, for instance. A different approach was necessary with the Medes and Persians, whose monotheistic worship of Ahura-Mazda as their god was alien to him, and who had been the ruling race for two centuries. He sought their co-operation by giving to their leaders high administrative positions as civil governors (satraps), both before and after Darius' death, these appointments including Babylonia, Persis, Susiana and Media. He left the moot (syllogos) of the Medes and Persians to govern their own affairs and to punish traitors to their own state. He adopted a mixture of Median and Persian dress in his dealings with Asians at his court, in order to show himself to be King of Asia. He made an attempt to persuade his Friends and close Companions to accept Asian practices at court, such as a kind of kowtowing (proskynesis); but when he came to realize how opposed they were to it, he abandoned the idea of working towards a fusion of Macedonian and Asian ceremonials. Thereafter he practised two forms of ceremonial, the Asian one involving Asian mace-bearers and guards.

The first attempt on Alexander's life in Asia was planned by Darius, who offered the Macedonian throne, a royal marriage and 1000 gold talents to Alexander, son of Aëropus, if he would murder Alexander. That at least was what a captured Persian agent said, and when Alexander convened a council of Friends they were convinced and wanted the son of Aëropus removed. Alexander kept him in custody (from winter 334/3). Then in October 330 a conspiracy was betrayed and those suspected of treason were tried by the Assembly of Macedones (some 6000 being present), with Alexander prosecuting. Parmenio, Philotas his son and commander of the Companion Cavalry, a Bodyguard, and some others were found guilty and were despatched; other senior officers were acquitted. A special order was sent for the killing of Parmenio before he could hear the verdicts, because he was in command of about half of the King's Army and a huge amount of treasure. The same Assembly demanded Alexander, son of Aëropus, for trial; he could not find words and was executed. In 327 a conspiracy by a number of Royal Pages was betrayed. They were found guilty of treason by the Assembly and executed. Investigation led to the arrest of Callisthenes, Alexander's official historian. As a Greek, he was not eligible for trial by the Assembly, and he was kept in custody 'to be tried in the Council [of the

Common Peace] in the presence of Aristotle [his uncle]'. He died probably of disease during the advance. There is no doubt that such conspiracies were in part the price which Alexander paid for his Asian policy. Nevertheless, he persisted with it.

In Asia the policy worked. For when the Macedonians marched on to Afghanistan and India, there was no serious rising in Susiana, Persis and Media. Indeed many Asians were fighting for him. That was essential, because the Macedonians and their supporting troops – Balkan, Greek mercenary and Asian – were no longer liberating settled populations from Persian rule but conquering very warlike and often nomadic peoples who had served in Persian armies. Three years of hard fighting ended in the subjugation and pacification of north-east 'Asia', bringing the army to the river Jaxartes, where Alexander founded 'the farthest Alexandria' (Alexandria Eschate at Khodjend now Leninabad) so named because it was at the border between his 'Asia' and his 'Europe' (see Fig. 12). In this area he recruited large numbers of fine cavalry – Bactrian, Sogdian and Scythian – for the next campaign.

The strain of continual fighting and the dislike of the Asian policy led in 328 to a fracas at a banquet given by Alexander to his leading Macedonians, at which there was the customary heavy drinking. Cleitus, who had saved Alexander from death at the battle of the Granicus river, mocked Alexander's Asian policy, and the two men had to be held back by their friends. Cleitus was taken away; but he returned alone, and Alexander, supposing him to be armed, killed him. When Alexander saw that Cleitus was not armed, he suffered terrible remorse. The Assembly of Macedones is said to have met and exonerated Alexander from blame. The rank and file were as loyal to him as ever; for they overawed the Sogdians by acts of spectacular daring. Three hundred men, using ropes and pitons, climbed the sheer face of 'the Sogdian Rock', reputedly impregnable, at night; thirty fell to their death, but the defenders surrendered. This was followed by the assault on 'the Rock of Chorienes' in bitter weather and deep snow. At the last stage Chorienes was allowed to consult the defender of the Sogdian Rock, Oxyartes, who praised Alexander greatly for his good faith and just dealing. Chorienes thereupon surrendered his position. Alexander left him in charge of the Rock and in command of the local tribes.

For the next campaign the Macedonians crossed the Hindu Kush (Caucasus) probably by the Kaoshan Pass (4360 metres) and six months were spent in the training of recent levies 'from all sorts of tribes'. Alexander believed the theory of Aristotle and other scientists that 'India' was the last peninsula of Asia, extending eastwards into the Ocean, and that the Ocean itself was visible from the top of the Hindu Kush. His concept of the inhabited surface of the three known continents and of the circum-ambient Ocean is shown in Fig. 12. He thought he was drawing close to 'the ends of Asia' (*ultima Asiae*). The tribes of Afghanistan put up a tough

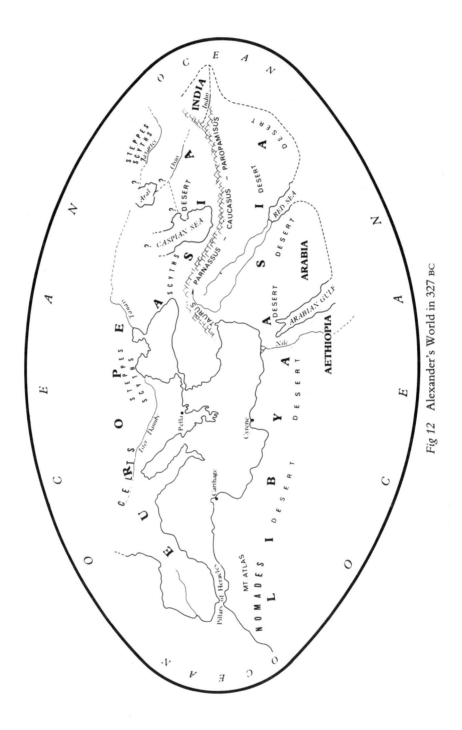

Fig 12 Alexander's World in 327 BC

resistance and were eventually overcome by another spectacular feat of daring, the capture of Aornus, achieved by 700 mountaineering Macedonians, who with Alexander in the lead climbed up the rock face at night. In May 326 he crossed the Indus with some 75,000 fighting men, of whom the Macedonians numbered not much more than a fifth. The first Rajah welcomed him and provided 5000 Indian troops. The second, Porus, opposed him on the bank of the river Hydaspes. Alexander crossed at night with a portion of his army and concentrated his attack on the left-hand part of Porus' line, where his Companion Cavalry and the Macedonian phalanx drove the enemy back on to the elephants. The Indian losses in the battle and during the pursuit were very great. But Alexander befriended Porus and even increased his kingdom. The victory was commemorated on a medallion (see Plate 25a: i–ii). The Assembly of Macedones promised to support the king in his advance now 'to the end of India'.

Disillusion came after more fighting during the monsoon rains, when the Macedonians reached the swollen river Hyphasis (Beas). Rumours were rife that huge armies and gigantic elephants lay ahead beyond the watershed of the Indus vally, and the Macedonians sat down to demonstrate that they would go no further east. Alexander convened a council of senior officers twice. Unable to persuade them, he hinted that others would follow him and he shut himself up in his tent for three days. The Macedonians stayed put. The bluff of Alexander was called; for he could not win set battles without the Macedonians. The omens at the sacrifice for crossing the river proved unfavourable. Alexander, attended by his closest Friends and leading Companions, announced that the army would turn back. The men cheered him with tears of relief. It was a remarkable feature of the Macedonian system that so momentous and so wise a decision could be reached without a rupture between king and Macedones.

The end of the eastern march (*anabasis*) was marked by the erection of twelve stone altars to the gods of Alexander's choice (Zeus Olympius and Zeus Ammon among them). They were analogous to the Pillars of Heracles at the Straits of Gibraltar, which had marked the western limits of Heracles' Labours. One of the altars was dedicated to Heracles, whom Alexander regarded as an exemplar and as a rival.

The conquest of the densely populated Indus valley was completed in seven months. The fleet which the Macedonians built and manned, to the amazement of the Indians, carried supplies and transported swift-moving assault groups. Strongpoints were captured by daring attacks. During one of these, Alexander led the way up a scaling ladder which broke and left him with three others on the battlement. Alexander jumped first into the fray, and the others followed. One was killed. Alexander was struck by an arrow which passed through his cuirass into a lung. He collapsed into his shield. Peucestas held the sacred shield from Troy over him, and Leonnatus fought on his other side. Both were wounded by the time that other Macedonians

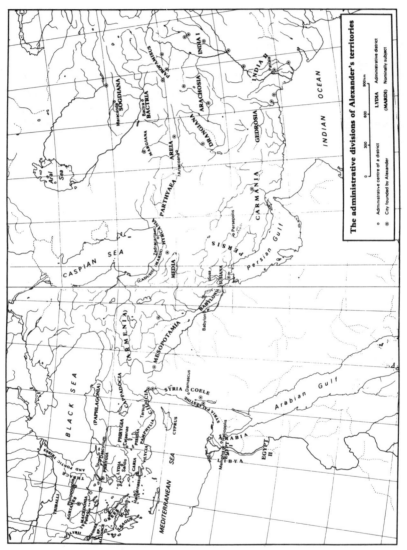

Fig 13   Alexander's territories

128

reached them. Alexander came near to death, but at thirty years of age, he was at his physical prime. When he recovered the Macedonians garlanded him 'with such flowers as India produced'. As Alexander approached the delta, a large-scale rising by tribes which had submitted was organized by the fanatical Brahmans. But the Macedonian forces, and especially the cavalry, were too quick for them. The rebellion was crushed with the killing of all who resisted and the selling of their women and children as slaves. The property was given as loot to the soldiers.

Alexander led the way out to sea and sacrificed to Poseidon with prayers for the safe passage of 'the expedition by sea', which he was already planning on the assumption that the sea was the Ocean and that circum-navigation to the Persian Gulf might be possible. Most of the army took a safe inland route, heading for Carmania, but Alexander kept on or near the coast, laying down supplies, digging wells and marking water-points for the fleet which was to follow. His army numbered some 12,000 men, predominantly Macedonians. When they entered the Gedrosian desert, the transport animals floundered in the scorching sand or were killed for eating, as supplies were running out. Alexander saved the army by finding water in the shingle of the beach; but most of the camp followers, who were hangers-on as traders, and their families died in the desert. The Macedonian losses were not in vain. The fleet of small warships under oar (triaconters) completed their voyage of exploration and adventure to the Persian Gulf. The maritime trade for which Alexander had built large harbours and dockyards in the Indus delta was now developed from India to Babylon and later to Alexandria in Egypt. Alexander and the Macedonians gave thanks to the gods in two festivals, one 'for the salvation of the army in Gedrosia', and the other in honour of Zeus the Saviour and Poseidon for the success of the fleet.

When the army and the fleet met near Susa in February 324, 'Asia' was all but conquered. The area east of the Hyphasis had been written off as that of another river (the Ganges). Arabia remained. While ships reconnoitred the Arabian coast as far as the Oman peninsula and others from Egypt approached Aden, Alexander planned to campaign across the neck of the Arabian peninsula in autumn 323 and to meet Macedonian reinforcements on the Mediterranean coast in 322. This presented no great difficulty. It was a matter of eight days by camel; and much was known of Arabian trade-routes both at Gaza and at Babylon, to which precious spices and perfumes were sent for export. Once the Arabs were defeated, 'he would allow them, as he had allowed the Indians, to govern themselves in accordance with their own customs'.

Let us consider the contribution of the Macedonians to the conquest of Asia. If we assume that one brigade of infantry and 200 cavalry from Macedonia accompanied Parmenio in the vanguard, the total number of Macedonians (including light cavalry) who campaigned in Asia was some

26,000 (3700 cavalry and 22,500 infantry). They were the spearhead in every major battle. They fought a huge number of actions, many being of a daring kind, during ten years of service from the Dardanelles to the Hyphasis, a distance as the crow flies of some 4000 kilometres. There was only one defeat, and that of a small force. No national army before or since can surpass the Macedonians in courage, toughness, discipline and loyalty, and none can rival the record of its achievement. When Alexander, in a boastful mood, claimed the limelight for himself, Cleitus gave the just rebuke, 'Those accomplishments were not yours alone. For the great part they are the work of the Macedones.'

IX

Macedonian Civilization in Relation to the Greek City-State and to the Persian Empire

Macedonian civilization partook both of Greek civilization and of Balkan civilization. Since the Macedonians of Lower Macedonia and of Upper Macedonia were by race and by language Greek, they shared much of the Greek outlook and they appreciated Greek art and literature, especially drama. At the same time they shared their enlarged kingdom in and after the reign of Philip with Balkan peoples – Illyrians, Paeonians and Thracians – and they had much more respect for Balkan institutions and for foreign religions than the Greeks who lived in city-states and despised any form of polity and deity other than their own. Situated as they were between the Greek peninsula and the Balkan land-mass, the Macedonians developed their own national characteristics and their own form of civilization. They were able to do so because their country had strong natural defences and favoured particular ways of life, and because they enjoyed a long period of cultural development, during which they staunchly maintained their independence, except for a short period of occupation by Persia c.510–480.

Macedonian civilization

The terrain of greater Macedonia has distinct characteristics. The high mountains provide timber, pasture and game, and the highest, Mount Olympus (2911 metres), made the entry from the south difficult (see Plate 3a). The defiles cut by the perennial rivers through these mountains rendered the entries from the hinterland difficult: typical are those of the Haliacmon by Beroea, the Axius at the Iron Gates (see Fig. 4), and the Strymon at Kresna (see Plate 3b). The contrast between the high country of Upper Macedonia and the plains of Lower Macedonia and north-east Thessaly is shown in Plate 4; and between the high country of Upper Macedonia and Epirus on the one hand and the plain of coastal Albania on the other hand in Plates 31 and 32. The country between the Axius river and the Albanian coast was ideal for transhumant pastoralism, which was widely practised by nomadic or semi-nomadic groups until recently. Plate 2 shows two leaders (*tshelniku*) with two rams near the headwaters of the Achelous, and sheep pasturing on the plain of Ioannina during the spring migration. Since the shepherds live in the open by day and night, men and

131

women wear thick clothing and the men a heavy cloak (*kāpa*). These need long pins and strong brooches; and wealth is carried by the women in the form of buckles, clasps and pendants. Examples of these from the Early Iron Age in greater Macedonia are shown in Plate 1. They include amulets and pendants of religious significance, and the double-bladed axes were probably inherited from the traditions of Minoan Crete.

There are large deposits of precious minerals in Macedonia, mainly to the east of the Axius. Metal was worked there from the Early Bronze Age. The ornaments of Plate 1 were mostly of bronze, and iron weapons were very numerous in the Early Iron Age cemetery at Vergina. Gold work of the highest quality has been found from the late sixth century onwards. Sindos, near the mouth of the 'gift-holding' river Echedorus (modern Gallikos), in which gold was panned, has yielded the objects of gold which are shown in Plates 5 and 6. Comparable pieces of late sixth-century date have been found recently at Vergina and at Aiane (in Elimeotis). The craftsmen, who excelled in filigree work, were no doubt indigenous to the area. Coining in gold, which began with Philip II, was of the highest standard (see Plates 9a: i, iv; 25b: i; 30a: i, ii). An extraordinary range of fine gold objects have come from the royal tombs at Aegeae (Plates 16 and 17); they were not peculiar to royalty, for similar pieces have been found in the burials of commoners elsewhere in Macedonia (e.g. Plate 24). The gilding of silver was skilful (see Plates 16 and 17). The outstanding quality of the gold work and the quantity of it are to be attributed to local craftsmen and the mining of gold, which was not present in the Greek peninsula.

Silver deposits in the Thraco-Macedonian area were exploited by Thracian, Illyrian and Paeonian tribes and by Greek adventurers from the mid-sixth century, when large numbers of heavy coins in silver were issued. The rather crude emblems were due to native craftsmen, and the coins were only rarely inscribed with Greek letters, the work no doubt of Greek-speaking craftsmen, for the Balkan tribes had no alphabet of their own. Examples are in Plate 7a: i, iii. The first coins of the Macedones were issued by Alexander I *c*.478 BC, when he captured the silver-mine of the Bisaltae and adopted the Bisaltic emblems (Plate 7a: ii, iv). His own die-engravers started the long series of superb royal coins with the octadrachm of Plate 7a: v. As the king alone struck and owned the coinage until the late second century BC, when some cities and regions issued silver and bronze coinages (Plate 26: v, vi), he had no hesitation in placing a representation of himself in Macedonian dress on some coins. Alexander I, Perdiccas II, Amyntas III and Philip II were shown on horseback (Plates 7a: v, 7b: i, v, 9a: vi), and from Alexander IV onwards the head of the king appeared as on modern coins (25a: iii, 25b: v, viii, 26: iii, vii, 30: i, ii, iv, v, vi, vii). His dress included the diadem, often of cloth with the ends hanging down; the *kausia* or 'warmer' (the characteristic Macedonian headgear); and the cloak (e.g. 7a: v, 7b: v, 9: vii). Alexander III on the Porus Medallion was shown standing, in cavalry uniform, with a thunderbolt in his hand; his face was hardly visible, but he was identified as the king by the ends of the diadem (Plate 25a).

The commonest device on the silver coins was a god or a hero: Zeus (9a: vi, 25b: ii, 26: ii), Apollo (9a: iii, 26: i), Athena (25a: iii, 25b: i, ix, 26: ii, iii), Nike (25a: iii, 25b: i, vii), Poseidon (25b: vii, viii, 26: i), and Heracles (9a: i, 25b: ii, iii, iv, vi), Perseus (26: iv), Rhesus (7a: iv), and probably Caranus (7b: iii) as the mythical founder of the Temenid house in Macedonia. The association of the king with the gods and heroes was of paramount importance. His interests were also represented. He hunted on horseback and had the privilege of killing a cornered lion (the mountain lion being then extant in Macedonia); hence the emblems on Plates 7a: v, 7b: i, v, and the frequent representations of trained horses on 7a: v, 9a: ii, v, vii; 7b: i, ii, iv, v, 25a: i, ii, 25b: v, vi, and 30: iii. There are references to war on the Victory coins (25a: iii, 25b: i, vii). Conquest was advertised by a deity wielding a thunderbolt or standing on the prow of a warship (25b: vii, ix, 26: i, ii, iii) and by Alexander III holding a thunderbolt on the Porus Medallion (25a: i, ii). A war of defence was indicated by the distinctive Macedonian shield (25b: ix, 26: v, vi).

Silver was used for fine utensils. Of the forty-seven silver vessels in the Tombs of Philip II and Alexander IV, two of exquisite shape are shown in Plate 18. Examples come also from non-royal tombs (e.g. the silver strainer of Plate 24). Tiny portraits were placed on some silver vessels (a Silenus on Plate 16). Of the bronze vessels the masterpiece is the Derveni Crater; it was sculpted with the vivid figures of the participants in a Dionysiac celebration (Plates 19–20). Bronze armour was of the highest quality. The finest examples of portraiture on a miniature scale are provided by the five ivory heads which were found as a group in Philip's Tomb (Plate 14); and the ivory relief showing a scene of Dionysiac revelry is charming (Plate 18). Iron weapons were developed very early in Macedonia. It seems that a form of mild steel was used for the making of Philip's iron cuirass and helmet (Plate 15).

Few statues in stone have survived, partly because suitable stone was rare in Macedonia, but mainly because the Romans removed a vast quantity as loot. An archaic Kouros of Kilkis reveals Ionian influence in the late sixth century BC. The head of Demeter had the severity of the archaizing style of the late fourth century (Plate 29a). The cult statue of Aphrodite from Dium in the second century is remarkable for the delicacy with which the folds of drapery are delineated and for the serenity of her expression (Plate 29b). A terracotta figurine of Aphrodite from Pella was found in a shrine of Cybele-Aphrodite; it stressed the sexual aspect of the goddess in the second century. The attitude of the shy young girl of the bronze statuette from Beroea, probably of the fourth century, is very appealing (Plate 27a).

The history of ancient painting has been revolutionized by the discovery of the Vergina frescoes (Plates 11a, 11b, 13). In the Rape of Persephone there is a remarkable sense of movement and a wonderful contrast between the ferocious aspect of Pluto and the desperate appeal of Persephone. The composition is more dramatic than that of the same subject on the Throne in Eurydice's Tomb (Plate 12), in which the four horses of Pluto's chariot were rendered in a more sophisticated manner. The immobility of Demeter in her grief is emphasized by the extension of the robe which swathes her head (Plate 11). If Tomb I was constructed for Amyntas III, as I have argued, the Rape of Persephone and Demeter Mourning were painted c.369 BC. The disposition of the figures in the Royal Hunt fresco (Plate 13) of Philip's Tomb c.336 BC, directs the viewer's eye to the right, where Philip is about to strike the lion with his spear; but the central figure is the young king, Alexander. The use of colour and the control of perspective in these frescoes is amazing (see Andronicus, *V* 87–116 and in *Eph. Arch.* 1987, 369 and 378). They are our earliest examples of a new school of painting which originated in Macedonia, inspired the painting of the Hellenistic period and was much copied at Pompeii and Herculaneum. We include as such a copy of the Boscoreale painting (Plate 21); the original alluded probably to Alexander's crossing of the Hellespont and his fixing of the spear in the soil of the Troad, while the philosopher Aristotle watched and Asia looked up at Alexander. The king wears the *kausia*. That form of hat is shown most clearly in the Relief from Aiane (Plate 10).

Macedonia pioneered the art of mosaic floors (Plates 28a and b). The mosaic Dionysus on a Panther was dated to 325–300 BC, and the others from Pella shortly afterwards. The subjects of these mosaics were taken from painting, as we see in comparing the Rape of Persephone fresco with the mosaic Rape of Helen from Pella (see Ph. Petsas, *Pella* (Thessaloniki, 1978) 99 and 120). The rounded pebbles of these mosaics imparts a greater illusion of movement than the flat tesserae of later mosaics, because the rounded surfaces reflect the light. It is probable that the figures in the Lion Hunt Mosaic were intended to be Alexander and Craterus (cf. Plu. *Alex.* 40, 5). The continuity in the tradition of mosaic composition is illustrated by the 'Alexander Mosaic' from Pompeii (Plate 22), portraying the Battle of Issus, in which a dead tree is used as in the Royal Hunt fresco (Plate 13). The portrait of Alexander (Plate 22) is probably truer to life than the famous Dresden Portrait; for the Alexander Mosaic was a faithful copy of a famous painting of the late fourth century BC (see Hammond, *AG* 329).

Another sphere in which Macedonia's originality enriched later generations is funerary architecture. The large vaulted tombs – of Eurydice 10.7 x 7.95 x 5.8 metres high and of Philip 9.5 x 6.56 x 5.3 metres high – are the earliest known examples of the type of tomb which was described c.350 BC by Plato in *Laws* 947 D (see p. 54). It originated in Macedonia after 369 (the probable date of Tomb I) and before 350. The problem of adding a pleasing façade to the open end of a vaulted rectangular building was brilliantly solved by making a temple-like rectangular front (Plate 13). A pediment was added later in the century. Both the funerary vault itself and the addition of a classical front to a building of a different style have been copied until very recently. Another architectural form which developed in Macedonia and was to have a long history was the large palace with an inner colonnaded court (Fig. 14). The combination of painting and architecture, which suited the brilliant Mediterranean light, was employed to great advantage on the façades of the vaulted tombs. Unusual sophistication may be seen in the painting on the back wall of Eurydice's Tomb, which created the illusion that there were further rooms beyond (Plate 12).

The contribution of Macedonia to the history of art was outstanding in metal-work (weaponry, armour and jewellery), coinage, silver and bronze vessels, ivory portraiture and reliefs, painting, mosaic and some forms of architecture. The level of achievement in these arts was much higher in Macedonia than in other Balkan countries, for instance when we compare the silver vessels of Rogozen and the fresco in the tomb at Kazanluk. When we look forward to the Hellenistic Age, Macedonia rather than Athens provided the models in many forms of art. One reason for the pre-eminence of Macedonia was the movement of leading artists to the court where patronage and financial rewards were available. Other reasons were the taste and the inventiveness of the Macedonian kings, the traditional skills of the population in metalworking, and the extraordinary vitality of the leading Macedonians in the age of expansion. Last but not least, Macedonian art was inspired primarily by the religious faith which provided scenes of Dionysiac ecstasy in this world and hopes of an afterlife.

Greek city-state civilization

The Greek world of city-states prospered through maritime trade. In the colonizing period (750–550) hundreds of city-states had been planted on the coasts of the Black Sea, the Mediterranean and Sicily, and they served as the middlemen in the exchange of goods between the relatively undeveloped hinterlands of Europe and Africa and the markets of Greece, Egypt and the Near East. The rivals of the Greeks were the Phoenicians of the Lebanon, who established their colonies on the western half of the North African coast, the south coast of Spain and the west coast of Sicily. Each had a virtual monopoly of the carrying trade in its own sphere, apart from an immediate rivalry in Cyprus, Syria and Egypt. The settlements of both peoples were small, with an adult male citizenship numbering hundreds and thousands, but they made up for their size by their amazing energy and inventiveness.

Interaction between Macedonia and the Greek world of city-states was limited to local contacts, until Athens came to dominate Aegean waters, first as the leader of an alliance of maritime Greek states and then in an imperial role as their master. For seventy years (475–405) Athens was the centre of the Greek world. She owed her position to her naval power, economic strength and cultural supremacy. Her warships (triremes, rowed with three banks of oars) were built with special timber, obtained mainly from Macedonia, and were rowed by expert crews of Athenian citizens and allied seamen. One of their tasks was to protect the merchant ships which brought grain from the Black Sea ports to Athens, where the population had outgrown its local produce. The economic strength which enabled her to maintain a navy of 200 or 300 triremes was based on slave labour and on foreign settlers in Attica, on her ability to direct merchant shipping to the Peiraeus and impose taxes on transit trade, and ultimately on the tribute she exacted from the subject states. She used her resources well, being the pioneer in the development of capitalism. As the centre of the Greek world she attracted the ablest thinkers, artists and craftsmen, and her own citizens were pre-eminent in tragedy, comedy, history, sculpture and architecture. Her cultural leadership was closely tied to her political leadership; for she was the pioneer of democracy. Her claim to be 'the school of Greece' was justified in terms of politics, economics and culture.

During this period Macedonia, being a land power, managed with difficulty to maintain its independence. Economically her timber, minerals and foodstuffs brought her modest revenues, and she developed a monetary economy; but she did not move in the direction of a slave-based capitalism, as most city-states had done. Politically she had nothing to do with democracy; for her salient characteristics were constitutional monarchy and a free population of peasants, shepherds and loggers. Culturally she was enthralled by Athens. The kings welcomed to the court many of the leading writers, artists and craftsmen from 'the school of Greece', and they led the way in the development of festivals of the Muses and the Arts at Dium, Aegeae and Pella.

The collapse of Athens and her maritime empire in 404 had little or no effect on the economic and cultural developments which had spread out from Athens and been adopted by most city-states. The next period (404–346) was an age of plenty. 'The Greeks today', wrote Demosthenes in 341, 'possess far more of the elements of city-state power – warships, manpower, capital and material assets – than their predecessors.' But it was an age of political chaos. Democracy and capitalism were unstable partners in a slave-based economy. The pursuit of wealth and power by unscrupulous individuals led to revolutionary strife between parties and in Sicily to long-lasting dictatorships. Continuing wars weakened the leading states (Sparta, Corinth, Athens and Thebes), and no one of them was able to impose its 'hegemony' – its military or naval leadership, on the others. Civilized standards declined. There was an increase in genocide (*andrapodismos*), expulsion, brigandage, piracy and atrocities, often associated with the employment of mercenary soldiers. 'It is easier', wrote Isocrates in 356, 'to raise a bigger and better force from the floating population than from the citizens.' His words were prophetic. Phocian generals hired mercenaries with the loot of Delphi and defeated the regular forces of Thebes and Thessaly.

Political thinkers proposed reforms. Plato, who saw for himself the signs of decline in Sicily, wanted to put the clock back to an ideal time when the laws governed conduct, citizens controlled slaves, commerce was restricted, and capitalism was so harnessed that the highest citizen income was only four times that of the poorest citizen. Isocrates was more forward-looking. The antidote to internecine wars was some form of union in which the city-states would guarantee constitutional procedures in their internal politics and establish a Common Peace with collective security. He was sufficiently practical to realize that such a union would not be self-generated but had to be induced or imposed by a leading state. By 346 he had despaired of Greece's traditional leaders. He turned to Macedonia. We have seen in chapter 7 how Philip imposed his military hegemony and used his authority to induce a form of union for the Greek city-states of the mainland.

In this period, 404–346, culture became more uniform throughout the Greek world with the spread of political democracy, commercial capitalism and a degree of urbanization. Athens was still the leader but she was now *prima inter pares*. Prose gained at the expense of poetry, oratory excelled as the means of persuasion in politics and at law, and philosophy flourished. As the book trade developed, literacy and reading became general among citizens and a standard form of Greek language evolved. Difficult times led to inventions in economics (banking, insurance, maritime loans, agronomics, mining, shipping, armaments and fortifications). The Greeks had much that was of value to offer to developing countries.

Macedonia was one of the lands which enjoyed the spread of Greek culture and benefited from Greek inventions. But she was independent in some ways. The political ingredient, democracy, was rejected. Capitalism was controlled by the royal monopoly of currency and of expenditure. Urbanization was planned. Movement of population was controlled, and slave-labour was minimal. Because the king disposed of enormous wealth, he made his court a centre of artistic excellence. As we have seen, by the time of Philip's death Macedonia was the leader in many forms of art, craftsmanship and architecture. Thus where Alexander conquered, he introduced a civilization which was fundamentally Macedonian and had been enriched by the spread of Greek culture.

The Persian Empire

Persia had held Macedonia in 510–480 as the westernmost province of its
farflung Empire, which then extended from the Indus valley to Mount
Olympus in Europe and to Cyrene in Africa. The Medes and Persians
excelled in cavalry, archery and siegecraft; they incorporated warlike
subjects in their armies; and they developed a Mediterranean fleet, to which
their Phoenician subjects provided the best flotilla. Their monotheistic
belief was reflected in the absolute power of the Great King, the representative on earth of Ahura-Mazda. The wealth of the Empire, partly issued in
coin but mainly hoarded, was in his hands, and he determined all policy.
His Kinsmen were his administrators, and he appointed the ablest of them
as satraps (governors) of the provinces. Imperial control was weakened
often by revolts; but the central forces, using a highly developed road
system and aided by the loyalty of the Phoenician fleet, were able to reassert
the authority of Persia in the long run. Beyond the limits of the Empire,
Persia used her wealth to good effect. In the west she hired the best infantry
in the world, the Greek hoplites, to serve in her armies, and her fleets were
often manned in part by Greek seamen. When a Greek city-state intervened
in Asia, she subsidized other Greek states of the mainland to create a
diversion. Thus she contributed to the defeat of Athens in 404 and to that of
Sparta in 394, and she posed as arbiter of Greek affairs in 386 and 366. When
Macedonia seemed to be a rising power, Persia subsidized an Athenian
commander, helped Perinthus, and sent funds to Athens. Her tactics
succeeded, for Philip withdrew.

When Philip united the Greeks and persuaded them to join Macedonia in
war against Persia, he capitalized on the traditional hostility which Greeks
felt towards Persia for her aggression. In 480–79 Xerxes' troops had
committed sacrilege against the Greek gods by destroying temples, and
they had committed atrocities against Greek women. The libertarian
principles of Greek democrats were outraged by the absolutism of the
Persian despot and the oppression of Greeks in Asia. Macedonians resented
also the subjection and occupation of their country in 510–480. There was
no particular clash of cultures. For the Persian Empire was multi-racial and
multi-cultural. But the Greeks of the city-states had always scorned the
non-Greek races and regarded them as servile by nature. Isocrates and
Aristotle thought in Greek terms of seizing Persia-controlled territories and
reducing the non-Greek peoples to serfdom. Alexander, brought up in a
multi-racial kingdom with religious and cultural tolerance of non-Greeks,
invaded the Persian Empire with a different attitude and a different aim
in mind.

As we shall see, Alexander showed an un-Greek respect for the civilizations which he encountered, for instance in Lydia, Caria, Phoenicia,
Egypt, Babylonia, Persia and India. He provided a form of administration

138

within which the native civilizations were to maintain their own identity and thus their self-respect. At the same time his intention was to introduce Macedonian civilization at three levels in the Kingdom of Asia: in the armed forces, in the higher administration, and in the new cities with the education of selected young Asians. That civilization had much in common with contemporary Greek civilization, because the two had a common language and participated in a common cultural heritage. But the distinctions between the two civilizations were to be more important in the Kingdom of Asia. For there Macedonian civilization was to be intrusive, not exclusive; tolerant, not contemptuous; and creative rather than inward-looking. We shall see in chapter 10 that Macedonian civilization was to penetrate more deeply into the customs and the outlooks of the conquered peoples of Asia than European civilization has penetrated into the customs and the outlooks of conquered peoples of Africa and Asia.

X

The Organization of the Areas
Controlled by the Macedonians

The Greek mainland and the Aegean islands

An indirect effect of the Macedonian conquests was emigration from the Greek city-states to Egypt and the East on a huge scale. Athens, the most prosperous city-state, shed a quarter of its citizen population during Alexander's reign, and some island-states might have shed up to a half. As Isocrates had foreseen, such an exodus eased the strains of overpopulation in the homeland and stimulated the growth of maritime trade. But it had little or no effect on internal politics; for the issue there was whether to co-operate with Macedonia in the person of Alexander as *hegemon* of the Common Peace or to reject that peace and go to war against Macedonia. Opinion swung to and fro, but generally caution prevailed. When Agis was encouraging revolt against the Common Peace, Demosthenes at first advised the Assembly to rebel; but later he backed down. In the same year, 330, Demosthenes' policy was acclaimed in general when he triumphed in court over his opponent Aeschines, who went abroad; yet the supporters of the Common Peace, such as Phocion and Demades, stayed in power.

In summer 324 a deserter from Alexander, called Harpalus, sought asylum at Athens, offering 5000 talents and 6000 mercenaries to help in a war against Macedonia. Demosthenes advised against granting asylum. In spring 323 he and other leaders were found guilty by the Assembly of having embezzled money deposited by Harpalus. Demosthenes was fined 50 talents; but he escaped abroad and was exiled. The internal politics of other states probably followed similar lines. The only recorded breach of the Common Peace after 330 was Aetolia's capture of Oeniadae and expulsion of its population of Acarnanians.

Diplomatic relations between Macedonia and the Greek city-states were governed by treaties of alliance with individual states and by an overall alliance with the Greeks of the Common Peace. Alexander was *hegemon* of the latter. The web of alliances with individual states was much more extensive; for the members of the Common Peace were only the states of the mainland (apart from Epirus) and some of the Aegean island-states. After the return of the Greek troops from Asia, Alexander dealt not with the Council of the Common Peace but with individual states in releasing prisoners and returning captured works of art to their original owners.

His attitude was conciliatory. For instance, he did not ask Athens to repay money deposited by Harpalus.

On returning to Susa early in 324 Alexander announced to his forces that all exiles from the Greek states were to be reinstated, except those under a curse and those exiled from Thebes. He hoped that this announcement would reach many who were serving or had served as mercenaries in Asia, and that they would go home. Then at the Olympic Games that summer the announcement was repeated by an officer of Alexander. It was not an order but a proposition, against which any state could enter objections; yet at Olympia it was made clear that Alexander meant the proposition to be adopted, if necessary perforce, and his name was cheered to the echo by the 20,000 exiles who were present. His aim was not to pack the states with his own partisans (for the great bulk of the exiles had been anti-Macedonian) but to create stable conditions and political reconciliation. We can see how enlightened a policy this would be in the modern world. The reaction at the time was that 'people in general welcomed the restoration of exiles as being for a good purpose'. Many states recalled their exiles, and Alexander provided guidelines for their proper treatment (for instance at Tegea, where the exiles were men who had supported Sparta in 330). The objectors included Aetolia, which would have to reinstate the Acarnanians in Oeniadae, and Athens, which had expelled all the Samians from Samos in 365 and would now have to surrender the island to them. Both were still negotiating with Alexander when he fell ill and died at Babylon.

In 324 Alexander's closest friend, Hephaestion, who ranked immediately after the king in the kingdom of Asia, died in a high fever. Alexander asked the Greek states to pay 'heroic honours' to him, and cults were established, for instance, at Athens; for this was merely a compliment, such as had been paid to benefactors. In the past Alexander had been accorded 'divine honours' by some Greek cities in Asia and by Thasos and Rhodes. He now asked that this should be done generally by the Greek states. There had been precedents, but not for the request by the recipient. 'Divine honours' were duly granted, with some sarcasm at Athens, where a cult was established before his death. It seems that Alexander as a Greek by blood wanted this form of recognition from the Greek states. There is no indication that it had any political significance.

Had Alexander lived to return to the eastern Mediterranean, where a huge fleet was being built, he would have imposed his will upon Aetolia, Athens and any other recalcitrant state; and the reinstatement of exiles would have created more settled conditions within the Greek world. It must have seemed to many that the Common Peace had succeeded during fourteen years in giving the majority of Greek states an opportunity to govern their own affairs, to liberate their kindred cities overseas and to gain in prosperity. Others felt that it prevented their state from dominating other states. From the point of view of Macedonia, the Common Peace provided a valuable alliance and made Macedonia's influence effective without drawing on Macedonian manpower. It would have had the same benefits if a campaign had been undertaken in the western Mediterranean, as Alexander intended.

Macedonia and the Balkans

Macedonia was all important as the source of the élite troops, the Macedones of the Companion Cavalry and the Phalanx. They were either recruited as young men or drafted from the militia. How numerous were they? In 335/4 there were some 3000 cavalry and 25,500 infantry, on the assumption that one squadron and one infantry brigade served in the vanguard in Asia. In 324/3 there were some 15,000 Macedones in Macedonia, 10,000 'veterans' on their way homewards, and 15,000 serving with Alexander. Thus there were more Macedones in 323 than in 334. How did this come about? Alexander drew as reinforcements 'fit young men from the countryside' – in other words not soldiers serving with Antipater. He thereby created new Macedones (altogether some 10,000 in two large batches). He also was able to promote to be 'Macedones' those serving in Asia who were native to Macedonia, such as the Lancers, the Macedonian Archers and the auxiliaries. And since the families of the phalangites often accompanied them, there were 'sons of Hypaspists' of serviceable age by 323. These figures show that our literary sources were correct in saying that the losses of the Macedones even in the great battles were very small. Did Alexander weaken the reserves of militiamen at home? It seems not, because Sippas, Leonnatus and Craterus were able each separately to raise large numbers of men inside Macedonia in 323/2.

Alexander was certainly anxious to maintain the birthrate at home; for he encouraged his 'veterans' to beget sons on their return. The kingdom entered upon a new level of prosperity. After the reign of Philip the respite from war favoured development, and very large amounts of bullion and coin were sent home from Asia. The mint at Amphipolis was the most prolific in the world. Local industries must have expanded to provide '25,000 sets of armour, inlaid with gold and silver' for Alexander's Macedones, and to build and maintain the Macedonian fleet. It was probably in this period of comparative peace that the cities of Macedonia began to increase in size and build circuit-walls. The Macedonians whom Alexander directed to settle in his new cities in Egypt and Asia were not thought of as lost to the home country. For they too would bear sons, who would join the forces and become Macedones in due course.

Peace reigned in the Balkans from 334 to 323 with two exceptions: a shortlived rebellion by the Macedonian general in Thrace with some Thracian support, and the combination of a disastrous campaign into the

Ukraine by his successor and a rising by Seuthes, an Odrysian king, *c*. 325–3. This peace helped the developing trade of the Balkans with the West, with Central Europe and with the areas surrounding the Black Sea. Damastium and the Paeonian kings continued to issue fine currencies in silver. The increase in prosperity was accompanied by 'Hellenizing' influences, emanating both from Macedonia and from Greek cities on the Thracian coasts and farther afield. Large drafts of Illyrian, Agrianian, Triballian and Thracian troops, including specialized units of cavalry and of javelin-men, served abroad under Alexander, and must have numbered several tens of thousands in all. Many stayed in the East, especially Thracians in the Indus valley. Others returned with riches in the form of pay and booty. The Balkan peoples had as their immediate overlords Antipater and the general of Thrace; but they also sent embassies to Alexander, for instance at Babylon in 324. Their willing co-operation with him was of great importance.

A related development was an invasion of southern Italy by the Molossian king, Alexander, at the invitation of the Greek cities, headed by Taras (Tarentum), in 334. His Epirotes, trained in the use of the pike, defeated the native tribes, and he entered into alliance with Rome; but his death in 331 ended the campaign. An Epirote Alliance was then formed, its members being only the southern tribes. The Chaones, Amantes and Dassaretii came under the control of Antipater. The widow of Alexander was Cleopatra, daughter of Olympias, and she acted as head of the Molossian state in some respects, from 331 being Queen Mother of the infant King Neoptolemus II.

We noted earlier (see p. 109) that Olympias as Queen Mother was head of the Macedonian State in religious and other matters. Unfortunately, she and Antipater quarrelled, although they sometimes had to act in concert, and she found an ally against Antipater in her daugher Cleopatra. They both wrote to Alexander. In 324 Alexander made new arrangements. Olympias took over the duties of Cleopatra in Molossia, and Cleopatra was given her mother's position as religious head of state; Antipater was to command the Macedonian reinforcements which would join Alexander in Syria in late 323, and Craterus was to take on the duties of Antipater on his arrival with the 10,000 veterans in Macedonia. We may infer from these arrangements that Alexander expected not to come to Macedonia in 322 but to conduct his campaign along the North African coast.

Whereas Philip had used the Attic standard in gold and the Thracian in silver, Alexander adopted the Attic standard for all his coinage (see Plate 25b). On the smaller silver coins and the bronze coins, which were used for local exchange in Macedonia and the Balkans, he did not add 'of the king' after his name, and the emblems were those of Amyntas III and Philip II, with special emphasis on a young Heracles. He continued to issue the gold *Philippeioi* and the tetradrachms of his father, which were particularly acceptable in the Balkans, the North and the West. The very great amount of coinage which was produced not only by Macedonia but also by Greek city-states at this time makes it clear that Europe was benefiting enormously from the conquest of Egypt and Asia, and that Macedonia was the richest state in Europe, and indeed in the world of Alexander.

The organization of the Kingdom of Asia

It was part of Alexander's genius that with every stage in his advance he was able to make permanent rather than temporary arrangements. Thus, on seeing that the Persian system of satrapies was satisfactory, he continued it, but with the crucial change that he placed civil, military and financial responsibilities not in the hands of the satrap (as Persia had done) but in those of three separate officers, each answerable directly to himself. Because Egypt was so wealthy and so difficult to control, for instance from Babylon, he made a more sophisticated separation of duties: two Egyptians as civil governors of Upper and Lower Egypt, two Greeks as civil governors of 'Libya' and 'Arabia', two Macedonians as generals of troops, a Macedonian as admiral of the fleet, two Macedonians as commanders of garrisons, and four officers to handle the mercenaries who were employed in Egypt. He used monarchy where it was traditional: Ada in Caria; kings in many city-states of Cyprus and Phoenicia; Taxiles, Porus and Abisares in the upper Indus valley; and four kings in the lower Indus valley, of whom three joined the Brahmans' revolt and were executed or fled.

There were some obvious reasons for making such arrangements. Alexander wanted the peoples of his Kingdom of Asia 'to govern themselves in accordance with their own customs', whether the manner of government was democracy in a Greek city-state or in an Indian community, aristocracy in a tribe (the Malli, for example), priestly authority in Judaea, Egypt and Babylonia, or various forms of monarchy. It was not just a matter of convenience. The devolution of authority enabled each people to retain its self-respect and develop its own resources, whereas in the modern world the extension of a central authority has often led to humiliation and stagnation. A particular instance was the administration of justice. Offenders were tried in accordance with their own laws. Alexander made a point of sending men accused of treason, such as the Persian Bessus and the tyrants of Methymna in Lesbos, to their own country for trial and punishment. A separate reason was the need for economy in the deployment of Macedonians on administrative duties. If he had appointed them at local levels as judges, tax-gatherers, education officers and political officers (or missionaries), he would have needed hundreds of thousands of Macedonians. As it was, his administrators operated only at the highest level and numbered a few thousand at most.

How did this system work? We are considering the first few years of its application, when Alexander and his army were engaged in further conquest. There was a danger that the king and his officers might seem unduly remote to his subjects in the Kingdom of Asia. This was offset by the right of appeal to the king which every subject possessed, and by the magnetic quality of a king and of his viceroys. Thus when Alexander returned in 324, appeals were made to him by soldiers and by Medes alike against officers and men of the garrisons in Media. Alexander heard the charges, investigated the cases, and condemned to death not just the officers but no less than 600 soldiers. 'This demonstration that the rulers could not maltreat the ruled in the kingdom of Alexander did more than anything else to maintain order among his numerous and widely differentiated peoples'. The impact of Alexander's personality upon his subjects was perhaps greater than that of any other ruler at any time. Already in his lifetime his heroic deeds and his love of others were being magnified in the accounts which came to be known as *The Alexander Romance*. The Macedonian satrap of Persis, Peucestas, who wore the native dress and spoke the native language, was commended by Alexander for his 'leadership'. Satraps who were incompetent or corrupt, whether Macedonian or Asian, were tried and imprisoned or executed, in one case by Alexander personally. During his absence in eastern 'Asia' rumours of his death led some satraps to break the rules and enlist mercenaries. On his return they were ordered to dismiss the mercenaries. Alexander's control of his administrators was strict.

To achieve co-operation Alexander wished to create equality of status between Europeans and Asians at two levels in particular: the higher ranks of commanders and administrators, and the military forces. We have seen that from the early years he appointed a number of Asians to be satraps, and although some proved unworthy he continued with that policy. He also appointed some Persians to military commands. His circle of Friends and close Companions included some Asians. In 324 a mass wedding was arranged at Susa, one of the Persian capitals. Alexander and some ninety of his European Friends married high-ranking women of the Persian, Median and Bactrian nobility, and the ceremony was performed with the Persian rites. In 327 Alexander himself had married Roxane, a Bactrian aristocrat, with whom he had fallen in love. He now married the eldest daughter of Darius and the youngest daughter of an earlier Persian king, Artaxerxes Ochus. He also converted into legal marriages the liaisons of some 10,000 Macedonian soldiers with Asians, and when he sent his veterans homewards he undertook to educate their children by Asian women and to fit them for Macedonian service at his own expense. Such consideration has not been apparent in the treatment of women and their children during warfare and withdrawal from Vietnam and Afghanistan.

The status of Asian military forces was a delicate issue. From 330 onwards Alexander had to recruit large numbers of Asian cavalry. At first they served as ethnic units, each equipped in its own style, and the most distinguished was the Persian Royal Guard, the Euacae. In 329 he drafted Asians into the Companion Cavalry and even Persians and Bactrians, some being sons of satraps, into the Macedonian Royal Guard. This admixture involved equipping some Asian cavalrymen with the Macedonian lance. Occasionally a distinguished Persian, such as Darius' brother, reached the highest Macedonian rank as a Bodyguard or a *hegemon*. Thus access to equal status became available to Asian cavalrymen. Asian infantrymen served in ethnic units with their own equipment until 324, when the 30,000 young Asians, trained as pikemen of the phalanx (see p. 123) came to Susa. Their drill on parade was superb. Alexander called them 'the new generation [*epigonoi*]'. The current generation of Macedonian pikemen were disgusted and alarmed; for Alexander was depriving them of their uniqueness.

Trouble broke out later at Opis, when Alexander announced to an Assembly of Macedones a redistribution of forces. His plan was to release from the current campaigning (but not from military service) those Macedonians who were unfit for combat through age or injury, and to send them home with a bounty; and to retain in 'Asia' 2000 Macedonian cavalry and 13,000 Macedonian infantry, whose pay would be so high that it would excite envy in Macedonia. Alexander had underestimated the resentment of his men; for they had hated his Asian dress, his Asian policy, and his adulteration of the cavalry, and now they saw that he would fill the gap in the pikemen–phalanx with his 'new generation' of Asians. His announcement was greeted with shouts demanding the release of all Macedonians and with jeers: 'Go to war yourself together with your father [Zeus Ammon].'

Alexander and his officers jumped from the rostrum into the crowd. He had his guards arrest the thirteen ringleaders, who were marched off to execution. His speech was heard in silence, and he ended by dismissing them all as deserters. After two days *incommunicado*, he sent for the leading Asian officers, made them commanders of cavalry and infantry units with the famous Macedonian names, and let the senior commanders kiss him as his 'Kinsmen'. This broke the spirit of the Macedonians. They ran to his quarters, threw down their arms and begged for an audience. He came out, wept to see them weeping, called them all his 'Kinsmen' and let them kiss him. They went away 'singing their victory song'. But the victory was Alexander's. He had ended the mutiny and made them accept the Persian system of 'Kinsmen' and kissing. And some 10,000 Macedones volunteered to return to Macedonia. They departed, each man with a talent as a bounty, under the command of Craterus; and to those who stayed with him he promised at some future date the same bounty.

In 323 Alexander completed his plans for the control of 'Asia' during the years when he expected to be campaigning in the Mediterranean theatre. The most unruly element, some 50,000 Greek mercenaries who had served many years in Asia, was to be settled with their Asian women and Eurasian children in Persis. In the place of mercenaries Alexander was to rely primarily on Asian troops. In May, 20,000 men of Persis, trained for a year and commanded by Peucestas, came to Babylon, where they were brigaded with Macedonian phalangites. The new phalanx had in each file four Macedonian pikemen on higher pay (they held the more dangerous positions in action) and twelve 'Persian' archers and javelin-men; it included also some trained Asians from Caria and Lydia. The phalanx was supported by 'no small number' of light-armed infantry from Cossaea and Tapuria, which bordered on Persis, and by 2000 Macedonian cavalry and large forces of Asian cavalry. The entire army of perhaps 40,000 men, in which the Macedonian phalangites numbered some 7000, was to maintain order and to deal with invaders or raiders such as the Scythians whose weapons were the bow and the javelin. In 323 it was stationed centrally and it could move outwards on all-weather roads.

'Alexander reckoned that he could control Asia with an army of modest size, because he had filled his new cities with settlers eager to preserve the status quo and he had posted garrisons at a number of places.' Numbers are difficult to visualize. In 1907 in British India the armed forces, including police, numbered over 400,000, of which the British element was some 75,000; they controlled a population of some 300 millions. Alexander counted on very large numbers of militiamen who had been and were being educated and trained 'in the newly founded cities and the rest of the spear-won territory' – by 323 already some 200,000 boys and young men in all. His faith was in the rising generation. The armed forces had a larger task in the kingdom of Asia than the British had in India. But there was a significant difference. Alexander promoted co-operation and partnership between Europeans and Asians, and he granted high military rank to suitable Asians, whereas as late as 1907 the king's commission was never granted to an Indian soldier. Alexander was organizing a kingdom in which all subjects of the king should have the same legal right, whereas the British were controlling an empire by the exercise of imperial power and privilege.

An army and a fleet were ready to undertake the conquest of Arabia, and his army was to meet Antipater and 10,000 Macedonian phalangites in Palestine in 322. By then a fleet of 1000 large warships would have been built in the South-east Mediterranean to deal with any trouble in the Aegean Sea and then to support his army in the campaign along the North African coast. For that campaign he would have plenty of Asian cavalry, 16,000 Macedonian phalangites and the 30,000 *Epigonoi*; for he reckoned that his most formidable opponents would be heavy-armed infantry. Death intervened. But the plans afford us an insight into the scale of Alexander's thinking.

Alexander believed in the city as the key to economic and cultural progress and to a degree of social integration. He therefore encouraged the growth of the Greek cities in Asia by exempting them from the payment of tribute, giving them additional land (as in the cases of Troy and Priene), and dealing with their envoys directly and not through the satrap. Where native settlements were small, he promoted the development of urban centres (for example in the lower Indus valley); and where populations were partly or wholly nomadic 'he founded cities so that they should plough and work the land, and that having a stake in the country they should not injure one another'. He himself founded seventy new cities (Seleucus later founded fifty in a much smaller area). For instance, at Khodjend (see p. 125) he directed the army to build the wall-circuit of Alexandria Eschate in twenty days, and he peopled it with Macedonians no longer fit for combat, Greek mercenaries, and volunteers from the neighbourhood. Where Macedonians were not available, he settled Europeans from the auxiliary services, and camp followers.

The average city founded by Alexander started with some 10,000 adult males, of whom at least 7000 were natives of the area. The model for these cities was Mecedonian, not Greek: in size, mixture of population, and inclusion within a kingdom. In some and probably most of the cities there were two grades of citizens, as in the cities of Macedonia (see p. 69): first, 'Macedones *and* [e.g.] Alexandrians': second, simply 'Alexandrians'. The first grade of citizens at the start consisted of European soldiers, still carrying arms and leading the development of the city, of which the institutions were those of a Greek democracy. The second grade consisted predominantly of other Europeans. The native peoples were subject to the laws of the city and to their own legal system; but they did not have the political franchise. The official language was standard Greek (*koine*). Natives of the city could learn Greek, rise into the lower grade of citizens, and if they entered the King's Army come back as members of the first grade.

The first function of the Alexander-cities was military. The leaders in the cities were soldiers and ex-soldiers. The young men of native origin, trained by Alexander's representatives (*epistatai*), formed the majority of the 30,000 Greek-speaking 'new generation' of pikemen, who became a part of the King's Army in 324. Other young men of European and of native origin were trained as militiamen, to keep order locally and to defend a frontier (such as Khodjend). The next function was economic; for the European element led the way in the development of agriculture, irrigation and stock-raising, and especially of trade and capitalism. Goods were carried on waterways and on the royal roads. The introduction of Greek culture, and especially of the Greek theatre (analagous to the cinema), led to the dissemination of Greek ideas and of the Greek language not only throughout the cities but also in the surrounding countryside. The term 'fusion' should be avoided. The two cultures, European and Asian, existed side by side, as in mixed marriages. The effect was rather one of stimulation and enrichment, in which the new factor was the European element.

The Persian kings had hoarded much of their wealth in kind, in bullion and in silver and gold coins (the latter called *darics*), with which they paid their mercenaries. Alexander converted this treasure into his own fine silver and gold coinages (see Plates 25a and 25b). Throughout his Kingdom of Asia, he encouraged a monetary economy instead of barter. His gold coins stressed the military triumph of the Macedonians with the helmeted head of Athena and a wreathed, winged Victory; and his silver tetradrachms showed the head of a young Heracles and Zeus enthroned, holding a sceptre and an eagle, which appealed also to the Asians to whom Heracles was Melkart and Zeus was Belus (Ba'al). A medallion, commemorating the victory over Porus, showed Alexander holding a thunderbolt, the symbol of the power of Zeus. The association with Zeus was dominant in Alexander's mind. Apelles painted the king 'bearing the thunderbolt' (*keraunophoros*).

In ten years Alexander and the Macedonians changed a rebellion-ridden and backward empire, suffering from a dictatorial and oppressive system of rule, into a Kingdom of Asia in which the victorious race gave leadership and the king aimed at the co-operation of the peoples of the kingdom. The signal demonstration of his purpose came at a banquet for 9000 guests after the end of the mutiny at Opis. The order of seating was Alexander and his leading Macedonians, then the Persians, and then 'any men of the other peoples who had precedence in reputation or some other form of excellence [*aretē*].' Alexander prayed publicly 'for the blessing especially of concord and partnership between Macedonians and Persians in the ruling [of the kingdom].' What he desired from and for his subjects in Persia was indicated in *The Alexander Romance*, which included a proclamation by Alexander to the Persians: 'You are each to observe the religions and customs, the laws and conventions, the feast days and festivities which you observed in the days of Darius. Let each stay Persian in his way of life, and let him live within his city . . . I wish to make the land one of widespread prosperity and employ the Persian roads as peaceful and quiet channels of commerce.'

'Alexander the Macedonian'

Alexander was a warrior-king, like his predecessors, and his Macedones were all warriors. He and they sought military glory, and they attacked reputedly impregnable strongholds with unlimited audacity. When they were not fighting, they engaged in the dangerous sport of hunting lions, bears, leopards and, in the East, elephants with a spear. The thrills of fighting and of hunting with hand-to-hand weapons had much in common. The Macedonians' history had been one of fighting for survival. Philip and Alexander led them through fighting to conquest and supremacy. There was no doubt in the mind of Alexander's engineer, Aristobulus, who was better able to understand Alexander than we moderns can, that 'Alexander was insatiable in his appetite for further acquisition'. Had he lived, he and his Macedonians would have campaigned along the African coast in 322/1.

Philip and Alexander were exceptional in their power of leadership, 'their own fearlessness in action banishing the fears of their men'; and their ability as generals in devising equipment, in strategy and in tactics knew no rival until Hannibal. And the fact that they were kings added a unique dimension to their relationship with their men. The brilliance of Alexander's intellect was most apparent in his prescience, precision and timing in the set battles in Asia. What made him much more than a conqueror was the use to which he put his power over others. For within ten years, during the continuing process of conquest, he created a type of association between conquerors and subjects that differed radically from the association between Athens and her subjects and was to differ from that between Rome and her subjects (see p. 79 and 203). Here too the power of kingship, especially when that king had the personality of Alexander, was a bonding factor, common to both conquerors and subjects, which was lacking in Athens and Republican Rome.

Alexander was typically Macedonian in the intense religious belief which was the mainspring of his activity. At the same time, he had the Macedonian tolerance of other peoples' religions and a willingness to accept their deities and diviners, especially in Egypt and in Babylonia. As a statesman, he applied to a constantly expanding area the principles of the Macedonian kingdom: co-existence, co-operation, regional self-government, an élite military–administrative overlay, development of cities (often socially mixed), imposition of peace, and furtherance of prosperity. The Macedonians understood those principles from their own experience in Europe, and they enabled Alexander to implement them in his settlement of Asia. What they would not willingly accept was the raising of Asians to their own level as the military–administrative controllers of Alexander's Kingdom of Asia. For they did not sympathize with the most daring of all Alexander's ideas, the ecumenical concept of a harmonious and integrated society. That idea was expressed by Plutarch in the following words:

> Alexander considered that he had come from the gods to be a general governor and reconciler of the world. Using force of arms when he did not bring men together by the light of reason, he harnessed all resources to one and the same end, mixing the lives, manners, marriages and customs of men, as it were in a loving-cup.

When Alexander fell ill (probably with *malaria tropica*), his first priority was to serve the gods of the Macedonian State. 'His fever being very high, he was carried on a stretcher to perform the sacrifices which custom

.(a) *Right*: Gold Quiver-cover
    (46.5 cm high)
 (b) *Below*: Gilded Pectoral
    (diameter 30 cm)

18.(a) *Left*: Dionysiac Revelry

(b) *Below*: Silver Vessels (30.5 cm and 24.5 cm high)

19.(a) *Left*: Derveni Crater (91 cm high)
   (b) *Below*: Seated Maenad

20.(a) *Left*: Satyr and
     Maenad
   (b) *Below*: Two
     Maenads

Asia looks up at Alexander who is planting his spear in Asian soil at the Hellespont. Boscoreale Painting (part only)

22. Alexander Mosaic (5.12 × 2.71 m)

23.(a) *Above*: Parmenio in Action
   (b) *Below*: Alexander Sarcophagus. The Sarcophagus, dated c. 325–300 BC, is named after
       Alexander, who is portrayed about to strike the lion from the left (6.3 m long)

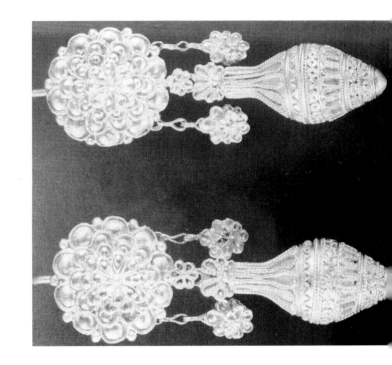

24. (a) *Left*: Silver Strainer (19.5 cm long)
    (b) *Below*: Gold Earrings (4.8 cm high)

a, ii

iii

25.(a) *Top*: Porus Medallion and *(centre)* Portrait of Alexander

(b) *Below*: Coins 336–240

b, ii

b, iii

b, iv

b, vi

b, vii

b, viii

b, ix

i

ii

iii

iv

v

vi

vii

26. Coins 240–167

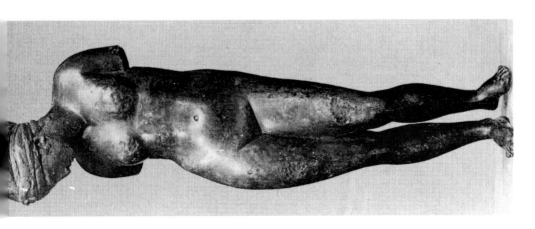

27.(a) *Left:* Girl of Beroea
(b) *Above:* Ptolemaic Queen (41 cm high)

28.(a) *Above*: Lion Hunt (4.9 × 3.2 m)
   (b) *Below*: Dionysus on a Panther (2.7 × 2.65 m)

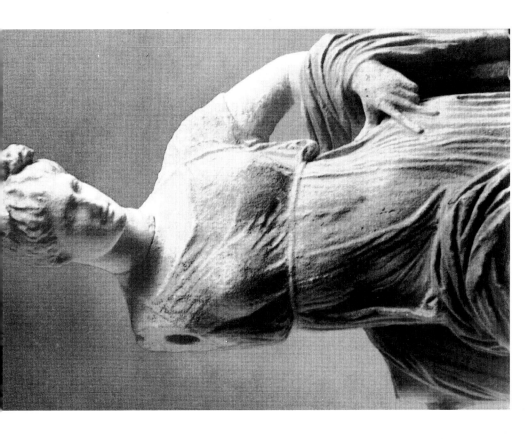

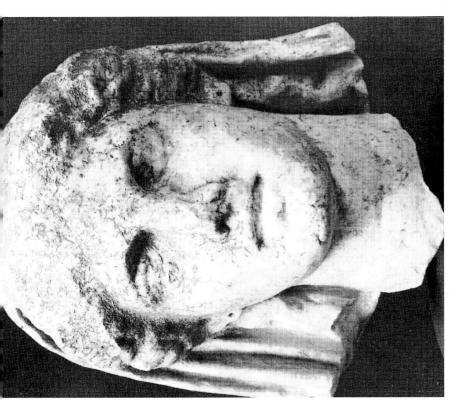

29.(a) *Above*: Demeter of Dium
(b) *Right*: Aphrodite below Olympus

i

ii

iii

iv

v

vi

vii

30. Coins of the Diaspora

Lake
Ochrid

Lake
Prespa

Corcyra

est Macedonia and Rome's Protectorate

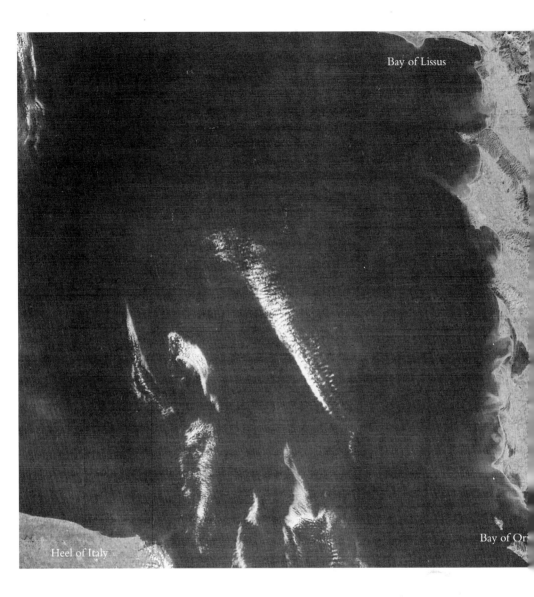

Bay of Lissus

Bay of Or[

Heel of Italy

32. The Strait of Otranto

prescribed for each day.' The gods who had saved him from so many perils and such serious wounds had promised, he believed, that he would conquer all 'Asia'; and it seems that he was entirely confident of conducting the campaign in Arabia. Then he lost his voice. His thoughts were of the officers and the men who had fought at his side. When the officers came in 'he knew them'. Then the Macedonian soldiers, fearing that his death was being concealed, 'in their grief and longing for the king pressed in to see Alexander . . . As they filed past, he greeted them one by one, raising his head with difficulty and indicating with his eyes'. He died later that day, June, 323 BC.

The personality of Alexander defies description. The strength and the directness of his emotions were devastating. His love for his strong-willed mother was such that he broke with his father and accompanied her into some form of self-imposed exile. When Antipater wrote criticizing her, Alexander remarked, 'He does not know that one of my mother's tears washes away ten thousand letters.' His father's stature was such that Alexander was always striving to become his equal; and only in the drinking-bout with Cleitus he claimed to have surpassed him. Throughout his life he was impelled by a love of glory and by a desire for all men to recognize his glory. He set no limit to his own endeavour. He would rival Achilles in battle and Heracles in his labours for mankind.

In relation to others, he was not self-seeking. He was generous to a fault in rewarding officers and men alike. He trusted his friends, at times beyond reason. His horror that he had killed Cleitus was as unlimited as his grief for the death of Hephaestion. His extravagance in honouring Demaratus and Hephaestion verged on megalomania, but not for himself. He had a spontaneous respect for others: for the royal Persian ladies, for the corpse of Darius, for the tomb of Cyrus, for the courage and dignity of Porus. When he fell in love with Roxane, he treated her not as a captive but as an equal, and in the weddings at Susa he arranged for the rites to be those not of Macedonia but of Persia.

He had a love of danger in the hunt, in personal combat, in being first into every action – a love which was not lessened by the wounds which made him face death. He saw as his destiny an endless series of conquests, and he did not count the cost in human lives except for those of his countrymen. What was his chief priority? Arrian was probably right in making the climax of his qualities 'attention to divinity'. Alexander was punctilious in carrying out the religious observances which were traditional and in his eyes obligatory, even in the last days of his illness. He believed that the purposes of the gods were revealed to him in dreams, oracles and omens, and he accepted those purposes without question. One purpose, he believed, was 'to reconcile the world' by placing men of worth on the same level in positions of authority and responsibility, whatever their national and racial origins, and by insisting on justice and mercy for all the people of

151

his kingdom, victors and vanquished alike. It was this side of his personality which inspired the creation of *The Alexander Romance* in many languages and held the imagination of so many generations.

XI

The Continuation of the Temenid Monarchy and the Macedonian State, 323–306

The decisions of the Macedonians, 323–321

The world of Alexander was inevitably shaken to its foundations by the sudden death of the king at the age of thirty-two. The chances that it would fall apart must have seemed very high. Philip and Alexander had never tried to disarm the peoples they had taken over or defeated; on the contrary they had armed and trained those peoples' best men and given them experience in war. It was particularly so in Greece. There Alexander had enabled the Greek city-states to unite their forces under the terms of the Common Peace; he had sent home their victorious troops, and his officers had led a Greek fleet of 160 triremes to success against Persia. Would the Greeks now turn their potentially huge forces against the army of 15,000 Macedonians and the small fleet which were stationed in Macedonia in 323? Would the Balkan peoples rise in support of the rebel king Seuthes and descend in swarms upon Macedonia? And in Asia surely the 15,000 Macedonians at Babylon would be swamped by the 50,000 Asian infantry and many thousands of experienced Asian cavalry, which were concentrated under arms at Babylon. Elsewhere in Asia what chance had the few thousands of Macedonians, mostly unfit for combat, of holding down the many millions of subjects?

The modern scholars who have seen the Macedonians as ruthless conquerors and Alexander as a hated autocrat, or even as a despotic successor of Darius on the Persian throne, have been quick to assert that by 321 the world of Alexander was 'dismembered', and that Alexander's ideas and achievements 'passed away'. It seems that they have been hypnotised by the personality of Alexander. They do not look beyond him to the Macedonians who created Alexander's world and who, as we shall see, held it firm against its enemies. It was almost miraculous that they succeeded; but it was less of a miracle to those who understood, as ancient writers reported, that 'the Persians mourned for Alexander as the justest of kings', the Queen Mother Sisigambis died of grief for him, and the inhabitants of his seventy new cities were eager to maintain the *status quo*. As we shall see, it was the Europeans who caused trouble, and not the Asians; and we may anticipate our narrative by remarking that the Asians stayed quiet not through 'oriental apathy' – their fighting had been far from apathetic – but through contentment with the changing conditions of their world.

The immediate problem was the succession. The decision lay necessarily with the Macedonians in Babylon; for they and the king, alive or dead, made up the Macedonian State. The leading Macedonian officers tried to impose the choice which they and the 2000 cavalrymen approved on the 13,000 infantrymen. But the latter stood out for their own choice. The ranks of the leading officers split. The real danger of an armed conflict was averted by the most senior officer, Perdiccas, who was not only a Bodyguard of the dead king and the successor of Hephaestion as the king's deputy in the Kingdom of Asia but also a member of the royal house. The full Assembly of Macedones, voting 'in the presence of the corpse of Alexander, so that his Majesty should be the witness of their decisions', adopted the proposal of Perdiccas, that Arrhidaeus (the half-witted half-brother of Alexander) be elected king, that Roxane's child *in utero* be elected king in the event of its being a boy, and that Perdiccas be appointed 'manager of the kingship'. The Assembly went on to make the following decisions: Arrhidaeus was to bear the name 'Philip' (for us Philip III), Antipater was to be general in charge of Macedonia and Greece, Craterus was to be 'protector of the kingship' in Macedonia (sacrificing, presiding, administering royal properties), Perdiccas was to be general of the King's Army in 'Asia'; and Meleager was to be the deputy of Perdiccas. The distinction between King of Macedones and King of Asia disappeared; for the Assembly of Macedones took decisions for the areas of both kingdoms.

On the negative side, the Assembly had chosen not to set up a republic, and not to elect Perdiccas (or Leonnatus, also a member of the royal house) king. On the positive side, it insisted on keeping the throne for the direct descendants of Philip, no doubt in the belief that the divine blessing was on that line, and it took steps to ensure that no one general could seize overall power. Antipater and Craterus were checks on one another; both were checks on Perdiccas; and Meleager was a further check on Perdiccas, because in the beginning Perdiccas had sided with the cavalry and Meleager with the infantry. The ultimate power lay with the Assembly, the king being a nonentity. This power was acknowledged by Perdiccas, when he brought before the Assembly of Macedones the plans of Alexander, which were recorded in the *Royal Journal*, and asked the Assembly to reach a decision. These plans included the Arabian campaign, the building of a huge fleet, the preparations for the campaign along the north coast of Africa, the construction of seven great temples, the creation of new cities (in Persis and Media especially), and the transplantation of Asians to Europe and Europeans to Asia. The Assembly decided not to proceed with these enterprises as being 'on an excessive scale and difficult to achieve'. There is no doubt that the Assembly was prudent, because Perdiccas lacked the necessary ability for conducting such campaigns.

Preparations for the funeral of Alexander included the traditional purification of the Macedonian army (see p. 32). In the course of it, Perdiccas, riding alongside Philip and commanding the cavalry and the elephants, arrested in the name of the king and executed some infantrymen who had broken into the royal quarters when the cavalry and the infantry had been at odds with one another. The next step was the appointment of a list of generals and satraps, allegedly drawn up by Philip but actually by Perdiccas. The list probably was confirmed by the Assembly of Macedones. The arrangements for the making of a funerary car which would carry the embalmed body of Alexander to Aegeae in Macedonia were entrusted to an officer named Arrhidaeus. Some days later Meleager was arraigned by Perdiccas, prosecuting on behalf of the king, and was executed for treason. A successor to Meleager was not appointed. In August Roxane gave birth to a boy. The Assembly of Macedones acclaimed him king and named him Alexander. The continuity of the Temenid house on the throne seemed to be assured. It lasted from 323 to c. 307.

A dangerous rising by 23,000 Greek mercenary soldiers in Iran was quashed by 3800 élite Macedonian troops and by Asian soldiers in the central satrapies, a success which showed that the Asians were loyal to the regime. In 322 Perdiccas, keeping Philip at his side and commanding the King's Army, defeated a native usurper in Cappadocia and wintered in Cilicia. Meanwhile, Antipater had been dealing with a major rising, led by Athens and Aetolia. His army of 600 Macedonian cavalry and 13,000 Macedonian infantry was defeated by a confederate army of 30,000, to which the Thessalian cavalry deserted. But the Macedonian phalanx, keeping formation, withdrew intact and held the fortified city of Lamia throughout the winter, the Greeks being feeble in siegecraft. In spring 322 an army of Macedonians and Asians, crossing from Asia and recruiting men in Macedonia, was defeated by the Thessalian cavalry but again the phalanx withdrew intact; and Antipater evacuated Lamia and returned to Macedonia, which was now well defended. The confederate fleet, led by Athens, was unchallenged in autumn 323; but it was not joined by the Aegean islanders, who had experienced Athenian methods. In 322 it was totally defeated in several engagements. Athens was eclipsed for ever as a naval power, and Macedonian supremacy at sea was established by Macedonian commanders and by crews of many races. For the decisive campaign Antipater's army, having been reinforced by Craterus, who brought 6000 veteran Macedonians and 1000 Persians and raised another 5500 men en route to Thessaly, amounted to 5000 cavalry and 43,000 infantry. The war was won by the charge of the Macedonian phalanx in August 322. Resistance was maintained only by the Aetolians that winter. Most states, and Athens in particular, surrendered unconditionally.

The other problem was Thrace, where Seuthes was still in revolt with 8000 cavalry and 20,000 infantry. The newly appointed general, Lysimachus, attacked with 2000 cavalry and 4000 infantry, of whom only a part were Macedonians, and inflicted heavy casualties. By the end of 322 his men had outfought Seuthes, who submitted and was left on his throne by Lysimachus. Thus in 323–2 Macedonian valour, supported by large numbers of Asian troops, prevailed on land and sea and gained a series of victories which were as remarkable as those won by Alexander. The three commanders – Perdiccas, Antipater and Craterus – had maintained Macedonian ascendancy in all theatres. Late in 322 they arranged marriage-ties with one another, when two daughters of Antipater (now seventy-five years old) were to marry Craterus and Perdiccas. And Antipater's policy towards Athens was supported by Perdiccas, who on behalf of the kings ruled that Samos should be restored to the Samians.

Antipater did not try to re-establish the Common Peace which had been shattered by the widespread rising. Instead, he imposed minority governments and where necessary, as at Athens, strong garrisons; and his agents executed or banished the leaders of the rising (among them Demosthenes, who had returned to Athens now and committed suicide). Heavy indemnities had to be paid, and the penalizing of democratic supporters was such that many emigrated, a large number of Athenians settling in Thrace. In abandoning the liberal principles of Philip and Alexander, and in adopting a traditional form of Greek imperialistic control, Antipater made conciliation and co-operation impossible, and he put an undue strain on Macedonia's limited manpower. Yet the success of Macedonian arms was plain for all Greek states to see.

The civil war of 321–306

The responsibility for the civil war lay partly with the royal house, in which Olympias and her daughter Cleopatra, as grandmother and aunt of the infant king, were at odds with Cynane, daughter of Philip by Audata and mother of Eurydice by Amyntas, the ex-king, who had been executed as a commoner in 335; and partly with three generals of the older generation – Antigonus the One-eyed (*Monophthalmus*), Antipater and Craterus. An added complication was the bitter enmity between Olympias and Antipater. Olympias' first move was to offer Cleopatra in marriage to Leonnatus, a member of the royal house, who was bringing an army to Macedonia and might oust Antipater; but he was killed in battle in spring 322. Her next plan was to marry Cleopatra to Perdiccas. Cleopatra went as far as Sardis early in 321. Meanwhile, Cynane had stolen a march on her rivals. She and Eurydice, aged about fifteen, had eluded Antipater's control and crossed to Asia, where Cynane was murdered on Perdiccas' orders by his brother. But the King's Army, outraged by the murder, insisted that Eurydice should marry Philip, as Cynane had intended. Thus Eurydice became a Queen, while Cleopatra waited.

The instigator of the generals was Antigonus, satrap of Phrygia. In 322 he disobeyed the orders of Perdiccas and was summoned to stand trial before the Assembly of Macedones. He escaped to Greece. There he told Antipater and Craterus that Perdiccas planned to marry Cleopatra, bring her and the two kings to Macedonia and oust Antipater and Craterus from their positions. True or not, the story caused them to patch up a peace with Aetolia, to approach Ptolemy as a son-in-law of Antipater for an alliance, and to lead their armed forces into Asia. Their aim was not to challenge the two kings, whom they and their Macedonian soldiers accepted, but to overthrow Perdiccas and his supporters.

The first action of the civil war, in Asia Minor, saw the death of Craterus, the most popular of Alexander's generals, in midsummer 321. Perdiccas had decided to deal first with Ptolemy, the satrap of Egypt, who had highjacked the corpse of Alexander in Syria and taken it to Egypt. He summoned Ptolemy for trial. Ptolemy presented his case before the Assembly of Macedones, who acquitted him and let him return to his satrapy. Perdiccas, who had the kings and the King's Army, unwisely pressed on with an invasion of Egypt, bungled a crossing of the Nile and was murdered by his own officers. The Assembly of Macedones offered the managership of the kings to Ptolemy; when he declined, it conferred the position on two officers, and after their resignation on Antipater. His list of satraps, nominally that of the two kings, was approved by the Assembly, which consisted now of the King's Army and the Macedones brought by Antipater from Macedonia. The Assembly went on to condemn to death any officers who were still supporters of Perdiccas in autumn 321.

Antipater, now nearing eighty, had a rough ride with the King's Army, which resented the quarrels of the senior commanders and clamoured for a bounty which Alexander had promised but had not paid. In spring 320 Antipater returned to Macedonia, taking with him all the royals except Cleopatra (she was under guard in Sardis), the Royal Pages, most of Alexander's Macedonians, and half of the elephant corps. Thus, after a gap of fourteen years, Pella was again the seat of the Macedonian State. But the centre of financial and therefore of naval and military power was now in the Kingdom of Asia.

We are concerned here with the characteristics rather than the details of the civil war. The kingship was not in dispute. All Macedonian soldiers and all commanders expressed their allegiance to the throne; and the soldiers had an affection for the women of the royal house. Thus, although Antipater distrusted Olympias and Cleopatra, he did not dare to lay hands on them. When Antipater's successor, Polyperchon, found himself opposed by Antigonus, Ptolemy and Antipater's son Cassander, he invoked the help of Olympias in 318. Oaths of allegiance to 'Olympias and the kings' were taken, and orders were issued in their names appointing Eumenes, a supporter still of Perdiccas, to be 'commander of all Asia with full powers', and instructing all satraps and officers to obey him. This intervention by Olympias enabled Eumenes to enlist the 3000 Hypaspists, now called the Silvershields, in her cause and to prolong the struggle. But it was a mistaken policy to commit the royal family to backing one commander against another.

In 317 Polyperchon's position deteriorated. He left Philip and Eurydice in Macedonia, but he sent little Alexander and Roxane to Olympias in Molossia. During his absence, Eurydice took the bit between her teeth: she announced that 'the king [Philip] had transferred the administration of the kingdom to Cassander', and she ordered Polyperchon and Antigonus to surrender their armies to Cassander. Because the announcement implied the deposition of Alexander, and because Cassander was her enemy, Olympias raised an army and entered Macedonia, where the Macedonian soldiers of Philip and Eurydice baulked at attacking the mother of Alexander the Great and deserted to her. Olympias had Philip stabbed to death, and forced Eurydice, now nineteen, to commit suicide in prison; she also killed some supporters of Cassander. Her cruelty shocked many Macedonians, and Cassander was able to confine her and the royal family to Pydna, which was stoutly defended. But famine caused her to capitulate on a promise that her life would be spared. Cassander did not keep his word. She was done to death by relatives of her victims in 316.

Cassander claimed to have liberated Alexander and Roxane, and he now married Alexander's aunt, Thessalonice, a daughter of Philip by a Thessalian queen. She probably became the boy-king's guardian, and Cassander was elected manager of the kingship by the Assembly of Macedones. He placed Alexander and Roxane in the garrisoned citadel of Amphipolis on the grounds that they might otherwise be seized by raiding forces, and he staged a magnificent funeral for the remains of Philip, Eurydice and Cynane. He was demonstrably doing his duty by the late king and the reigning king.

A break in the civil war occurred in 311. The main contenders agreed to a settlement which was to last 'until Alexander, son of Roxane, shall come to maturity' – in other words until 305, when at the age of eighteen Alexander would rule in person and make his own distribution of powers. The next disaster was due to Polyperchon. He got control of Heracles, a natural son of Alexander by Barsine, a Persian aristocrat, who was about to be eighteen; his plan was to make Heracles co-king with Alexander and to let Heracles rule in person. In 309 he brought Heracles and Barsine with an army of some 20,000 men to the frontier. Cassander feared that his own Macedonian soldiers might desert to Heracles. He therefore persuaded Polyperchon by arguments and promises to murder Heracles and Barsine. These murders alarmed Cleopatra, still in Sardis, who had hitherto kept clear of the contestants in the civil war, but now she tried to escape and marry Ptolemy. Antigonus arranged her murder. Death overtook Alexander and Roxane in the citadel of Amphipolis; but their demise was kept secret until 306/5. The analysis of the bones in Tomb III at Vergina has now revealed to us that they belonged to a youth not yet sixteen, and thus that Alexander died not later than 308/7. The male line of the Temenid house was now defunct, and the bond which had held the Macedonians in a common allegiance, wherever they were, was snapped, as it proved, for ever.

The bitter animosities of the civil war were reflected in propaganda for and against members of the royal family. Cassandrites blackened the name of Olympias, who was said to have instigated the murder of her husband Philip, and the supporters of Olympias claimed that Antipater and his sons Cassander and Iollas had engineered the poisoning of Alexander the Great. These items of propaganda have been accepted by some scholars – wrongly, in my opinion. The deaths of Alexander IV and Roxane were certainly said by his opponents to have been ordered by Cassander. On the other hand, they may have been due to disease or have been passed off as such. At any rate, the gifts in the tomb of Alexander IV were magnificent. The truth about their deaths is unascertainable.

The contenders in the civil war had soldiers and money at their disposal, because they disregarded Alexander's division of civil, financial and military responsibilities. Ptolemy was the first to do so: he appropriated the revenues from the financial officer Cleomenes (who was executed), took command of all troops in the satrapy and attracted Macedonians by offers of high pay. Other satraps followed suit. Macedonian élite troops were what they wanted; for the officers became their administrators, and the Companion Cavalry and the Phalanx were the spearhead of attack, as they had been under Alexander. Each ambitious contender set up replicas of Alexander's military system: for instance, Leonnatus in 322 had a Guard of Companion Cavalry (*agema*), Persian chargers with gold bits, and personal hairstyle and equipment like that of Alexander; and Eumenes had an Infantry Guard, Companion Cavalry and a squadron of Pages, and he distributed purple caps (*kausiai*) and cloaks to his Macedonians.

The supply of such Macedonians varied over 323–307 with the movements of veterans and others to and from Macedonia. The bulk of Alexander's pikemen went home; but some 3000 veterans stayed with Antigonus, and the 3000 Silvershields served in Asia to the end. Antipater brought perhaps 3000 young pikemen to Asia, who stayed. New accessions were the sons of Asian women born to Macedonian soldiers, whether during active service (for example, the sons of 10,000 in 324, and 3000 sons of the Silvershields) or when stationed in cities; and Alexander's seventy cities continued to produce militiamen and recruits for Macedonian units of cavalry and infantry alike. Losses of Macedonians in action were small. Desertion was often preferable to combat, and set battles were rare. The infliction of heavy casualties at Gabiene in 316 by the Silvershields was a unique event, and they suffered no loss themselves.

All contenders depended on very large numbers of front-line Asian troops. For instance, at Paraetacene in 317 Antigonus had 8000 Asian pikemen, and Eumenes had 5000 such; and most of the cavalry on either side was Asian, armed usually with native weapons but sometimes with lances. The bulk of Ptolemy's army in 313 was Egyptian. Antigonus employed 9000 mercenary infantry at Paraetacene, and Eumenes 6000; they were mainly obtained from Greece and the Balkans. Losses of Asians and mercenaries seem to have been easily replaced. The support services for the armies were supplied predominantly by Asians.

The need for the satraps to win the co-operation and develop the resources of the native peoples was greater than ever; for they depended on the loyalty of their Asian troops and on the revenues. An outstanding example was Peucestas, satrap of Persis, who trained large numbers of Persian troops and gave a huge banquet at which Macedonians and Persians of high rank received equal honour and sacrifices were made to the gods, to Philip and to Alexander, the analogy being with Alexander's banquet at Opis (see p. 149). Peithon, satrap of Media, and Seleucus, satrap of Babylonia, were also successful in winning the affections of their subjects. Ptolemy developed the resources of Egypt and added Cyrenaica, 'won by the spear'; and in the East the Macedonian Tlepolemus, the Cyriote Stasanor and the Bactrian Oxyartes were dependable governors of Carmania, Areia and Paropanisadae respectively. As the cities founded by Alexander took root and prospered, they developed commercial exchange and provided troops. The treasure accumulated by Alexander in Asia was kept intact for the kings and their representatives until 316, when Antigonus began to confiscate large sums. Coinage was issued with the name of Philip III in gold, silver and bronze, and there were posthumous issues of Alexander's gold and silver coinage. Some half-drachmae in silver and some bronze coins for circulation in Europe carried the name of Alexander IV (see Plate 25b: v). No contender in the civil war issued coinage in his own name, although Ptolemy and Antigonus acquired great financial resources.

The effect of the civil war on Asia and Egypt was superficial. While it employed large numbers of men who were becoming professional soldiers through long service, it did not lead to massacre, enslavement, destruction of cities or impoverishment of civilian populations (as wars between Greek states had often done). Below the surface, everything which Alexander had planned continued to develop: the co-operation of Macedonians and 'Asians' at various levels, the growth of cities, the expansion of commerce, the conversion of specie into currency, the education of selected Asians, and the spread of the Greek language. The sufferers in the civil war were those city-states of the Greek mainland which were defeated in the Lamian War and then became pawns for rival Macedonian contenders, who backed one side against the other in party-strife. Macedonia continued to be a rich kingdom in its own right.

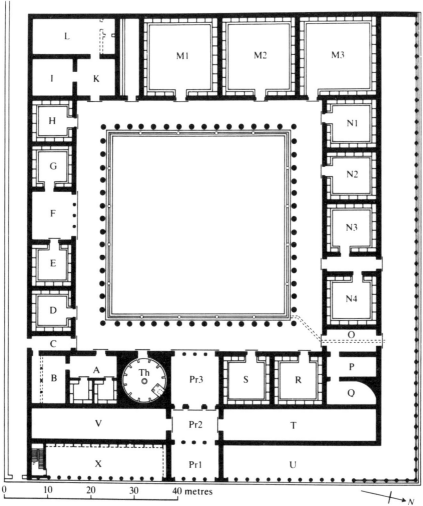

Fig 14 The Palace at Aegeae

The posthumous coinages of Alexander were widespread in Europe. Bullion and coin were sent from Asia to Pella from time to time, until Antigonus began to confiscate the treasuries for his own use. Cassander made some short-term gains in the west, where he probably founded Antipatrea (Berat in central Albania), but he lost them when he was distracted by events in the civil war. He strengthened the manpower of the country by planting large numbers of Autariatae (an Illyrian tribe) within his frontiers in 312 and 310 and using some of them as soldiers, and he improved his trade and his defences by founding two great cities, Thessalonica and Cassandrea, into which neighbouring populations were transplanted. Cassandrea was treated at first as a Greek city, because the Greeks of the Pallene peninsula were transplanted and Greek refugees – from Olynthus, for example – were reinstated there as citizens. The magnificent palace at Aegeae was built by Cassander in the last decade of the century. Macedonia's prestige was maintained as the centre of the Macedonian world, the seat of the Temenid kings, until the death of Alexander IV was made public.

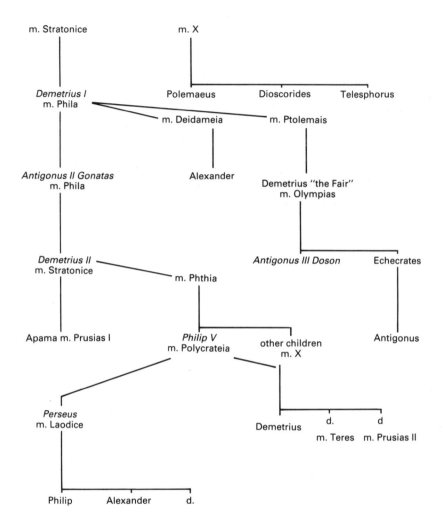

Note: names of those who became king of Macedonia are in italics.

Fig 15 The descendants of Antigonus Monophthalmus

XII

The Macedonian States of the Hellenistic Age, 306–200

The Formation and Character of the Macedonian States

As soon as the death of Alexander was known, Antigonus stepped into the vacancy. He had prepared the ground in 315, when he had convened in Phoenicia an Assembly of Macedones, which consisted of soldiers and ex-soldiers, and had publicized its decisions as 'the decree [*dogma*] of the Macedones with Antigonus', a form of words which implied that it was an act of state. But in the publication he had emphasized that he was under the overall authority of Alexander, whose true 'manager' he (as opposed to Cassander) claimed to be. Now that that authority was gone, the Assembly of Macedones with Antigonus, meeting at his headquarters in Syria, acclaimed Antigonus and his son Demetrius as kings. Thereby a Macedonian State was created, complete with its to-be-hereditary constitutional monarchy. Whether Antigonus said so or not, it was clear to his rivals that he intended this to be *the* Macedonian State and himself to be 'King of Macedones' wherever they were. They therefore followed suit. Ptolemy, Seleucus, Lysimachus and Cassander were acclaimed individually as kings by an Assembly of Macedones in the area over which each exercised control. But because all four formed an alliance against Antigonus, they had to respect each other's position and did not claim kingship over all Macedones. Thus four more Macedonian States were born, and the existing Macedonian State in Europe acknowledged their birth as separate entities. It was the dawn of a new age.

The move from satrap or general to king was simple. Each of the five already had his Infantry and Cavalry Guards, Companion Cavalry, School of Pages and élite Macedonian units, which now became his 'King's Army'; and each had a group of Friends and Companions which he had been accustomed to consult on matters of strategy and policy. He had only to put on the diadem and call his headquarters a palace; for the mechanism of his Macedonian State was already in position. The members of the Assembly in all five states were 'the citizen soldiers [*politikoi stratiōtai*]' and the ex-soldiers, who together possessed the political franchise. They elected or deposed a king, voted on matters he brought before them, and tried cases of treason. Their numbers were maintained by the king, who admitted recruits to his King's Army and made them 'Macedones'. They were bound to the king by an oath of allegiance; and he was bound to them by self-interest, since they were the spearhead of his army and the implementers of his authority.

Each king was anxious to claim a connection with the Temenid house or at least with a related divinity. Cassander was in the strongest position; for he was married to Thessalonice, a daughter of Philip II, and he named his three sons Philip, Alexander and Antipater. His statue was erected at Dium, alongside the statues of the Temenid kings, and the dedication on the base has been discovered: 'King of Macedones Cassander, son of Antipater, to Zeus of Olympus'. His coinage, issued only in bronze (see Plate 25b: vi), was marked 'of King Cassander' and used the emblems which Amyntas III and Philip II had favoured – especially those of Heracles and his weapons – in order to stress the continuity of his rule with theirs; and the gold and silver coinage of Alexander the Great was still in vogue. Ptolemy hinted that he was a natural son of Philip II or at least a second cousin once removed through Arsinoe, and he claimed descent from Heracles and from Dionysus; and his coins 'of King Ptolemy' portrayed himself with the aegis of Zeus (see Plate 30: ii), an eagle on a thunderbolt and Alexander the Great in a car drawn by elephants. Lysimachus, who was probably Thessalian by origin on his father's side, emphasized his close personal association with Alexander the Great; and his coins 'of King Lysimachus' bore a fine head of Alexander as a god wearing the horn of Zeus Ammon and on the reverse a victorious Athena, goddess of war (see Plate 25a: iii). Seleucus claimed descent from Apollo, who placed his mark in the shape of an anchor on Seleucus' thigh at birth; and his coins 'of King Seleucus' continued the issues of Alexander the Great, commemorated his horse Bucephalus as a horned horse, and showed an Indian elephant above an anchor (see Plate 30: iii). Later Seleucid kings claimed Heracles as an ancestor. Antigonus and his descendants, who later became kings of Macedonia, claimed kinship with the Temenid house, and the last king, Perseus, called his sons Philip and Alexander. In Macedonia they were members of the royal tribe, the Argeadae (see p. 31), as the Temenids had been. Thus the two dynasties – Temenid and Antigonid – could be called Argeadae. The coins 'of King Antigonus' were in the image of Alexander's coins and suggested that Antigonus was the successor of Alexander throughout the Macedonian world. The coins 'of King Demetrius' celebrated a great naval victory over Ptolemy by showing a Poseidon with poised trident and on the reverse a Victory on a ship's prow (see Plate 25b: vii, viii).

The theory and the practice in the homeland (see p. 34 and 109), that the king owned 'the spear-won land' and exercised direct rule over 'peoples conquered by the spear [*ethnē dorialōta*]', were applied in the new Macedonian states. Ptolemy and Seleucus, for instance, made the claim that they ruled over territory 'won by the spear', and they were capable of extending that territory by further conquests. The king sequestered land by right for himself and for the foundation of new cities or military settlements, and he gave estates to deserving Friends. He owned the deposits of precious metal within the kingdom, and he worked the mines with convict- or slave-labour, usually under inhuman conditions. He governed the indigenous peoples by *fiat*, fixing taxes, directing labour, controlling agricultural production and carrying out the reclamation of land by drainage and by irrigation (such as the Fayum in Egypt). The kings had need of Greek settlers as well as Greek mercenaries; for the Greeks and the Macedonians gave the lead in the new cities, of which Seleucus alone founded fifty, and Greeks often acted as civil servants in the royal administration.

The kings accorded favoured status to existing Greek cities and to the new cities, in order to attract Greek immigrants and encourage growth. Both types of cities tended to develop cosmopolitan populations of many races, but the official language was always the *koinē*, the language alike of Macedonians and Greeks. In both, the Macedonian system of education, of which the gymnasium was the symbol, was soon well rooted. As in Macedonia, the cities provided for the King's Army the recruits who became Macedones, and the king also promoted distinguished Greeks or natives to the rank of Companion and Friend. Thus it was possible for men of 'excellence' (to use Alexander's term *aretē*) of whatever race to rise to high positions.

Monarchical states on the Macedonian model were created elsewhere from time to time. Pyrrhus, for instance, formed a kingdom which extended at one time from Acarnania to Lissus (on the Albanian coast) and included part of Macedonia; his own descent from Achilles gave him a divine ancestry and a bond with Alexander the Great. Philetaerus and his adopted son Eumenes founded the Pergamene kingdom. Their successors kept the head of Phile-taerus on their coins but without the title 'king', and they claimed descent from Telephus, a son of Heracles (see Plate 30: v, vi). They based their administrative system closely on that of the Ptolemies. A separate monarch-ical state arose in Bactria through the secession of a Seleucid satrap, Diodotus (see Plate 30: vii). His coins 'of King Diodotus' showed Zeus and a thunder-bolt in the manner of Alexander's coins, and the founder of the succeeding dynasty placed on his coins the elephant-scalp headdress of Alexander. The Macedonian model with a Greek bureaucracy was adopted by native dynas-ties which established themselves on the fringes of the Macedonian world in Bithynia and Pontus (the dynastic names being Nicomedes and Mithridates), and to a lesser extent in Cappadocia, Meroe (Sudan) and Parthia.

In the Macedonian kingdom there had certainly been worship of individual kings after death (for instance Archelaus, Amyntas III and Philip II), and also collective worship of all past kings at the state festival known as the Xandica (see p. 32), which was held annually down to the fall of the Macedonian king-dom. During the period of the civil war sacrifices were made to 'the gods and Philip and Alexander' by the Macedonians and the Persians at Persepolis (see p. 160); and the Macedonian soldiers believed from 323 onwards that

Alexander survived death and exercised some power over Macedonian affairs. When Ptolemy brought the corpse of Alexander to Egypt, he set up a cult of Alexander as founder of Alexandria (a 'hero-cult', like the hero-cult of Philip II at Philippi). When the new Macedonian states came into being, Ptolemy established an official worship of Alexander as a god throughout his kingdom; and after their deaths Ptolemy himself and his queen were worshipped as deities at the instigation of Ptolemy II. The worships of Alexander and Ptolemy were combined at the annual festival of the Ptolemaic dynasty, the *Ptolemaieia*. Similar cults developed for Seleucus after death as a god, and for Philetaerus likewise. These forms of worship had religious meaning particularly for the Macedonians, since they believed that the favour of the gods was transmitted through the kings, generation after generation.

Deification of a living king was something different. It seems that Amyntas III and Philip II received 'divine honours' in Macedonia and were worshipped there during life (see pp. 94 ff.); on the other hand, such honours were denied to Alexander by the Macedonians. The first known example of such deification in a new Macedonian state was the inclusion of Ptolemy II and Arsinoe as 'sibling gods' (*theoi adelphoi*, Ptolemy being married to his sister) in the *Ptolemaieia* (see also Plate 30: i). The earliest evidence for a similar cult in the Seleucid kingdom occurs in the reign of Antiochus III; but it probably originated earlier. The precedents in Macedonia suggest that these deifications were intended to influence the Macedonians in Egypt and Syria primarily.

The kings in the new Macedonian states represented themselves as the protectors and benefactors of all their subjects. Like Alexander, Ptolemy collaborated with the Egyptian priests, and carried out some traditional ceremonies as ruler of Egypt, and he and his successors helped Egyptian temples financially. From the start he treated the Egyptians 'humanely' (*philanthrōpōs*) according to a contemporary historian, Hieronymus; and the right of appeal, which Alexander had granted to every subject (as traditionally in Macedonia), was continued by Ptolemy and his successors. Seleucus 'won the goodwill of the masses' in Babylonia to such an extent that he regained the satrapy with a tiny force of Macedonians (200 cavalry and 800 infantry). He and his successors gave generous donations to the native temples in Syria and Babylonia. Where kingship traditionally had a divine right and divine aura, as in Egypt and Babylonia, the authority of the Macedonian king was enhanced. The Greeks stood apart from the indigenous peoples. Because they were treated favourably, they responded, both as communities and individuals, by honouring spontaneously the commanders in the civil war and then the kings with the whole gamut of honours up to worship as deities (for example, Scepsis in the Troad worshipping Antigonus in 311, and Priene King Lysimachus later). Such honours were little more than expressions of gratitude, acknowledgements of superior authority, and superlative compliments in the minds of donors and honorands alike.

Although the Macedonian states often fought one another, they were efficient in many respects. They provided for their inhabitants long periods of peace within the frontiers of each kingdom (continuous for almost three centuries in the case of Egypt), and they attained a high level of material prosperity (see Plate 30: ii). The government was streamlined, in that the king and his Macedones took all decisions, policed the kingdom, and defended or extended its frontiers with the help of indigenous and mercenary troops. The cities, whether Greek or indigenous in origin or royally founded within a kingdom, had no foreign policy and were in consequence not subject to the Greek disease of party-strife (*stasis*). At the same time they felt themselves to be enjoying 'liberty, autonomy and democracy' in accordance with royal charter, and they combined and competed with one another in many fields of activity. Their enterprise contributed very greatly to the prosperity of the kingdom.

There were opportunities for advancement for the native peoples in the cities, the armed forces, and economic life, except where they were tied to royal estates or rigidly directed, as at times in Egypt. The central government was economical in that the governing class was small and the élite forces were tiny in relation to the total population. The distribution of wealth within each state was pyramidal. The king and his courtiers were immensely rich, the cities were well to do, the peasant workers were mainly at subsistence level, and the slave population was considerable but not always impoverished. When we consider recent events in Eastern Europe and in the lands extending from Lebanon and Sudan to Afghanistan and Pakistan, we may conclude that the Macedonian States succeeded in maintaining civilized standards and a high degree of internal peace and prosperity for a remarkably long time.

Economic and cultural developments

The area under the control of the Macedonian States fluctuated in extent, especially in the East. There all lands east of Kandahar in Afghanistan were ceded by Seleucus to Sandracottus (Chandragupta Maurya) *c*.303 in exchange for a treaty of friendship, of which a clause legalized intermarriage between Europeans and Indians, and for 500 elephants, which enabled Seleucus to defeat Antigonus at Ipsus. The Bactrian Kingdom (including Sogdiana) grew rapidly to have 1000 walled cities and expanded briefly into Sinkiang, then on the Chinese border. Later, *c*.150–130, it was swamped by migrating 'Scythians' (Sacae and Tochari). But the Bactrian kings had by then recaptured most of the Indus valley; and they even penetrated down the Ganges valley as far as Patna. At a high social level Europeans and Indians co-operated, as the legality of intermarriage indicated, and coins were sometimes marked with bilingual inscriptions (Greek and Brahmi or

Prakrit) and Greek and Buddhist religious symbols. The last European king in the Indus valley disappeared at the end of the pagan era. In the area south-east of the Caspian Sea, the Parthians became independent c.240. Antiochus III recovered all the lost provinces in 209–4, but his successes were ephemeral. The Parthian king Mithridates I (175–38) acquired Media and finally Babylonia. Most of the areas west of Media were to fall victim to the advance of Rome, with which we shall deal later.

One remarkable expedition was undertaken to the West. Pyrrhus, who had created a Macedonian type of kingdom (see p. 167), was invited first to liberate the Greek cities of southern Italy, and later to save the Greek cities of Sicily from barbarian aggression. Pyrrhus saw himself as a second Alexander the Great. He appealed to the four Macedonian kings, probably in the name of Alexander, for help in the cause of Greek freedom, and he obtained ships, money and some Macedonian pikemen and also a holding force for Epirus during his absence. It was the one and only occasion, in 280, of common action by the Macedonian world. An army of 3000 cavalry, 25,000 infantry and 20 elephants won remarkable victories; it advanced to within 60 kilometres of Rome, and it expelled the Carthaginians from all Sicily except Lilybaeum. The almost invincible quality of troops trained in the Macedonian manner and led by a brilliant general was amply demonstrated. But the Greek states even turned against him; Rome and Carthage became allies; and his victories proved to be 'Pyrrhic', in the sense that his losses were more decisive, since he had no reserves. In 275 he and half his original army returned to Epirus. Thereafter the advance of Rome in the West was relentless.

The area of trade did not fluctuate so much. For even when the Mauryan kingdom or the Parthian kingdom was strong, or when Syracuse was annexed by Rome, the area of the Macedonian kingdoms was still the richest centre of exchange in the ancient world. Goods continued to enter it overland from China and Arabia, and by sea from India via the Persian Gulf and sometimes via the heel of Africa. Luxury goods and animals came from Central Africa to Egypt. Greek and Phoenician seamen sailed beyond the Straits of Gibraltar, and Pytheas of Massalia (Marseilles) circumnavigated Britain and probably reached Scandinavia c.300. Maritime trade developed rapidly with bigger ships, navigational handbooks, lighthouses (one 300 feet high off Alexandria in Egypt), riverine harbours, canals and artificial basins. The monetary economy with which the Greeks and the Macedonians were familiar was established throughout the Macedonian world; and the gold and silver coinages of the Macedonian kings, being of real value, were universally accepted. The increasing volume of trade was matched by developments in banking, insurance, bottomry (maritime loans) and arbitration. The strongest centres of wealth moved from Macedonia and the Greek mainland to Syria and Egypt. For example, the state procession at Alexandria in 271/70 included a parade by 23,000 cavalry and 57,600 infantry under arms, and Ptolemy's navy then was the greatest in the world. Even in 166, when a huge indemnity was being paid to Rome, the procession at Daphne in Syria included a parade by 9000 cavalry and 41,000 infantry. There was an extraordinary display of gold at both festivals.

The court of Alexander was a cultural centre. During his campaigns he was accompanied by philosophers, geographers, scientists, actors and writers, who responded to a new world of ideas and actualities. There were native Macedonians and naturalized Macedonians among them (Marsyas, Ptolemy, Aristobulus, Nearchus), but most were Greeks, who had often left their city-states. Alexander himself was the patron of the arts, holding festival after festival of music, drama and athletics, and he employed the leading artists and actors. Outstanding among his successors was Ptolemy, who in 294 founded 'the Home of the Muses' ('Museum') at Alexandria and attracted to it the scholars of the Greek-speaking world, who were paid by him generous salaries to engage in research under ideal conditions. Poetry, which had withered in Greece in the fourth century, revived at Alexandria; and new genres appeared in the hymns of Callimachus, the pastoral of Theocritus and the artificial epic of Apollonius of Rhodes. Prose too found new interests in romantic love, antique themes, local history and adventure; early examples were *The Alexander Romance* and the romantic novels.

For his 'Museum' Ptolemy founded the first public library, funded by the state. His example was followed by other kings, and by many cities. Second in importance was the library of Pergamum, which invented parchment (*pergamene*) as a rival to papyrus, and its scholars specialized in antiquarian research and linguistics. With the spread of Greek literacy, native scholars recorded in Greek the learning and the history of Egypt, Babylonia and Jerusalem. At Alexandria and at Syracuse great advances were made in mathematics, mechanics, astronomy, hydraulics, optics and other sciences. Alexandria was the great centre of literary scholarship and librarianship. Thus the world created and maintained by Macedonian arms was a forerunner of the modern world in many of its interests and skills.

The city was the cultural nucleus in the Macedonian kingdoms. Because it was racially open and not, like the classical Greek city, closed, its culture was to some extent cosmopolitan. We have learnt much from excavation. Xanthus, a Lycian city, grew to have a Greek acropolis alongside the older Lycian one. At the other end of 'Asia', at Ai Khanum in eastern Afghanistan, a city founded by Alexander as Alexandria-on-the-Oxus (Amu Darya) grew to have fine houses of Macedonian type near the river and very much more numerous small houses on higher ground for native inhabitants – all within the city's defences. The Greek temples were overshadowed by an imposing Asian stepped shrine, and Delphic mottoes were paralleled by an ivory statuette of a Bactrian goddess. Macedonian features were a heroon (cult building in honour of the founder), a theatre, a library, a swimming pool, a palaestra (school-centre) and *gymnasion* (wrestling school). The governor's residence had a colonnaded central court for ceremonial in the Macedonian manner and a treasury and workshops as at Persepolis. Stores included olive oil (from the Mediterranean), incense (from Arabia), mother of pearl (from Pakistan) and gold and silver ingots (one inscribed in an unknown language). Macedonian coins were struck on a standard set by a state official (*dokimastes*), and rectangular coins minted in Pakistan were current. In the library area fragments of papyrus and parchment included a treatise on Plato's theory of ideas and of a poem otherwise unknown.

At another site in Afghanistan, Tillya Tepe, a cemetery of AD *c*.100 yielded remarkable evidence of the co-existence and fusion of Macedonian and Bactrian ideas among the ruling class. A gold diadem with elaborate palmettes, gold Erotes riding on dolphins, gold and ivory necklaces, fluted dishes of gold, and gold facings on women's clothing are reminiscent of the grave goods in the royal Macedonian tombs at Vergina. A gold belt-clasp portrays a warrior or war-god armed in Macedonian style with helmet, tunic and kirtle of a traditional kind. On another gold belt-clasp Dionysus fondles Ariadne (as on the Derveni crater), and a drunken Satyr gestures towards them. The influence of China can be seen in the dragon on which Dionysus rides, and that of Scythia in the sacred trees and snarling animal-heads facing the warrior. An Aphrodite in gold shows the fusion of ideas. She stands in a Macedonian pose, naked to below the navel, with swirls of drapery below; she wears wings in the local style; and on her forehead there is an Indian tattoo-mark.

The founders and benefactors of the cities were the kings. A prominent feature was the palace of the king or of his deputy. Examples have been excavated at Aegeae (late fourth century BC) and at Demetrias (late third century BC). They have the same plan – inherited from Philip II, as we may infer from Alexander taking to Asia a 100-couch marquee for banquets. The kings preferred to build large cities (the circuit-wall being 6 kilometres long at Pella and 8 kilometres long at Demetrias) often on level or undulating ground and sometimes enclosing a fortified riverine harbour (Pella and Dium), with broad streets on a grid-plan, large insulae for housing, and drainage channels. Temples to gods and goddesses in the Greek tradition were found sometimes together with fertility cults, associated with an abundance of water (at Dium) or with spirits of the earth (a circular pit at Pella being similar to one in Samothrace), and with cults in honour of Isis and Sarapis. In religion, as in most corporate activities, the king set the example and provided funds.

The distinctions between Macedonian culture and Greek culture dwindled with the spread of state-organized education. The Macedonian form of education for boys from fourteen to eighteen which Alexander had instituted in his cities in 'Asia' was soon adopted in the Greek cities of Asia and the Aegean islands, and even to some extent in states of the Greek mainland. Here too the kings led the way. Seleucus, for instance, paid 'the horsebreakers, drill-sergeants and all educators in the arts of warfare' from the funds of his War Office at Apamea; and Attalus II of Pergamum funded the salaries of teachers of the children of Delphi. Their example was followed by wealthy citizens throughout the Hellenistic world. The kings gave a high priority in state expenditure to education in the cities. It was an education not in local or 'ethnic' languages but in Greek literacy as the basis of an intelligent and cultured life, and it was fostered because the educated citizens of whatever racial origin were providing the basis of economic, cultural and military strength in the Macedonian States.

XIII

The Macedonian Kingdom:
Disasters and Recovery, 301–205

Wars for the throne and invasions by Gauls

The main currents of trade from all points of the compass ran towards Egypt and the western coast of Asia, so that Macedonia lay on the periphery and not at the centre of exchange. Consequently, Cassander had smaller financial resources than Ptolemy, Seleucus, Lysimachus and even Demetrius, the son of Antigonus, who had inherited his father's hoarded wealth and a powerful fleet. What made Macedonia important for the other kings was its prestige as the heartland and its army of cavalry and phalangites, which approached 30,000 men c.300.

When Cassander and his elder son died of disease in 297, the Macedonian Assembly elected the two surviving sons, though minors, as joint kings. One murdered his mother, Thessalonice, and quarrelled with his brother. One sought help from Demetrius and Pyrrhus, and the other from Lysimachus. The result was foreseeable. Each was killed in the struggle for power. Demetrius reigned from 294 to 287; then Pyrrhus and Lysimachus were both elected, and each ruled half the country until 285; finally Lysimachus drove Pyrrhus out and ruled into 281, uniting Macedonia with its lost province of Thrace and controlling most of Asia Minor. But Seleucus felt threatened. He defeated and killed Lysimachus in battle, crossed into Europe, and was murdered there by Ptolemy Ceraunus, the eldest son of Ptolemy (he had died in 283 and been succeeded by a younger son). Whereas Alexander had held his world together, his three contemporaries – the Bodyguards Ptolemy, Lysimachus and Seleucus – perpetuated its division into rival kingdoms. If Alexander had lived some forescore years as they did, how different that world would have been.

Ptolemy Ceraunus led the forces of Lysimachus and Seleucus towards Macedonia, defeated Antigonus 'Gonatas' (? 'Knock-Kneed'), a son of Demetrius, and was elected king late in 281. His powerful neighbour, Pyrrhus, who was about to invade Italy, exacted a loan of some Macedonian soldiers from Ptolemy Ceraunus and obtained help from the other kings. Pyrrhus sailed in May 280. Ptolemy turned his attention to possible pretenders. Committing perjury (for he had taken an oath in the temple of Zeus to respect their lives), he murdered two of Lysimachus' sons, and made plans to attack another son, who was backed by Illyrians. At that moment a new storm broke on the strife-torn kingdom.

Late in 280, huge numbers of Gauls set out from central Yugoslavia in three groups to raid Thrace, Paeonia and Macedonia. The king of the Dardanians warned Ptolemy and offered with 20,000 men to make a common stand. Ptolemy rejected the offer. The king then joined the Gauls, who had a clear passage into Upper Macedonia. Although Ptolemy's Friends advised him to buy time by paying danegeld and letting the Gauls go on into Thessaly, Ptolemy fought with such troops as he had available at the moment. 'The whole Macedonian force was destroyed.' Ptolemy was captured and decapitated.

Lower Macedonia was saved by a general, Sosthenes, who managed to deflect the Gauls westwards towards Illyris. As successors to Ptolemy Ceraunus the Assembly elected and soon deposed as incompetent first a brother of Ptolemy, and then a nephew of Cassander. A Macedonian army tried to break the tradition of electing to the throne only a member of some royal family and hailed the commoner Sosthenes as king; but he insisted on the oath of obedience being taken to him simply as general. Two minors – probably sons of Lysimachus – were then elected, one succeeding the other.

In 279 Brennus invaded from Illyris with a huge force of Gauls. They were ferocious warriors. The cavalry fought in formation with two reserves for each cavalryman, and the infantry, fighting individually and not in formation, carried a door-like shield and wielded a long sword so sharp that it could sever a pike at one blow. Sosthenes seems not to have modified the Macedonians' equipment or tactics in any way. He led the Macedonian army in its traditional formation into a set battle and was totally defeated. The Gauls ravaged the length and breadth of Macedonia, killing all who failed to find refuge in the walled cities, and passed on towards Delphi. There they were defeated and withdrew in disorder, harried by the Aetolians, who won a great reputation as fighters, but not by the disorganized and demoralized Macedonians. Antigonus Gonatas, eager to take advantage of the chaos, landed on the coast of Macedonia; but he was repulsed. Early in 277 he happened to have landed his army near Lysimacheia in the Thracian Chersonese, where a band of Gauls was on the rampage. By some ruse he attacked them when they were laden with loot, and he won an outright victory. Presenting himself as the conqueror of the dreaded Gauls, he won the throne of Macedonia by defeating his rivals and liberating Cassandreia from a tyrant. The grandson of Antigonus Monophthalmus, he was the first of a consecutive line of 'Antigonid' kings, which was to end with the deportation of Perseus.

The reigns of Antigonus II Gonatas (276–39) and Demetrius II (239–29)

Antigonus found himself king of a devastated, debilitated kingdom, which had lost almost all its first-line soldiers in two total defeats. The record of the Macedonian phalanx as invincible was shattered. To restore the manpower of the kingdom to its former strength might take fifty years. The outlook for the economy was grim, because the Gauls had created havoc throughout the Balkan peninsula from the Adriatic coast of Illyris to the Dardanelles and from the Danube to the Aegean littoral, and they had established two states – of the Scordisci and of Tylis – as bases for further raiding. They were not the only menace. Pyrrhus returned from Italy and invaded Macedonia in 273. He out-generalled Antigonus, overcame all resistance, and boasted that the Molossians had reduced Macedonia to subjection. This boast and the sacrilege committed by his Gallic mercenaries at Aegeae, where they robbed some of the royal tombs, rallied the Macedonians in support of Antigonus. When Pyrrhus was killed at Argos and his son Alexander was distracted by a war with the Illyrians, Antigonus regained possession of Macedonia, in 271. But it was a diminished kingdom in the west; for Tymphaea and Parauaea were ruled by Alexander.

The power of Antigonus, before he became king of Macedonia, had lain in his fleet and in the bases in Greece which his garrisons and his puppet-governments still controlled: Demetrias, Chalcis, Athens, Megara, Corinth, Argos and some places in the Peloponnese. The cost of paying garrison-troops and crews of oarsmen may have been more than offset by the revenues which he exacted on the trade of these cities. But the policy had two serious defects. The hatred engendered in the city-states encouraged other kings to interfere (as Pyrrhus had done and Ptolemy II was shortly to do); and when Antigonus was king of Macedonia his sending of men to the fleet and to the Greek cities resulted in a disregard of Macedonia's northern and eastern frontier areas.

During his long reign (276–39), Antigonus struggled against the break-away of some Greek cities, the rival naval power of Ptolemy II who supported Greek dissidents, the growth of the hostile Achaean League in the Peloponnese, and the overrunning of Macedonia by Alexander II of Molossia when the main Macedonian army was in Attica. The economy of the country was crippled. Antigonus was able to issue only a small amount of silver coinage, which had a very limited circulation (Plates 25b: ix and 26: i, ii). He encouraged internal exchange by issuing a lot of bronze coinage. To the Macedonians he was a generous and charismatic king, a convivial entertainer of his Friends, and a cultured man. Each year he held a festival, the *basileia*, which was a celebration of kingship, and his greatest service to Macedonia was that he restored the prestige of the monarchy and left a thirty-five-year-old son to be elected to the throne as Demetrius II in 239.

176

While Antigonus struggled to salvage Macedonia and keep his holdings in Greece, the balance of power in the West had shifted decisively. There Rome had become the leading naval power. She had defeated Carthage in 241, and had brought the Greek states of Sicily and South Italy into the orbit of her authority. Rome's concerns seemed to be with the western Mediterranean; but Italian ships sailed in the Adriatic Sea, and during the long Punic War (264–41) there had been lively trade with the kingdom of Alexander II, who ruled from central Albania to the mouth of the Corinthian Gulf. In the East, Ptolemy II and Antiochus II were engaged in the Second Syrian War (260–53), and their successors Ptolemy III and Seleucus II in the Third Syrian War (246–1). Antigonus was connected by marriage with Antiochus II and he fought at sea against Ptolemy II, who countered by supporting Antigonus' enemies in Greece. Ptolemy III emerged from his war as the leading naval power with bases as far afield as the Thracian coast. While the Seleucids were weakened by the Syrian Wars, Scythian nomads broke into Parthyene and laid the foundations of the later Parthian state, and the satrap of Bactria broke away and established his own kingdom. Thus the endless wars between the rival Macedonian kings were leading to a shrinkage of the areas under Macedonian control in Europe and in Asia.

For ten years Demetrius II struggled to maintain his garrisons in Greece, but he lost ground overall to the Aetolian League and the Achaean League, which entered into an alliance. First he sought the help of the Epirote League by marrying Phthia, daughter of the widowed Molossian queen, Olympias, and by supporting it in Acarnania againt the Aetolians. But the Molossian house, weakened by problems of succession, was brought to an end by assassinations and by a popular rising, which led to the birth of the Epirote Alliance with an anti-royalist bias in 232. Then he sought the help of the Ardiaei, an Illyrian group of tribes, which was based on Kotor and had become a naval power. During the troubles of the Molossian dynasty they had acquired the northern part of Epirote territory and they now occupied Lissus and the Mati basin. Demetrius and the Ardiaei feared their common neighbour, the Dardanians.

About 232 the Macedonian army was routed with heavy losses in a set battle by the Dardanians. Thereupon Demetrius paid money to the Ardiaei, whom he engaged to attack his other enemy, the Aetolians in Acarnania. A band of Ardiaei, landing from their light warships (*lembi*, each rowed by fifty men who fought as warriors), surprised the Aetolians, defeated them and departed with much loot. Returning in 230 and engaging in acts of piracy, they captured by treachery Phoenice, the richest city in Epirus, and inspired such terror that the Epirote Alliance made disadvantageous terms and even entered into alliance with the Ardiaean kingdom. But the Greeks were not the only victims. Italian ships had been attacked. Rome sent envoys to protest. They were told by the reigning queen, Teuta, that piracy was a private matter and not a concern of the Ardiaean State.

Macedonia becomes the leader of Greek states

In spring 229 Demetrius died a natural death. His nine-year-old son Philip
was elected king, and 'the first men of the Macedones' arranged that a
cousin of Demetrius, called Antigonus, was appointed 'guardian and
general'. At this time an Ardiaean fleet captured Corcyra and laid siege to
Epidamnus (Dyrrachium). In the summer Rome acted. Massive forces
sailed unheralded from Italy (see Plates 31 and 32). A fleet of 200 large
warships descended on Corcyra, which was surrendered without a fight and
was received into Rome's 'friendship'. Another fleet, carrying the main
army, took Apollonia into Rome's 'protection'. This army, 2000 cavalry
and 20,000 infantry strong, went on to relieve Dyrrachium, and then
received two Illyrian tribes, the Parthini and the Atintani, into 'friendship'.
The naval and military forces defeated some Ardiaean tribes farther north
and freed the island-city Issa (Vis), which was being attacked by the
Ardiaeans. This exercise of Roman naval and military power reduced
the Ardiaeans to impotence. Yet the Roman forces did not enter the Gulf
of Kotor.

During the winter one Roman consul, based on Dyrrachium, organized
what we may call 'the Roman Protectorate'. At sea it extended from Issa to
Corcyra, and on the coast it included the only good harbours of what is
now central Albania, namely Dyrrachium and Apollonia (see Plates 31 and
32). Thus the lower Adriatic Sea and the entry into the Sicilian Sea became a
Roman lake, protected by ships based in Italy and guaranteed by the
Ardiaeans' undertaking not to send more than two warships south of
Lissus. On land the Protectorate consisted of the rich coastal plain, which
was used for winter pastures by inland tribes, and of two tribal groups
which held the Shkumbi valley (the Parthini) and the area north of that
valley up to the Black Drin (the Atintani). These groups cut the lines of
communication between the Ardiaeans and the Macedonians, and between
the Ardiaeans and the Epirotes. To the north of the Protectorate Rome
set up a client-kingdom and entrusted it to Demetrius of Pharos, the
commander of the garrison which had surrendered Corcyra. Finally,
the Ardiaei agreed to pay an indemnity. They were then accepted by Rome
as her 'friends'. Late in 228, all Roman troops returned to Italy. Defence was
left to local volunteers, who were to be trained, and reinforcements could
be brought across the Adriatic at short notice.

These arrangements were reported by Roman envoys to the Aetolian
League and the Achaean League, which had tried to help Corcyra against
the Ardiaeans, and to Athens and Corinth, which bestowed honours in
return by admitting the envoys to the Eleusinian Mysteries (a religious
festival) and by opening the Isthmian Games to Italian athletes. On the
other hand, Rome did not enter into diplomatic relations with either
Macedonia or Epirus, which had become immediate neighbours of Rome's

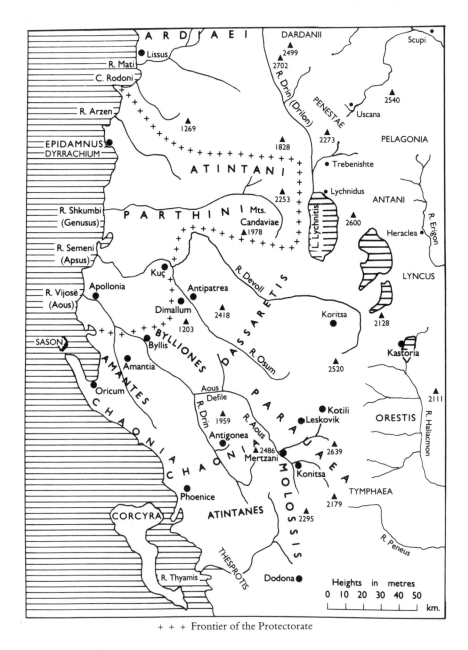

+ + + Frontier of the Protectorate

Fig 16 The Roman Protectorate and its neighbours

Protectorate; nor did they open negotiations with Rome. The purpose of Rome's actions was clear. It was not to incapacitate the Ardiaean kingdom, of which the heartland was unaffected, but to acquire control of the Lower Adriatic, occupy Corcyra as a strategic naval base, and provide an extensive staging area on land for any Roman army which might wish to operate in the Balkan area. But that was not all. For as long as the Protectorate held firm, no hostile power in the Balkans could mount an invasion of Italy, as Alexander and Pyrrhus had done within the last hundred years.

Antigonus, the guardian and general of the young king, was a passive spectator of these events. His army was little – if at all – larger than that which Rome had deployed, and he had no fleet in western waters. He attacked two enemies who might be tempted to approach Rome: the Dardanians whom he defeated thoroughly, and the Aetolians, who were being subsidised by Ptolemy III. He defeated them also, so successfully that peace was made. But in the south he lost ground; for revolts by Athens, Argos and Aegina made it virtually impossible for the Macedonian fleet to reach the Peloponnese. In 227 that fleet sailed to Caria, where Antigonus was the friend of a local ruler (Olympichus), and good relations were established with Priene and Samos. On his return young Philip was deposed and Antigonus was elected king as Antigonus III 'Doson' ('About-to-give'). His aim in the Aegean may have been to strengthen his fleet through alliance and to control the Hellespont, so that he could force Athens to submit by threatening its food supply. But details are lacking, and in spring 224 he embarked on a new policy, accepting an alliance offered by the Achaean League and taking a field army of 1400 cavalry and 20,000 infantry overland to the Isthmus of Corinth. Co-operating with the Achaeans, he forced their enemy, Cleomenes of Sparta, to evacuate Corinth and Argos, in each of which Antigonus placed a Macedonian garrison.

It looked as if Antigonus was about to follow the unwise policy of Antigonus Gonatas. Instead, in autumn 224, he set up a coalition of which the members were Macedones, Epirotes, Acarnanians, Thessalians, Boeotians, Phocians and Achaeans, the last including all members of the Achaean League. Each elected its own representatives to sit on a Council, which voted on the admission of new members and on other matters. In the past, when a Macedonian king had advised the Greek states to form a coalition, Macedonia had not been a participant; for example, in 337 the Greek states of the Common Peace as an entity had entered into an alliance with the Macedonian State. Now Macedonia was a member of the coalition, having no more rights than Phocis, for instance, or than any new member, however small. That Macedonia accepted such a status was a guarantee of its sincere wish to unite the Greek-speaking peoples of the mainland against any violator of the peace.

At the moment the violator was Sparta, supported by Ptolemy III; in the future it might be some outside power. For their part, the Greek states recognized the revival of Macedonia's military strength and they trusted Antigonus to abide by the terms of their agreement. The coalition was called 'the Symmachy', the word meaning 'alliance', which was its legal basis. The first task was to allocate the 'hegemony' – the command of the allied forces. The Council awarded it to the Macedonian State, which appointed its experienced and permanent commander, Antigonus. The Symmachy suffered from one serious limitation: while the Council might pass a majority vote to go to war or to make peace, the decision had to be taken by each allied state.

In 222 the allied forces, consisting of 600 cavalry and 18,000 infantry from Macedonia (including mercenaries), 600 cavalry and 8000 infantry from the other allies, and 1600 Illyrians as allies of Macedonia, inflicted a devastating defeat on Sparta at Sellasia near the Laconian border. Antigonus treated the Spartans humanely, but required Sparta to become a member of the Symmachy. He and his army hastened back to deal with an Illyrian invasion of Macedonia. He defeated the Illyrians but suffered a fatal haemorrhage. Tributes were paid to him by many Greek states. At home the Assembly elected as king Philip, aged sixteen, and appointed five leading men to carry out specific duties during his minority. One of them, Taurion, was to act as commander of the Symmachy's forces; but he was ineffective. The Aetolians attacked many members of the Symmachy with impunity until Philip came of age at eighteen in summer 220. Taking over from Taurion, Philip convened a meeting of the Council, which agreed to recommend to the member-states that they should all declare war on Aetolia. They did so early in 219. By then a new situation was developing in the north-west, which led to the second Roman campaign east of the Adriatic Sea.

The client-king whom Rome had established, Demetrius of Pharos (see p. 178), joined the court of the Ardiaei and became their effective leader. He detached the Atintani from the Roman Protectorate, made alliance with Antigonus Doson, and brought the Illyrian troops who fought with distinction at Sellasia. Illyrian warships sailed south of Lissus, despite the agreement with Rome, and in 220 Demetrius and his fleet joined Aetolia and then changed to Macedonia; on the way home they ravaged some lands within the Roman Protectorate. During the winter Philip arranged that another Ardiaean leader, Scerdilaidas, should bring 30 *lembi* south and join in a planned attack on Aetolia. Early in 219 Philip and a Macedonian army of 800 cavalry and 15,000 infantry defeated Aetolian forces and captured two naval bases, Ambracus and Oeniadae. All was ready for the arrival of Scerdilaidas. But a report that the Dardanians were about to invade Macedonia caused Philip to return up the west coast, and at Actium he met Demetrius of Pharos, who informed him of a Roman intervention. A consul commanding a fleet and army had reasserted Roman authority in Corcyra and the protected area, including Atintania, and captured Pharos, from which Demetrius had escaped on a *lembus*. The consul

Fig 17   The Peloponnese

was accorded a triumph for achieving his objective. He did not make any attack on the Ardiaean homeland.

Although the help of an Ardiaean fleet was now a forlorn hope, Philip accepted Demetrius of Pharos as an ally and honoured him at his court. He had to weigh any offence this might cause at Rome against the value of the Ardiaei, if they should join him in an attack on the Roman Protectorate at some future date. The immediate problem was Aetolia; for their forces had raided as far as Dium in southern Macedonia and Dodona in Epirus (the latter after Philip's return home from Actium). In a series of brilliant campaigns as commander of the Symmachy's forces and with the help of Scerdilaidas, who sent fifteen *lembi*, Philip sacked the Aetolian capital Thermum, ravaged Aetolia's western lands, defeated Aetolia's ally Sparta, and concentrated the fleets of Macedonia and the other members of the Symmachy in the Gulf of Corinth. In 217 Aetolia accepted peace terms perforce. Philip was praised for 'his beneficent policy', which now brought a form of unity embracing the Macedonian kingdom and the Greek states and a peace which was to last for six years.

Alliance with Carthage and war with Rome

Some weeks before the peace was made, a courier from Macedonia informed Philip that Hannibal had won a great victory over the Romans at Lake Trasimene. Writing with hindsight, Polybius thought that this news caused Philip to make peace; but it was the Aetolians, not Philip, who were pressing for peace. In the north-west area, Philip had established a city of Macedonians early in 217 at Bylazora (Titov Veles), from which a Paeonian population was displaced, and thereby 'almost freed himself from fear of the Dardanians'; for the Dardanians' easiest route into Macedonia was through Polog into the Axius valley near Bylazora. Philip's ally, the Ardiaean Scerdilaidas, treacherously attacked some Macedonian ships at Leucas, and on returning home he invaded Pelagonia, ravaged other parts of Upper Macedonia, overran much of Dassaretis and captured Antipatrea, a Macedonian city founded by Cassander (Berat). After the conclusion of the peace, Philip chased Scerdilaidas out of that area and took it over himself, so that he came close to the frontier of the Roman Protectorate. Rome showed her hostility to Macedonia in two ways: she demanded from Philip the handing over of Demetrius of Pharos – a demand which he as head of an independent state refused – and she accepted Scerdilaidas as an ally.

During the winter Philip hired Illyrian shipwrights and built 100 *lembi*, which were suitable for raiding but could not engage the large warships of Rome, and he trained Macedonian infantrymen to row. He planned, while Hannibal was in the ascendant in Italy, to attack Apollonia (the southern port of the Protectorate) by land through Dassaretis and by sea, which involved a voyage of some 700 miles, rounding the Peloponnese. In 216 the fleet – by night and undetected, surprise being essential – reached Sason, an island near Apollonia. But Philip was then informed that Scerdilaidas, already at Apollonia, was expecting some Roman quinqueremes (large warships). These ships were rowed by oarmen in three banks, as in a trireme, but the oars of two banks were rowed by two men each. He withdrew at once – wisely, because the report was true and if he had sailed upriver to Apollonia he and his fleet would have been trapped. But his intended act of war was now public knowledge. Later in the year, when Hannibal had destroyed another Roman army at Cannae, Philip opened negotiations with Hannibal. Early in 215 a treaty of alliance for all time was concluded between Carthage and the Symmachy (Philip having acted with the concurrence of its Council). It was a diplomatic triumph for Philip that he had carried his Greek allies with him; for the treaty contained a clause that in the event of Rome seeking terms she had to evacuate the whole Protectorate, Pharos and Corcyra included, which was the concern more of Macedonia than of the Greek states, at least in the short term. Rome learnt of the treaty and declared war on the Symmachy.

In 214 Philip repeated his attempt on Apollonia with a fleet of 120 new *lembi biremes* (with two men to each oar). He was within an ace of success when a Roman fleet reached Oricum and passed 2000 men unobserved at night into Apollonia. A sortie succeeded. Philip lost siege-engines, 3000 men and much of his fleet. Rome added Oricum to the Protectorate, stationed a fleet there and named as a theatre of operations 'Greece and Macedonia' (the Greek part of the Symmachy being implicated). But her forces were needed in Italy. The initiative lay with Philip. He won the Parthini and the Atintani to his side, captured Dimallum within the Protectorate, and by a remarkable feat of arms took and garrisoned Lissus, whereupon the tribes of the Scodra region joined him. He began late in 212 to build a new fleet there with Illyrian timber, and he hoped that a Carthaginian fleet might reach him; for Hannibal held the heel of Italy across the Adriatic (see Plate 32). But Rome made a countermove: in autumn 211 a large Roman fleet sailed into the Gulf of Corinth and asked the Aetolian League for alliance against the Symmachy. Terms were agreed: Aetolia to keep any captured city east and south of Corcyra. Rome to take the bulk of the loot (including humans), and neither party to make a separate peace with the Symmachy. The Roman fleet captured Oeniadae (Philip's naval base); and the Rome–Aetolia pact was joined by Sparta, Elis and Messenia, and across the Aegean by Attalus, the king of Pergamum in Asia Minor, who was hostile to Philip.

Rome succeeded in her primary aim, which was to prevent the fleet of Philip and his allies from making contact with Carthaginian fleets (one reached Tarentum, and another the mouth of the Gulf of Corinth). Her own fleet captured Aegina, where it was joined by the fleet of Attalus; but the two fleets were outwitted by Philip, who brought seven quinqueremes and twenty *lembi* to the Isthmus, where they were hauled overland into the Gulf of Corinth. The Romans terrified the Greeks by ruthless sacking of any cities which resisted. People were slaughtered, 'dogs were cut in two, and limbs hacked off animals.' On the other hand, Rome did little to help her allies on land. The army of Attalus was defeated and he withdrew to Asia; Aetolia was ravaged as far as Thermum; and her plea for military aid met with little response. In 206, when Rome failed to honour her original undertaking to send twenty-five quinqueremes each year, Aetolia made a separate peace 'on the terms which Philip wanted'. The absence of Macedonian forces in the south had been an opportunity for the Dardanians; in 209 they had carried off 20,000 prisoners and huge quantities of loot from Orestis. In 205 a peace was concluded at Phoenice between the Symmachy and Prusias (the ruler of Bithynia) on the one hand and Rome, the Ardiaei and Attalus (he had been at war with Prusias in Asia Minor) on the other hand. Both sides were escaping from a stalemate. On balance Philip could claim that the terms of peace were in his favour, since he was granted Atintania and had gained Lissus and Scodra.

Since 220 Philip had proved to be a strong and capable king. In 218 he dealt firmly with indiscipline by the Royal Infantry Guard and with unruly and mutinous behaviour by some leading Macedonians, who thought they could dominate the young king. At each step Philip consulted his Friends and was supported by them in decisions which led some officers to commit suicide; and when he charged the commander of the Guard with treason the Assembly of Macedonians sentenced him to death. As a commander in the field Philip rivalled Alexander in personal dash and courage, and his army operated with extraordinary speed of movement, summer and winter alike. At sea his fleets showed initiative and daring. Within the Greek peninsula the reputation of Philip and of his armed forces stood very high, and he had kept the majority of Greek states on his side. It was chiefly in the north-west that the Macedonians had suffered losses. There Philip had failed to eject the Romans from their foothold on the Adriatic coast. This failure was to be critical in the years to come.

XIV

Relations with Rome:
Resistance, Collaboration and Defeat

The disintegration of the Symmachy
and the defeat of Macedonia at Cynoscephalae

The world situation in 205, the year that peace was made at Phoenice, was becoming relatively clear. Rome was about to defeat Carthage and so to become the only great power in the western Mediterranean. In origin a city-state, comparable to Athens or Carthage, Rome had established her military supremacy over all Italian peoples in a series of hard-fought wars. But, unlike other city-states, she had progressively expanded the number of her citizens, sometimes granting full rights but often withholding political and electoral rights, and she had devised a graded system of alliances with less-dependable communities and with backward tribes. Rome decided all matters of foreign policy. In the event of her declaring war, she conscripted her citizens for service in the legions and her allies as cavalrymen and auxiliaries, and she required naval service from maritime peoples. Thus she had huge reserves of manpower. In the Second War against Carthage, despite very heavy losses, Rome maintained armies of some 200,000 men and fleets of 125 large warships with crews and marines totalling some 50,000 men. Conscription from the whole of peninsular Italy continued after the defeat of Carthage. Armies and fleets were deployed for the conquest of the Gauls and Ligurians in north Italy, the disciplining of Sardinia and Corsica, and the creation of two provinces in Spain. In the same decade, 200–190 BC, Roman forces were sent across the Adriatic Sea.

The direction of Roman policy in and after the Second War against Carthage was firmly in the hands of the Senate, which was to a great extent a self-perpetuating body of landowning administrators. Within the Senate, a group of families whose members had traditionally held major offices and military commands played a preponderant part in deciding and implementing policy. The Senate had a close affinity with a similar class of landowners, who were the controlling force in the allied communities. Thus in Greek terminology the Roman and Italian system was that of a close oligarchy. Yet at Rome itself, the form of a democratic element survived in the Assemblies (*comitia*), of which the decisions were in theory sovereign, final and binding on the Senate. The substance was different. Those who attended meetings were a tiny fraction of all Roman citizens, namely those resident in or near the city, who were often susceptible to various forms of bribery. The Senate went through the motions of a democratic procedure, but it was confident of enforcing its will sooner or later on the electorate.

It was at first difficult for Philip and his Friends to understand the workings of the Roman constitution and to see through its quasi-democratic façade to the controlling hand of an élite group within the Senate. Diplomatic procedures and 'war or peace' negotiations seemed to be conducted in an unfamiliar manner. On the other hand, Philip and his advisers were well versed in the affairs and the techniques of their Macedonian rivals in Asia and in Egypt. In 205 they were greatly impressed by the successes of Antiochus and by the resources of Ptolemy, to which we shall now turn.

Ptolemy IV, a few years older than Philip, had succeeded to a very powerful kingdom in 221, and defeated Antiochus III at Raphia in 217 and had annexed Palestine. His army of some 75,000 men and 73 elephants at Raphia had included well-trained Egyptian and Libyan troops. But in the following years his kingdom was weakened by a series of native risings, so that the fleet became unable to maintain control of distant bases in the northern Aegean. Antiochus III, a contemporary of Philip (he succeeded in 223 at the age of eighteen), recovered from his defeat at Raphia and gained spectacular successes, campaigning from 209 to 205 with an army of 20,000 cavalry and 100,000 infantry and re-establishing control over all Alexander's satrapies from Armenia to the Hindu Kush. He crossed into Afghanistan and northern Pakistan, where he established friendly relations with the local Indian ruler and received rich gifts and many elephants. On his return through the south-eastern satrapies to Babylonia, he was greeted as Antiochus the Great, a second Alexander. His fleet as yet was small.

The eastern Aegean was the scene of conflicting interests in 205. Philip held a few western islands and was influential at Delos, where he had dedicated a portico and founded a festival called *Philippeia*; and he enjoyed the alliance of many cities in Crete. Attalus of Pergamum and Rhodes were the leading seapowers of the east Aegean, and Attalus was the ally of the Aetolian League, which had enrolled among its members some Greek cities by the Hellespont and the Bosporus. Philip's ally and relation by marriage, Prusias of Bithynia, held some Greek cities in that area; he was hostile to Attalus and Aetolia. The chances that the Peace of Phoenice would last there were slim.

In comparison to the great powers, Philip was relatively weak in resources. He had operated with a field army of less than 20,000 men and a fleet of five quinqueremes and 120 *lembi*, which had been no match for Rome's twenty-five quinqueremes and the fleet of Attalus. To these he could add the forces of the Greek states of the Symmachy, potentially as numerous, if each member-state voted to undertake a war proposed by the

Council of the Symmachy. He had other troops which were stationed to protect Macedonia against hostile neighbours, especially the Dardanians and the Illyrians. Such being the state of affairs, Philip had to decide to concentrate his manpower either on a military campaign or on a naval campaign, if it was to be of any magnitude; for he lacked the men for both simultaneously. In 205 he had learnt the lesson that the combination of a Roman fleet, a Greek ally with well-placed harbours, and the fleet of Attalus constituted a deadly danger to the Symmachy and ultimately to Macedonia. On the other hand a Roman army, operating from the Protectorate, would be cut off from any Greek ally and would find it difficult to penetrate the western frontier of Macedonia. Considerations such as these led Philip to decide on a naval offensive in the Aegean, in the hope that he would eliminate Attalus, control the Hellespont and the Aegean Sea, and keep the Greek states loyal to the Symmachy. In winter 205–4 he laid the keels of large warships, which would be ready for a major offensive in 201.

Meanwhile, he strengthened his northern frontier by inflicting a crushing defeat on the Dardanians. Then advancing along the coast he won over Lysimachea, Chalcedon and Perinthus from membership of the Aetolian League, joined forces with Prusias and helped him to win (and destroy) Cius and Myrlea. On his way back he captured Thasos by treachery and sold the population into slavery. This was a departure from his usual treatment of a defeated enemy. The reason for it is not known. In spring 201 he launched his naval offensive. He and a few allies produced some forty-five large ships from quadriremes upwards to one *dekeres*, 150 *lembi* and 'sawfish' (small craft), of which the total crews numbered some 25,000 men. (The quadrireme resembled the quinquereme (see p. 183), except that only one oar of one bank was rowed by two men. We do not know how a *dekeres* was rowed.) For this large-scale operation he had prepared the ground diplomatically by leading Ptolemy and Antiochus each to believe that he would join him. Winning over the Cyclades and some Egyptian ships at Samos, he fought an indecisive major battle against the fleets of Attalus, Rhodes and Byzantium, and then some successful engagements against them individually. Landing his troops, he defeated Attalus' forces but failed to take Pergamum by assault; occupied Rhodian territory on the coast opposite the island; and campaigned inland in Caria. But his enemies bottled up his fleet. In spring 200 he tricked them and sailed home, leaving some troops to hold what he had acquired in Asia. It was a disastrous campaign. Instead of winning naval supremacy in the Aegean and bringing most Greek states to his side, as he had hoped, he had lost not only many Macedonians (as marines) and crew personnel but also credibility in the eyes of the Greek states. Moreover, the fleets of Attalus and Rhodes were free to advance to Attalus' base, Aegina, and to make contact with Aetolia and Rome.

Between spring 201 and spring 200 the news leaked out that Philip had entered into alliance with Antiochus and that the two kings intended to divide the external possessions of the infant king Ptolemy V. In the course of 201 Antiochus was besieging Gaza, Rome imposed her peace terms on Carthage, and envoys from Attalus and Rhodes asked Rome to intervene against Macedonia. The Senate prepared the way for intervention by allotting 'Macedonia' as a 'province' (theatre of war) to A. Sulpicius Galba and by authorizing him to propose in the Roman Assembly that war be declared against 'King Philip and the Macedonians'. But the war-weary Assembly refused 'to pile war on war'.

Meanwhile, the Senate had despatched three Roman commissioners, whose duties were to collect charges against Philip and ascertain the sympathies of each state in the event of a war between Rome and Macedonia. The envoys themselves enjoyed diplomatic immunity because the Treaty of Phoenice was in force. They reached Athens when a war was raging between Athens, helped by ships of Attalus and Rhodes which were based on Aegina, and Acarnania, helped by some Macedonian troops. The presence of the envoys was an encouragement to Athens. She declared war on Macedonia. The result for her was disastrous. Her countryside was devastated; and her food supply was cut, as Philip seized the Thracian Chersonese, laid siege to Abydus and controlled the passage of ships through the Hellespont (Dardanelles). Her allies – Attalus, Rhodes, Aetolia, some cities in Crete, and Ptolemy V – proved useless. In late summer 200 Athens asked Rome for help.

At Rome, the Assembly had agreed to go to war. The next step in Roman procedure was to deliver the ultimatum, that the offending state would make reparation or else receive a declaration of war. One of the three commissioners reached Philip at Abydus in August and delivered Rome's demand that Philip should compensate Attalus and Rhodes, respect Ptolemy's possessions, and 'not make war on any Greek state'. When Philip pointed out that Attalus, Rhodes and Athens had made war on him, he was cut short. This was not an occasion for dialogue but an ultimatum: the alternative was war. Philip's reply was a request to Rome 'not to break the treaty' and the assurance that, if Rome should go to war, 'we shall defend ourselves bravely, calling the gods to our aid'. The declaration of war came with the advance of Roman forces: an army from the Protectorate capturing Antipatrea and massacring its population, and a fleet from Corcyra occupying the Peiraeus and with Rhodian and Athenian ships raiding a Macedonian base at Chalcis.

Philip made no reply at sea. He ravaged Attica, attended a meeting of the Achaean Assembly at Argos, and asked the Achaean League to help him against Rome. The Assembly refused. It was obvious that the Symmachy was fatally split. Would Antiochus and Ptolemy support Philip, as their predecessors had helped Pyrrhus? The three commissioners arrived first in Syria and then in Egypt. They were hospitably received and they gave assurances of Rome's friendship to the two kings, who were hard at war with one another. If Philip made any approaches, he was rebuffed. Macedonia was virtually alone in facing Rome, and even her claim to protect the Greek states had been usurped by Rome when she ordered Philip not to attack any Greek state.

In 199 most states watched as neutrals while the Roman army, aided by the Ardiaeans and other Illyrians and by the Dardanians, invaded and ravaged the western cantons of Upper Macedonia. Philip, commanding a smaller but more mobile army, blocked and harassed the Roman army, which on its return to the Protectorate mutinied. The Roman tactics appealed to the Aetolians and Athamanians. They now joined Rome and ravaged Thessaly; but while the Roman army was mutinous Philip routed the Dardanians and then the Aetolians, inflicting heavy losses. In 198 Philip held a strong defensive position in the defile of the river Aous and drew the Roman army southwards. The first Roman commander failed to break the position, and the second, Titus Flamininus, discussed terms of peace with Philip, who refused to accept evacuation of all Greek cities outside the kingdom and payment of compensation to Rome's allies. Some Greek shepherds then guided a turning force and Philip withdrew into Thessaly. There he prepared his next line of defence, which ran from Atrax on the river Peneus to Phthiotic Thebes (renamed Philippopolis as a city occupied by Macedonians). The holders of the line were to be supplied from Larissa, Demetrias and Phthiotic Thebes.

The Aetolians looted and massacred in south-west Thessaly, and Roman forces tried but failed to storm Atrax. The fleets of Rome, Attalus and Rhodes captured and sacked any Greek cities which resisted, notably Eretria which yielded 'statues and works of art' beyond expectation. The Roman army moved into Phocis, where it was supplied by a fleet in the Corinthian Gulf. The proximity of these forces overawed the Achaean League, which abandoned its alliance with Macedonia, allied itself with Rome and provided troops to attack the few Greek states which still supported Macedonia. In November a two-month truce was agreed in order that Macedonia and Rome's allies should propose conditions for peace to the Senate. The hearing at Rome was a farce; for the Senate was interested not in rights and wrongs nor in conditions of peace, but only in defeating Macedonia quickly. Attalus had complained that Antiochus was invading his kingdom and might be about to cross into Europe. The Senate sent envoys to say that both kings were friends and allies of the Roman people and should make peace. Antiochus withdrew his army from the territory of Attalus 'in respect for the Roman envoys' authority', but he continued his advance towards the Hellespont.

For his field army in 197, Philip had to enlist some boys of sixteen and men over age in order to bring his phalangites up to 18,000. That was due both to losses in 201/200 and to the fact that he was still maintaining garrisons at Corinth and Chalcis, and in Thessaly, Thrace and Caria; and other troops were needed to guard his frontiers against Illyrians, Dardanians and the enemy fleet. The rest of his army consisted of Illyrian, Thracian and mercenary light-armed infantry, 5500 strong, and 2000 Macedonian and Thessalian cavalry. His only active ally, Acarnania, was far away. Flamininus, whose command had been prolonged, out-generalled Philip and cut him off from Demetrias and Phthiotic Thebes; for he encamped just south of Pherae, when Philip, unaware of his presence, was just north of Pherae. Both armies moved west, Philip heading for the road from Pharsalus via Crannon to Larissa, and Flamininus following the Enipeus valley. The Karadagh ridge lay between the two armies, which were out of touch with one another. At dawn on the third day a thick mist halted Philip's army; had it been clear, he would have reached his objective, because Flamininus delayed in his camp. Each commander sent a detachment to the top of the intervening ridge, and there by chance the detachments met and fought. The ridge itself and the parallel spurs running south from it were called the Dog's-heads, (*Cynoscephalae*). The battle, in June, was to be so named.

The strength of Flamininus' army lay in two legions, each of 11,000 men. His 8000 or so light-armed men were mainly Italian, Aetolian and Athamanian; his cavalry, part Roman and part Aetolian, numbered 2500; and he had some elephants, which the Macedonian and Thessalian cavalry had not been trained to face. Of the two commanders, Philip aimed, as in the past, to wear his enemy down by blocking and harassing tactics and then to obtain tolerable terms; but if chance should offer a favourable opportunity for a charge by his pikemen-phalanx he intended to take it. He would have to be very confident of the outcome, because he had no reserves at all. Flamininus wanted to force a decisive battle and to inflict maximum casualties, even at the risk of defeat; for Rome had limitless reserves.

When the fighting began on the ridge, Philip had sent some troops off to forage as the mist lightened. Each commander reinforced his troops on the ridge with light-armed and cavalry and kept his heavy-armed infantry standing to arms beside his camp. A message came back to Philip, who knew the lie of the land but could not see over the ridge from his camp: 'the enemy are on the run, now is your chance.' Philip set off with half of the phalanx, and ordered 'Jumbo' Nicanor to follow closely with the other half. Meanwhile Flamininus, who could see the fighting from his camp, was leading one legion forward into the fray, while the elephants and the second legion waited on his right. On crossing over the intervening ridge, Philip's phalangites adopted a close formation, sixteen men deep, with a flank guard on the right, charged downhill into the looser formation of the legion, and with lowered pikes drove it back. Realizing that this legion would be defeated, Flamininus switched to the second legion. He led the elephants and the men up the parallel ridge in battle order and routed the second half of the phalanx, as it came over the intervening ridge in disorder. A link

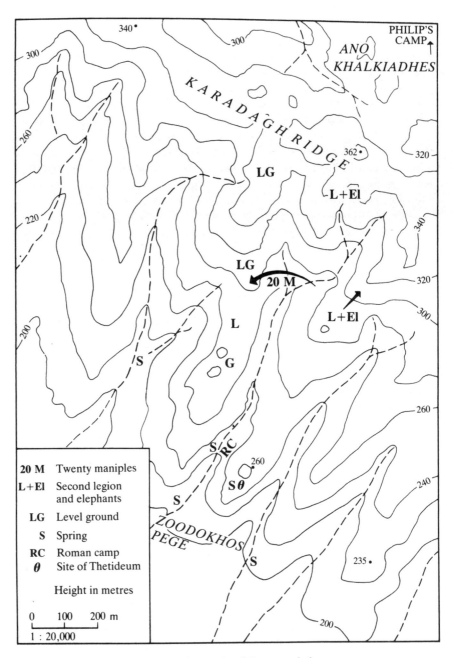

Fig 18 The Battle of Cynoscephalae

between the two battles was made by a Roman officer, who led 2000 legionaries from the advancing legion on to the other ridge and then charged downhill into the rear ranks of the victorious phalanx, throwing it into disorder. In the close hand-to-hand fighting which followed the break-up of the phalanx formation, the pike was useless. The phalangite's short sword and shoulder-shield were no match for the legionary's heavy javelin (*pilum*), long sword used with gladiatorial skill, and door-like shield. Most of the phalangites fell fighting; those who tried to surrender were massacred; and a minority escaped, the king among them.

Defeat was total, for the cavalry had not been able to face the elephants and had fled. On the field of battle 8000 Macedonians lay dead, and in the pursuit 5000 prisoners were taken, while the Roman casualties were in hundreds only. Philip detached an officer to burn his *Journal* and other papers at Larissa, and adopted an almost imgregnable position in the Vale of Tempe. Victory in battle being now impossible, Philip asked for terms of peace, hoping to save his kingdom from invasion and occupation. Flamininus and the Aetolians were at variance, neither trusting the other. Flamininus wanted to make peace, before Antiochus could cross to Europe and perhaps support Philip, whereas the Aetolians were eager to 'expel' Philip and sack Macedonia. Philip was granted a four-month truce on the *status quo* but on payment of 200 talents and the surrender of his son Demetrius and some leading Macedonians, who were to be held in Rome as hostages. During the truce the Dardanians invaded and ravaged parts of Macedonia, until Philip conscripted 500 cavalry and 6000 infantry and drove them out. At this moment the people of Orestis defected to Rome. They had suffered much in recent years from Dardanians and Romans, and they realized that Philip had little chance of protecting them. But the other cantons of Upper Macedonia stayed loyal.

In Rome the Senate received reports that Antiochus was close to the Hellespont. It decided on the following peace terms. Philip was to pay 1000 talents (half forthwith), surrender his fleet apart from a flagship and five *lembi*, withdraw his garrisons from Greek cities and recognize the independence of Orestis. He accepted, protesting at Rome's bad faith in breaching the terms of the truce. At least Macedonia had been saved from invasion and her army had not been disarmed. The Aetolians believed that Macedonia had been let off lightly. They resented the fact that Rome alone had decided the terms of the peace, and they protested publicly that Rome was succeeding Macedonia as 'the tyrant of Greece'.

Collaboration and recovery

There was truth in the Aetolians' protest that Rome was behaving as 'the tyrant of Greece'. Rome's presence in Greece had been incidental to her war

193

with Macedonia; and in the course of the war some states had joined her as allies, most had remained neutral and a few had opposed her. Yet after the victory, Roman military and naval forces stayed in Greece (not in Macedonia) until 194. They were there to support and, when necessary, to enforce the rule of pro-Roman political leaders in individual states (at Thebes, for example) and the Senate's awards of territory to this or that state or League (e.g. of Leucas to Acarnania and Corinth to the Achaean League). The political changes were resented; for instance, the methods employed at Thebes led to a popular rising, during which 500 of the hated Roman soldiers were killed. The awards were from the Greek point of view arbitrary and tyrannical. When Sparta refused the order to hand over Argos to the Achaean League, the Roman army ravaged Laconia and enforced compliance. When the Roman forces left in 194, they took with them huge quantities of loot which had been seized not from Macedonia but from Greek states. In consequence, the claim of Rome at the Isthmian festival of 196 that she was the liberator of Greek peoples rang hollow for most Greek states.

Roman forces stayed in Greece for a further reason. At the Isthmian festival of 196 a decree of the Senate was announced: 'the Greeks in Asia and in Europe are to be free and use their own laws.' Antiochus' envoys who were present at the festival took back an order from the Senate: Antiochus was to respect the freedom of the (Greek) city-states in Asia, withdraw from city-states previously held by Ptolemy and Philip, and not cross to Europe with an army. Antiochus then invaded Thrace and replied to the Senate that Rome had no *locus standi* in Asia, Thrace was his by inheritance from Seleucus, and Ptolemy was about to become his son-in-law. There was clearly a danger that Antiochus' army and fleet, being now in Europe, might obtain support from Macedonia and invade Greece or/and the Protectorate. The Senate therefore advised Philip to consult Rome 'on the matter of alliance', and the result (details are not known) was a sworn treaty of 'peace and friendship', in which Macedonia agreed unilaterally to support Rome in war. In 195, when Rome attacked Sparta, her army was reinforced by 1500 Macedonian soldiers, as well as troops of Thessaly and Achaea and ships of Eumenes (the successor of Attalus) and Rhodes. Even so, the Macedonian hostages were retained in Rome, and instalments of the indemnity had to be paid; for Rome was afraid that Philip, 'friend' though he was, might join Antiochus.

Rome acted with Antiochus as she had acted with Philip. Her final ultimatum was that he must either depart from Europe and do what he pleased in Asia, or stay in Europe and have Rome defend the liberty of Greek city-states in Asia. While Antiochus hesitated, Aetolia invited him 'to liberate Greece' from Rome, and her own forces captured Demetrias and attempted without success to seize Chalcis and Sparta. Thereupon Antiochus sailed with 6 elephants, 500 cavalry and 10,000 infantry from the Hellespont to Demetrias, where he was given supreme command by Aetolia. It was now the autumn of 192. Roman forces could not arrive in strength until the spring. Help was offered to Rome by Ptolemy, who feared Antiochus, and by Carthage and Masinissa, a Numidian king. Should Macedonia join Antiochus? If she did so, reinforcements from Asia would be able to march overland through Macedonia instead of having to be transported by sea in the spring; and the combined forces of Antiochus, Philip and the Aetolian League would then have every chance of capturing the Roman Protectorate (Hannibal, a refugee at the court of Antiochus since 195, was said to have recommended such a course). Philip decided to stay on the side of Rome, perhaps because he did not wish Macedonia to be the battlefield between two great powers, and perhaps because he distrusted Antiochus personally and militarily. During the winter he and a Roman commander, advancing from the Protectorate, captured Larissa.

In 191 a Roman army of 15 elephants, 2000 cavalry and 20,000 infantry trounced Antiochus, who had wasted the winter months and not yet received his main army by sea. He fled to Asia, made various offers which were refused, and mustered 75,000 men. In 190 a Roman army, rejecting Philip's offer of troops, marched to the Hellespont, crossed unopposed into Asia, was joined by the army of Eumenes and, although half as numerous, won an outright victory. Antiochus' Macedonian phalanx of 16,000 men fought in close formation and held its ground until Antiochus' elephants stampeded and broke its ranks; thereafter the Roman legionaries went in for the kill, as at Cynoscephalae. Rome's terms for peace were that Antiochus should renounce his claim to all lands west of the Taurus range, surrender all his elephants and most of his fleet, and pay an indemnity of 15,000 talents. Antiochus accepted. Rome made awards of territories and city-states in Asia to Eumenes and Rhodes as her allies. In 188 she withdrew her forces, leaving a 'settlement' backed by her authority.

Rome had handled Philip carefully. At first he was assured that he could keep cities which he captured while fighting for the common cause, but Roman commanders soon outmanouevred him by making a truce unilaterally with Aetolia. In winter 191/90 the hostages were sent back to Macedonia. In spring 190, as the Roman army marched through Macedonia, further instalments of the indemnity were cancelled. In 189, at the request of Rome, Macedonian troops, commanded by Perseus, the elder son of Philip, joined in the attack on Aetolia. However, when Rome imposed terms of peace on Aetolia, Philip was not consulted, and when she made awards of places she did not honour her original assurance to him. The principle of her so-called 'settlements' was clear: to balance one power against another (for example, Aetolia against Macedonia, Philip against Eumenes) and control them by her authority, and if necessary by armed force. It was unrealistic, given this policy of *'divide et impera'*, to expect that past services to Rome would be rewarded.

Greek states were quick to exploit the Roman system of control. They kept sending complaints against Philip to Rome, and they regularly received decisions in their favour from the Senate. Then, in order to see that these decisions were implemented, the Senate sent commissioners to the disputed places and to interrogate Philip. Eumenes played the same game with regard to Greek city-states on the Thracian coast; decisions were in his favour, and Philip was warned 'not to appear to be acting against the wishes of the Senate'. When Philip sent his son Demetrius to intercede for him at Rome, Flamininus and others made it clear that they wanted Demetrius, not the elder son Perseus, to succeed to the throne. The Senate implied that punitive measures had been averted only through the influence of Demetrius.

During these trying years, when Philip had to turn the other cheek, he was rebuilding the strength of Macedonia. 'He compelled the Macedonians to beget children and raise them all'; 'he transplanted a great multitude of Thracians to Macedonia'; and he settled 5000 deserters from Antiochus' army and many refugees in his kingdom. As his coasts were no longer threatened, he rearranged the disposition of his Macedonians. He transplanted 'citizen families' (i.e. Macedonians proper) from their coastal cities to sites which he chose for defence against Dardanians and Illyrians, and he filled the cities they vacated with Thracians, Gauls and other immigrants, who worked the land as subjects of the king. The speed of recovery from the crippling defeat at Cynoscephalae seemed almost miraculous. It was due to the spirit of the Macedonians and the diligence of the immigrant workers (they were not 'guests' but permanent settlers); to the natural resources of the kingdom; and above all to the immunity from raids and from war, which resulted from the alliance with Rome. Philip husbanded the increasing revenues from taxation, 'redeveloped old mines and opened new mines in many places'; and exported the fine timber, of which he had the royal monopoly. Whereas Antigonus Doson and Demetrius had coined only in bronze, Philip was now issuing coinage in gold and silver (see Plate 26: iii, iv) as well as in bronze; and for a number of years he had been paying the indemnity to Rome in silver bullion.

During Philip's reign coinage was issued for the first time by the Macedonian Assembly, the Macedonian citizens of two regions (Amphaxitis and Bottiaea; see Plate 26: v, vi), the Paroraei (mainly Thracian-speaking), the Paeonian Doberi (in the Strumitsa valley), Pella, Thessalonica, Apollonia (in Mygdonia), Aphytis, and Amphipolis. The first two coined in silver and bronze, and the others only in bronze. These coinages had no political significance. The king provided the minerals, and the purpose was to encourage the adoption of a fully monetary economy and to stimulate internal exchange and export. Thus 'he increased the revenues of his kingdom . . . by harbour dues.'

Under the ongoing terms of the Roman settlement, Macedonia was limited on the west by the Ardiaeans, Dassaretis and Orestis; on the south

196

by the Thessalian League; and on the Thracian coast by Maronea. But no limit had been set to the north-east and the north, and it was in those directions that Philip deployed his armed forces. In a series of successful operations he gained control by subjection or by alliance of inland Thrace as far as Byzantium, which he protected from Thracian attack, and he entered into alliance with the Scordisci, a Gallic tribe north of the Dardanians. The next step was to form friendship with the Bastarnae, a powerful Germanic tribe which had settled on the north bank of the lower Danube, and to invite them to join in a campaign against the Dardanians. A diplomatic mission was established with them, and Perseus married a princess of their royal house. Agreement was reached on an ambitious plan. An army of Bastarnae, accompanied by their families, was to meet Philip's army in the middle Strymon valley, defeat the Dardanians, and plant a settlement of Bastarnae near the Macedonian frontier, probably in the Polog region. In 179 the Bastarnae were approaching the Strymon, and Philip was waiting with the main army at Amphipolis. At that crucial moment Philip was taken ill and died.

His last years had been saddened by dissension within his kingdom. In 183 three leading Macedonians and their associates were executed for treason, no doubt after trial, and their sons and daughters were imprisoned 'in accordance with a royal order'. Tension between Perseus, who was Philip's intended successor, and Demetrius, who was *persona grata* at Rome, led to an open quarrel at the purification of the Macedonian army in spring 182; and each prince had supporters at court, who favoured policies of ultimate resistance to Rome or continuing appeasement. Philip trusted both his sons. He left Demetrius as his deputy in 181, when he and Perseus were on campaign, and in 180 he sent Demetrius on a mission to Paeonia. There Demetrius died. Rumours were spread that Perseus was responsible for his death, and that Philip intended to disown Perseus and commend Antigonus as his successor. The truth is not ascertainable.

The defeat and the partition of Macedonia

Perseus' first act was to be elected king by the Macedonian army. He then took the corpse of Philip, escorted by the army, to Aegeae for burial. A member of the royal house, who had probably been a rival for the throne, was executed, presumably on a charge of treason. During Perseus' absence the Bastarnae quarrelled with the Thracians; some of their leaders were struck by lightning during a terrifying storm; and they found no Macedonian vanguard at the rendezvous. Most of them went home; but 30,000 went on, defeated the Dardanians and settled on captured land. Meanwhile a Thracian king, Abrupolis, invaded eastern Macedonia, ravaged up to the walls of Amphipolis and retired with loot. Perseus, returning with the army, invaded the kingdom of Abrupolis and expelled the king. He then sent an envoy to Rome, asking that he be recognized as king, and that the treaty of 'friendship' made with Philip be continued with him; and he explained why he had punished Abrupolis, who had an alliance with Rome. The request was granted in 178. He took in this year a second wife, Laodice, daughter of Seleucus IV (the successor of Antiochus). Because Rome had banned the fleet of Seleucus from the Aegean, the bride was escorted by the fleet of Rhodes, to which Perseus supplied timber as a gift.

Perseus maintained the influence of Macedonia in Thrace, sometimes by military action. He had particularly close ties there with the Agrianians; with Cotys, who was king of the strongest tribal group, the Odrysians; and with Byzantium, which controlled the entry to the Bosporus. Unlike Philip, he fished in the troubled waters of the Greek mainland. In Thessaly and central Greece, Rome's support of the well-to-do had enabled them to introduce harsh laws of debt and to delay the workings of the courts, so that both Rome and the well-to-do were hated by the mass of the citizens and party strife was frequent. Perseus advertised his policy by cancelling debts to the crown, liberating past offenders, and recalling exiles to Macedonia. Then he helped the Aetolian League to put the same policy into effect by providing financial aid. Some city-states in Thessaly and Boeotia followed suit. In addition, Perseus supported the federalists in Boeotia; and when they came into power, a treaty was concluded between Macedonia and the Boeotian League. He was hailed as a philhellenic benefactor and philanthropist. But the extension of his influence southwards was blocked by two bitter enemies, Athens and the Achaean League.

The first attempt to pit Rome against Macedonia was made in 177 by the Dardanians, who sent envoys to Rome to announce that Perseus and the Bastarnae were in league and to ask for help against them. Rome sent commissioners to the Bastarnae on the lower Danube and to Macedonia, where they noted the prosperity and preparedness of the kingdom. As nothing was proven, the Senate merely warned Perseus 'to be seen to be being puncitilious in respecting the treaty he had with Rome'. Later the Dardanians managed to dislodge those Bastarnae who had settled near Macedonia. Complaints soon flowed in from Greece, and the Senate sent out one commission after another, because it was clear that Perseus might oust Rome as the protector of liberty and social justice. Sometimes a commission ameliorated the position of the debtors, or arranged a reconciliation (taking hostages in Aetolia to ensure that the reconciliation was honoured). In 173 Eumenes of Pergamum informed the Senate that Perseus was preparing for war, and the Senate sent a commission to Macedonia. In 172 Eumenes addressed the Senate in a secret session on this theme, urging Rome to attack Perseus before Perseus could cross to Italy. On his way back an unsuccessful attempt was made on his life at Delphi. He claimed that Perseus was responsible.

The Senate now started on the long process of preparing for war against Macedonia. Alliances were made with three Thracian tribes 'in the rear of Macedonia', friendships or/and alliances were reaffirmed with cities in Crete, Rhodes, Ptolemy VI and Antiochus IV, and envoys visited Carthage and Masinissa to arrange for supplies and elephants. In autumn 172 a strong fleet and 5000 soldiers were sent into the Protectorate, and five envoys with 1000 soldiers – an unusual accompaniment which suggested military aid – began to tour Greece with a summary of charges against Perseus. Their aim was to help pro-Roman politicians, recruit allies and secure bases for action. They persuaded the Epirote League to send troops into Orestis and the Achaean League to send 1000 troops to garrison Chalcis. Most of the envoys reported to the Senate in spring 171.

During this process the protests of Perseus and the arguments of the envoys he sent to Rome were of no avail. When the five Roman envoys were leaving Corcyra for their tour, they received a letter from Perseus which asked why Roman troops were crossing from Italy to the Greek cities (of the Protectorate). They gave an evasive verbal reply and hastened on their way. At Larissa, where two Roman envoys had just persuaded the Thessalian League to side with Rome in the event of war, envoys from Perseus arrived, conveying his request for a personal interview. The king and Marcius Philippus met in November. As their fathers had been guest-friends, Perseus was overtrusting, and he was tricked by Philippus into believing that, if he should send envoys to Rome, any differences would be settled reasonably. The envoys whom Perseus then sent were not given an audience by the Senate until March 171. Their arguments that Perseus had acted properly and kept the treaty with Rome fell on deaf ears. The Senate was not interested in arguments of right or wrong, or in its treaty of friendship with Macedonia. It simply ordered the envoys to leave Italy within thirty days. By then a Roman army of some 37,000 men would be on the frontier of Macedonia, and its purpose was the destruction of the Macedonian State.

Perseus had tried to counteract the political propaganda of the Roman envoys (of which a part is known from a text inscribed for public view at Delphi) by sending a self-justifying memorandum to the Greek states. Many sympathized with Macedonia, but very, very few dared face the hostility of Rome and the danger of being ruthlessly sacked by her legions or marines. He had asked Eumenes, Antiochus and Ptolemy to join him against the common enemy of all the Macedonian kingdoms, but without avail. In fact Macedonia stood alone except for some Balkan allies. Because Perseus had trusted Philippus and kept the terms of the treaty, whereas Rome had acted treacherously, he had been outmanoeuvred strategically; for while he awaited the hearing of his envoys at Rome, Thebes and Chalcis were being occupied by Roman and pro-Roman troops, so that a naval and military offensive could be launched, not as in 199 from the Protectorate and Corcyra, but from Thessaly and Chalcis. But by waiting he demonstrated to his own people that justice was on their side. A Council of Friends at Pella recommended not appeasement but war, and when he addressed the army the soldiers roared out a demand for action. Macedonia was united in going to war. The gods, they believed, were on their side.

A Roman fleet of fifty quinqueremes met that of Eumenes at Chalcis, unopposed because the Macedonian fleet had been surrendered in 197 and not reconstituted. The main Roman army, by forced marches, reached Larissa, where it was joined by troops from Eumenes, the Aetolian League, the Achaean League and some Thessalian cities. Meanwhile Perseus was mustering his army at Citium. The Macedonian citizen forces were 3000 cavalry and 26,000 pikemen – numbers comparable to those of 336, which indicates the extent of Macedonia's recovery. The Odrysian allies, led by Cotys, provided 1000 cavalry and 1000 infantry. Other infantry were 8000 Thracians, Paeonians, Gauls and Agrianians (being mainly from within the kingdom, apart from the Agrianians), 1500 Greek émigrés and 3000 Cretans. Unlike Philip in 199, Perseus had no far-flung garrisons; but he still had to defend his land frontiers with local militiamen, and he had regular troops supporting the local militia at harbours such as Demetrias and Pella to resist the marines of the Roman fleet. His resources were stretched to the utmost. He had amassed supplies in advance, but a long war would exhaust them. His aim, like that of Philip, was to weaken the morale of the Roman army by harassing tactics, engage in a set battle only when sure of a victory, and hope for a peace on honourable terms.

In 171 those tactics succeeded. The Roman forces had to withdraw from Larissa and seek supplies elsewhere. Perseus, with the approval of his Friends and commanders, sued for peace with a return to the *status quo ante* and with Macedonia paying all expenses incurred by Rome during the war. The Senate demanded only one thing: the unconditional surrender of Macedonia. Several later requests, even with higher financial payments, were refused, and the same demand was made. In 170 the Epirote League split, Molossia joining Macedonia, and Chaonia and Thesprotis staying in alliance with Rome. That winter Perseus conducted two remarkable campaigns in severe weather: one in the north-west, where Rome had considerable losses and Perseus took 1500 Romans prisoner; and the other in the south-west, which failed to draw Aetolia away from Rome. Looting by the Roman forces, even of Chalcis, caused increasing hatred of Rome. On the other hand, Perseus was negotiating for alliances with the Ardiaean king (Gentius) and with the Bastarnae.

In 169, for the first time, the Roman army penetrated the strong southern defences of Macedonia and reached Dium; but shortage of supplies enforced a withdrawal to Heracleum. That winter Perseus, whose requests for peace were rejected, persuaded Rhodes and Prusias of Bithynia to intercede at Rome. When the usual reply was made, he appealed to Eumenes and

Antiochus on the ground that they would be the next victims of Rome's imperialism. They refused, Antiochus being now at war with Ptolemy. Alliances were concluded with Gentius, who received a prepayment of 10 talents, and with the Bastarnae. The latter entered the Strymon valley with 10,000 cavalrymen and 10,000 reserves, and their commander demanded full pay in advance. With the approval of his Friends and commanders, Perseus replied that he needed only 5000 of them, whereupon they all departed in a huff. Just before the campaigning season a navy of forty *lembi* which Perseus had built escorted fifty grain-carrying Macedonian merchantmen from the Black Sea to Macedonia and then captured a convoy of transporters carrying Eumenes' Gallic troops. But the successes of Perseus only stiffened the determination of the Senate.

For the campaigns of 168, Rome deployed 30,000 men against Gentius, some 5000 marines and 20,000 oarsmen against the Macedonian coast, and a squad of elephants, 4000 cavalry and 39,000 infantry (the only Greeks being Cretans) against Perseus, who was holding a strong defensive position to the north of Heracleum. Gentius surrendered at Scodra; Roman forces this time captured and looted the Ardiaean cities of the coast to and beyond Kotor. The Roman fleet was staved off by perhaps 10,000 troops (2000 Macedonian 'Peltasts' holding Pella, and Illyrians, Gauls, Thracians and Agrianians stiffening the local militia elsewhere). The Roman commander, Lucius Aemilius Paullus, unable to penetrate the defensive position of Perseus, captured the Petra Pass by surprise at night. As Perseus' defences were now turned, he withdrew at night to just south of Pydna. Paullus, advancing without reconnaissance, suddenly saw the Macedonian phalanx ready to attack on level ground rather more than a kilometre distant. This was Perseus' opportunity. The phalanx advanced, but not fast enough to deliver its charge; for Paullus managed to withdraw his army westwards on to a steep-ended ridge. Luck was with him, in that the ridge had a strong spring of water; but Perseus moved his army on to the plain between Paullus and the coast, so that the Roman fleet was unable to supply Paullus directly. It looked as if Paullus would soon have to retreat under very difficult conditions in order to find supplies.

The battle which ensued developed out of a clash between some advanced troops at a time when the 24,000 phalangites and the 26,000 legionaries were in their respective camps less than a mile apart. As more troops became engaged, each commander brought the infantrymen out of his camp and deployed them into line with light-armed and cavalry forming the wings. A Roman officer saw the Royal Guardsmen, who formed the left part of the Macedonian phalanx, 'dazzling in gilded armour and newly dyed purple cloaks' and next 'the Bronze-Shields by brigades . . . making the hills resound with harsh battle-cries'. The Macedonians formed line on the level ground more quickly, lowered their pikes and charged with devastating effect; their pike-points pierced shield, cuirass and opponent alike. They

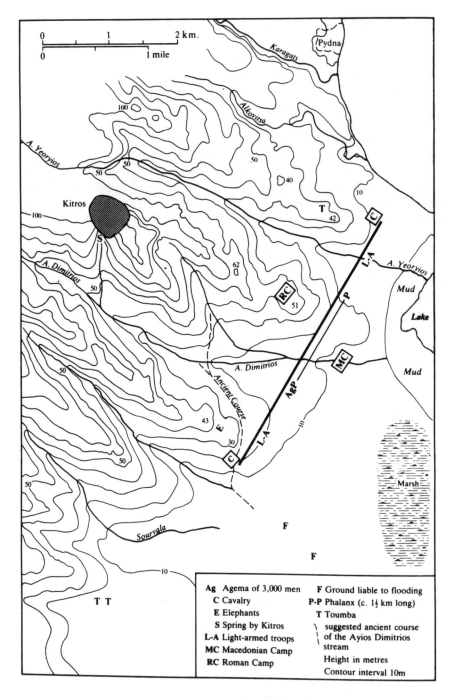

Fig. 19 The Battle of Pydna

were, however, too successful and impetuous; as their line drove the legionaries back, it hit uneven rising ground and crumpled, with the result that many gaps appeared. Into these gaps Aemilius sent his legionaries in small groups, and once inside they took the disordered pikemen in flank and rear, cutting them down with their long swords. Against the Macedonian left Aemilius sent elephants charging downhill into the cavalry, whose horses stampeded in terror (they had been trained to the sight of cardboard elephants and simulated trumpeting, but not to the smell of the beasts). A special anti-elephant unit of infantry with spiked shields proved ineffective. Then the elephants, cavalry and light-armed infantry routed their light-armed opponents and surrounded the 3000 Royal Guardsmen, who 'fought in formation until the last man was cut down'. Meanwhile, the whole phalanx was outfought, as the pikemen's little shields and short swords were no match for the legionaries' long sword and door-like shield. Those who swam out to the Roman ships and tried to surrender were slaughtered in the water, and the wounded on the battlefield were killed. The dead were estimated at 20,000.

Perseus commanded the cavalry on the right of the 3.5-kilometre line. From there he had no control over the development of the battle, and when the phalanx collapsed he and the Macedonian cavalry fled 'almost unscathed'. The Roman pursuit inflicted further casualties. The 11,000 who were taken prisoner later in the open and at Pydna were sold on the slave market. Apart from the cavalrymen, the Macedonian army ceased to exist. Perseus and some Friends, with an escort of the Royal Pages and Cretans, reached Samothrace and asked for terms in vain. The Friends and the Pages accepted an offer of a pardon with retention of their property. Perseus and his eldest son gave themselves up. The Macedonian monarchy was at an end.

Aemilius permitted the spoiling of the dead and the sacking of Pydna, Aegeae, Pella and some other cities in the Roman manner, and he gave the Roman cavalry *carte blanche* to ravage the countryside and plunder as far afield as the Strumitsa valley. Further sacking and spoliation, as if Rome was still at war, continued in 167, until the final settlement was announced to a meeting which consisted of ten leading men from each Macedonian city. The country was to be divided into four states, on which Aemilius imposed a Roman code of laws. Between them there was to be no intermarriage and no trade in building material or agricultural produce. Salt was not to be imported (this probably to prevent transhumant pastoralism). Arms were forbidden except for frontier guards facing Balkan peoples. Gold and silver were not to be mined, ship-timber not to be exported, and the royal estates not to be cultivated. Half of the taxes previously paid to the king were to be sent out of the country to Rome, the other half remaining for internal services. Any stocks of grain and oil which the Roman forces had not consumed were distributed to Greek states. These measures, coming on top of the looting, ravaging and loss of people and stock, ensured that any economic recovery would be slow. The other step was to remove the administrative or officer class. Aemilius read out a list of men who, with any sons over fifteen years of age, were to be deported on pain of death to Italy. It is unlikely that they ever saw Macedonia again; for of 1000 leading men of the Achaean League deported at this time only 300 – among them the historian Polybius – lived to return seventeen years later.

At Rome the state loot was so enormous that all direct taxation of the Roman People was abolished for more than a century. In the procession celebrating the triumph of Aemilius, '250 carriages carried the statues, sculptures and paintings' which had been taken mainly from Macedonia. In front of the triumphant general walked Perseus, dressed as a peasant and in chains, and with him his children. Soon afterwards, either from self-starvation or from persecution by his guards, the last 'King of Macedonians' died in solitary confinement.

XV

The Significance of the
Macedonian Achievement

By any standard of comparison, the scale of the Macedonian achievement is remarkable. The original homeland, Pieria, was tiny, being no larger than County Durham and much more mountainous. The early kingdom (Pieria, Bottiaea, Almopia and Eordaea) was smaller than Yorkshire. When Upper Macedonia was incorporated by Philip II, the whole area from which the Macedonian phalangites were recruited by Alexander the Great was no larger than England from the latitude of York to the Scottish border. When the British Empire was at its peak, it was fashionable to contrast the size of the British Isles with the size of the British dominions. The contrast between the recruiting ground of the Macedonian phalangites and the areas which they conquered and their descendants controlled is much more astonishing.

The land plays a part in shaping a people's character and qualities. The remote uplands of Olympus and Pieria bred a consciously distinct people, relatively safe in their fastnesses from invasion. Then a ring of high mountains and a great river – the Axius – gave a natural protection to the early kingdom; and an even higher ring – in places rings – of mountains and the Axius surrounded the recruiting ground. The Macedonians endured great extremes of climate from an intensely cold winter to a torrid heat in summer. The combination of mountain and plain suited a wide variety of activities: transhumant pastoralism, lumbering and afforestation, stock-raising, fruit-growing, vegetable-growing and cereal production. The inhabitants had to be physically tough to withstand such extremes of climate and versatile in making a living. We have seen this toughness in the open-air pastoral life, and their versatility in adopting a settled life and developing cities in the early kingdom; and even more vividly in the continual endurance of Alexander's Macedonians and their ability to climb rock-faces with ropes and pitons, construct siege-engines of great height, bridge wide rivers, build rafts and ships, and lay out cities with amazing speed. No ancient Greek army, based on largely slave labour, and no modern army, relying on machinery, has possessed all those abilities. They were a very healthy people, not debilitated by malaria and consumption (as in Turkish times and up to the Second World War) and not weakened by the effects of pollution. That this was so is proved by the vigorous longevity not only of such commanders as Antipater, Parmenio, Antigonus, Seleucus and

Lysimachus, who fought as cavalrymen on either side of eighty years of age, but also of Alexander's 3000 Silvershields who were invincible in battle long after reaching the modern retiring age of sixty.

As members of the Greek race and speakers of the Greek language, the Macedonians shared in the ability to initiate ideas and create political forms. They differed from the southern Greeks in two vital respects: they preserved their early institutions and they maintained their early religious beliefs throughout their history as a free people. One consequence was the Macedonian form of constitutional monarchy, in which the king's religious duties were of paramount importance; and another was the participation of the Macedonians *en masse* on royal occasions such as a wedding or a funeral, at numerous state festivals, at burials with military honours and in thanksgivings. The king was regarded by the people as their intercessor with the gods. He had special access, as a Temenid descended from Zeus (later kings advanced similar claims). Every day, in sickness and in health, he made 'the prescribed sacrifices in the traditional manner'; in addition he made sacrifices or oblations on numerous occasions, such as entering a Macedonian city's bounds, preparing for battle, and giving thanks for salvation. Many festivals were conducted by the king and the people together, and on these occasions the king led the service and supplied sacrificial victims for the men. The oath of allegiance to the king which each soldier took individually was sworn with the gods as witnesses. Great kings were worshipped after death, and their spirits were thought to be present at ceremonies of state; and the arms of all past kings were carried in a religious procession, because they had some numinous power.

The bonding force of religious unity in a national society is difficult to comprehend today in an age dominated by sectarianism, agnosticism and atheism. Yet we can appreciate that shared religious beliefs inspired the Greek city-states to unite in opposing the Persians and the Carthaginians, and led them to the conviction that the gods were on their side. So too the Macedonian soldiers wore wreaths of laurel in facing the 20,000 Greek mercenaries of Onomarchus, and they believed that Apollo gave them the victory. Nor did their faith weaken with time. For the bronze coins which Philip V minted for internal exchange portrayed Zeus, Poseidon, Athena, Artemis, Helios (the sun god), Pan, Heracles and Perseus; and the coins of the 'Macedones', of regions and of cities in the reigns of Philip V and Perseus portrayed even more deities, adding Apollo, Demeter, Dionysus, Hermes, Strymon and Maenads (see Plate 26). In 171 it was at the ritual purification of the army that the Macedonians declared their determination to follow their king in fighting on behalf of their gods and their country.

The powers of the king in secular matters were far-reaching. He granted the higher citizenship of being a 'Macedon' to those whom he chose. In the event of war he exercised supreme command, conscripted men, provided arms and enforced discipline; and he promoted, demoted or punished at his discretion. He controlled the distribution of the population; thus, if he wished to found a new city, he transplanted an entire community from an existing city to a new site, and he was able to import foreign communities and settle them in the kingdom with permanent rights. His control of the economy was also far-reaching. Where we may 'nationalize' some natural assets, he owned all mines and forests outright and took the profits; he issued the currency of the realm with his own minerals; and he used the timber to build a navy or to sell abroad. He possessed all land which was 'won by the spear', and he laid down the conditions under which that land would be settled and worked, whether by Macedonian citizens or by those who became subjects of the king. He received the bulk of the taxes. He was in many cases the final judge of appeal.

Such powers vested in the head of a modern state would be thought to negate personal liberty. In Macedonia it was not so. A Roman writer, who viewed monarchy with distrust, remarked of the Macedonians that 'while they are accustomed to the command of a king, they live with a greater semblance of liberty than any others'. To the Macedonians this was not a 'semblance' but a sense of liberty. For they had the rights of free men. Under the constitution they elected or deposed a king, appointed a guardian to act if the king was a minor, and judged any case in which the king charged a Macedonian with treason. In their Assembly they responded to the king's proposals, and they decided on such vital matters as war and peace. The individual citizen was able to express his view directly (not through a representative) in the Assembly, whether in debate when he removed his helmet if he addressed the king, or in a trial for treason; and every subject was entitled to appeal to the king. Socially there was no barrier between the king and the Macedonians; for he marched, fought and suffered alongside them, and many anecdotes show that he spoke to them and they to him as man to man. This familiarity, combined with 'the people's inborn reverence for their kings', was a distinguishing feature of the Macedonian form of monarchy.

While the king took the decision in many cases, he usually consulted a group of Friends and/or commanders beforehand, and he used them as a sounding-board of what the Assembly was likely to feel, for instance in stopping at the Hyphasis river or going to war with Rome. He had, as it were, a Cabinet and a Chiefs of Staff Committee to advise him from their experience; and the members were not elected or permanent, but of his own choice. These associates were regularly in the company of the king, and some of their sons were educated together with the boys of the royal family in the School of Pages. Thus a king knew his leading citizens intimately. This was essential, in that he alone appointed men to what we might call 'ministerial posts', in which they had to act without the guidance of any civil service. Thus the system of government was extremely direct, immediate and unbureaucratic, more so than any European system today.

Scale 1:2,500,000

These qualities of government were possible because the king granted the Macedonian citizenship (which gave admission to the Assembly) to those who in his opinion were fitted to serve him in the army or in a similar capacity. This restriction was known to Aristotle in some undeveloped Greek states, such as Malis, where 'the citizen-body consisted of soldiers and ex-soldiers, and holders of office were elected from those on active service'; and he observed that such forms of government were fitted primarily for war. In fact, the situation of Macedonia was such that the state was either fighting for survival or trying to control other states during the centuries of its freedom. It was logical that those who were to fight should be those who took or contributed to the decisions of the state.

The substructure was no less important. Every member of the kingdom, male and female alike, was a citizen either of a *polis* or of a regional community. These local bodies had their own assembly, officials and militia, and with the reservation that the king exercised the overall rule they decided many matters, such as grants of citizenship, admission of outsiders as residents, financial taxes and disbursements, education of citizens' children and military training. The king issued directives through his appointed 'overseers'. In most respects the local bodies were independent. For instance, in 171, the cities sent deputations to Perseus with offers of money and supplies for the war against Rome. Internally they seem to have been free from the violent party strife which weakened the Greek states, partly no doubt because foreign policy and national defence were not in their hands. Their relations with the central government were not complicated by any form of party politics. The vigour and the stability of the cities and the regional units contributed greatly to the strength of the state.

If the Macedonian kingdom had not expanded beyond its early frontiers, its institutions would still be worthy of study. What makes that kingdom so exciting is its ability in dealing with other peoples. Decisive steps were the readiness of the Macedonians to accept into full equality as citizens the men of Upper Macedonia who were chosen by the king to serve in the army, and the willingness of Macedonian communities to be transplanted to sites in Upper Macedonia and of communities from Upper Macedonia to be settled in cities of Lower Macedonia. To the areas east of the recruiting ground, the substructure of *polis* and of regional community was applied but without any imposition of language, religion or custom. Paeonians, Thracians and Bisaltae continued to speak their own languages, practised their own worships, and preserved their own institutions (even monarchy in the Paeonia of the middle Axius valley); and they raised and trained their own militia. Their obligations to the king were clear-cut. They were subject to the king's overall policy, obeyed directives conveyed through his overseers or his generals, and paid land-taxes and other taxes to the king. Some élite forces, small in number, served under the king as light-armed cavalry and infantry; and the portrayal of such cavalrymen on Paeonian coins shows that such service was regarded as prestigious. It was this Macedonian tolerance of other peoples' idiosyncracies which enabled Philip II 'to make from many tribes and nations a single kingdom and people'. The English treatment of Welsh, Scottish and Irish peoples was very different in the formative stages of the United Kingdom. It has to be emphasized that unity and uniformity were not and are not the same thing.

As members of the Greek-speaking world, the Macedonians differed from other states in that they did not set up a 'trophy' – a public record of victory – to humiliate the vanquished. Victory gained, they considered how to regulate the situation and if possible to win the vanquished people's collaboration. The solution was not always the same, because conditions varied and kings gave different leads. Philip II was able to absorb, for instance, the Odomantes living east of the Strymon and the Greek city-states of Chalcidice, apart from Olynthus, into the Macedonian kingdom and let them manage their own affairs locally. After the victory at Chaeronea he initiated the establishment of the Common Peace and won the co-operation of its members in the war against Persia. An even closer association with a large number of Greek states – the Symmachy – was achieved by Antigonus III Doson and Philip V on similar principles to those of Philip II. The workings of the Common Peace and of the Symmachy are of interest in relation to those of the European Community and the coalition known as NATO. There were also less enlightened policies, such as the imposition of minority governments and the intervention or the threat of intervention by armed forces; these were the policies which Athens, Sparta and Thebes had employed, and the resentment which they bred tended to weaken the position of the ruling state, as in modern times.

Alexander and the ablest of his generals and of the subsequent kings set up kingdoms overseas in which the Macedonian principles of racial tolerance and practical co-operation were carried further. Within each kingdom, the king and the Macedonians formed the inner kernel, and they determined the policy of the state. But because they were a tiny fraction of the population within each kingdom, they needed to obtain co-operation on a much greater scale than in the past within the Macedonian kingdom. There was no attempt to impose their own language, religion or legal system throughout each kingdom; and Alexander in particular showed his respect for other cultures in praising Peucestas for learning Persian and adopting some Persian practices, in presiding himself in some religious ceremonies of the Egyptians and the Babylonians, and in sending criminals to their own community to be tried in accordance with its legal practice. This policy, instead of demeaning native cultures, helped to preserve the self-respect of those who had been made subject to the king.

The substructure of the overseas kingdoms was based on that of Macedonia. The peoples of the lands won by the spear were generally left to practise their own religions, customs, laws and forms of organization; and Alexander wished that to continue, because he intended to let the Arabs 'govern themselves according to their own customs, like the Indians'. At the same time, Alexander peopled more than seventy new cities with wounded or unfit Macedonian soldiers, other Europeans (Greek, Thracian and Illyrian), and indigenous communities, transplanted from the vicinity. Because he wanted these cities to support the Macedonian régime, he intended that their mixed population should be led by the Macedonian and Greek elements, and that it should develop some characteristics of the Macedonian way of life. Accordingly, from the outset the institutions of the new cities were modelled on those of the cities in Macedonia, and the language of administration and instruction was Greek. Mixed marriages in these cities were inevitable. They were indeed encouraged by the example of Alexander and eighty of his Companions in marrying Asian women (they observed the wedding customs of their brides), and in adopting and educating the Eurasian children of the Macedonian soldiers. For the future, the introduction of a Macedonian form of education was all-important. It was provided for selected indigenous boys in the cities and to a lesser extent in other communities, and it was designed to equip them for positions of leadership. The priorities were the learning of Greek literacy, an understanding of Greek literature and ideas, and the physical and mental training which would fit a young man to take his place in a Macedonian phalanx or in the local militia. This system of education was soon adopted by all the cities of the overseas kingdoms and of the Macedonian kingdom itself, where the regulations for the 'gymnasiarch' have survived in inscriptions at Beroea and Amphipolis.

That this system of education overseas led to the progressive Hellenization of the cities was vividly expressed by Plutarch: 'when Alexander was civilizing Asia, the reading was Homer, and the tragedies of Euripides and Sophocles were being sung by the boys of Persis, Susiana and Gedrosia [learning Greek as a foreign language]'. The military aspect was equally important. Whereas in the Macedonian kingdom the cavalry and infantry which supported the Companion Cavalry and the Macedonian phalanx were a tiny fraction of the whole, the non-Macedonian element had to be much larger in the overseas kingdoms. We hear most of indigenous soldiers 'of all races', 'armed in the Macedonian manner', who formed the phalanx of Alexander's 30,000 Epigoni with their own command system and in later reigns fought in phalanx formation alongside the Macedonian phalanx; it is evident that they had all been educated in the Macedonian manner in the cities. Before Alexander died, his Companion Cavalry included large numbers of selected Asians, and it is probable that the Companion Cavalry of his successors was similar in that respect.

In addition to their Macedonian and quasi-Macedonian troops, Alexander and his successors employed very large numbers of indigenous cavalry and infantry, which were brigaded in ethnic units and were equipped in their ethnic style. They represented the principle of collaboration with and respect for indigenous peoples. The overall command was vested in the king, and the command of large units in the king's deputies, normally Macedonians by birth or by adoption.

On two occasions our sources report a ceremony to celebrate the principles of collaboration and mutual respect. At Opis, where the 9000 guests were men of many races but predominantly Macedonians and Persians, all chosen for their 'excellence' (aretē), Alexander prayed especially for 'concord and sharing in the rule [of the kingdom] between Macedonians and Persians'. At Persepolis in 317, when Peucestas supplied animals for sacrifice by the army (of over 40,000 men) and provided a banquet, he placed in the circle of highest honour both Macedonians and Persians. The ideas of 'concord' and 'excellence' run through much that our sources report about Philip and Alexander. The Common Peace of the Greeks which they led in war was based on reconciliation between the member-states. When Alexander asked the Greek states to restore exiles (including the Samians expelled from their island by Athens forty years earlier), his purpose is revealed in inscriptions at Tegea on the Greek mainland and at Mytilene on Lesbos; for the citizens residing at Tegea had to swear an oath to be not resentful but at peace with the returnees, and at Mytilene the two parties are to be 'in concord with one another'. The concomitant of concord is peace within the group, whether that group is a single state or a family of nations. He claimed to have established peace in Greece, and he had done so in 'Asia' at the time of his early death.

That the Persians understood his purpose is implied by *The Alexander Romance*, in which Alexander was represented as ordering them to observe their own laws, customs and religions, and as expressing his wish that peace and prosperity should be thenceforth the characteristics of Persia. His Macedonian successors, when they founded their kingdoms, made every attempt and were often able to achieve peace and prosperity, each within his own kingdom. A Greek author of the Hellenistic period lies behind the statements of Plutarch that, having conquered 'Asia', Alexander proceeded to establish for all men in his kingdom 'concord and peace and partnership with one another', and that his mission from the gods was to be 'a general governor and reconciler'. These concepts were not new. They had been expressed by political theorists such as Isocrates with reference to the Greek world, and they were to reappear in Hellenistic philosophical thought. In modern times they have been the dreams of the founders of the League of Nations and of ecumenical Christian thinkers. What was remarkable about Alexander and the Macedonians was that they put those concepts into practice and that they established conditions of 'concord, peace and partnership' within their kingdoms for considerable periods of time.

There are, of course, limitations to be observed. 'Concord' was sometimes broken by Macedonian oppression and native risings, in Egypt particularly. 'Peace' within a kingdom was disrupted by conflicts over the succession. 'Partnership with one another' was sometimes prejudiced by the nationalistic attitude, for instance, of Antigonus Monophthalmus. The level at which this partnership was practical was between men 'of excellence' (*aretē*) of whatever race or colour in a king's army and administrative service and in the cities. That excellence was to a great extent the product of education, because excellence included the intelligence, courage and honesty which would enable the leaders of society – Macedonian, Greek and Asian – to develop concord, peace and partnership within their cities and their kingdom.

In spite of these limitations, the Macedonians created the conditions under which Graeco-Macedonian civilization infused the East with new life and brought greater economic prosperity at all levels. This achievement may be compared to that of Rome which brought Graeco-Roman civilization to the West. We owe to this gifted people, so small in number but so capable, our inheritance of Greek literature and scholarship and its own ideas of racial tolerance and collaboration which they, more than any other people, put into practice on an unparalleled scale.

Specification of the Coins in the Plates

Note: The coins are silver unless otherwise described; the 'stater' is the standard coin of which other coins in the series are denominations; where possible coins are enlarged to twice the actual size.

Plate 7a: i   'Goat' stater of the Bisaltae.

            ii   'Goat' stater of Alexander I, who replaced the monogram of 7a: i with the first two letters of his name in reverse order, *c*.478 BC.

            iii   Stater probably of the Letaei, prior to 500 BC. A Silenus is courting a Nymph.

            iv   Octadrachm of Alexander I, *c*.475–52 BC, showing the mythical hero of the Bisaltae, Rhesus.

            v   Octadrachm of Alexander I, *c*.475–52 BC. The king rides to the hunt with two spears and a hunting dog. He wears a cloak, a *kausia* and a cloth diadem, of which the ends hang down his back.

Plate 7b: i   Tetradrachm of Perdiccas II, similar to Plate 7a: v.

            ii   Tetrobol of Perdiccas II. The horse has been trained for dressage and the club below it is the club of Heracles.

            iii   Didrachm of Archelaus. The head is probably of Caranus, the mythical founder of the Temenid house in Macedonia; he wears a diadem-circlet.

            iv   Didrachm of Archelaus in the tradition of ii.

            v   Didrachm of Amyntas III. The king, wearing *kausia* and cloak, is about to strike (the lion in vi).

            vi   The lion on the reverse, gnawing a spear.

Plate 9a: i   Gold half-stater of Philip II, *c*.356 BC. The head of Heracles, wearing a lionskin cap, was adopted from the coinage of Philippi.

            ii   Tetradrachm of Philip II, portraying the racehorse and jockey which won at the Olympic Games of 356 BC.

            iii   Tetradrachm of the Chalcidian League. Head of Apollo, long-haired and wearing a laurel wreath.

            iv &

            v   Gold stater of Philip II. Head of Apollo, wearing a laurel wreath / two-horse chariot victorious at the Olympic Games of 348 BC. This coin is the famous 'Philippeios'.

            vi &

            vii   Tetradrachm of Philip II. Head of Zeus, wearing a laurel wreath / a bearded rider, wearing *kausia*, tunic and cloak, and in some issues a cloth diadem, and raising his right arm in a salute. The rider is Philip. He was always portrayed from the left, because he had lost his right eye.

215

Plate 25a: i   The Porus Medallion, a decadrachm. Horseman with flying cloak, plumed helmet and long lance, is attacking King Porus and his mahout on a war-elephant. The mahout is hurling a javelin. The horseman may be Alexander, holding his horse firmly as it rears in alarm / Alexander, equipped as a cavalryman with his sword in a scabbard carried high, cuirass with kirtle, and hand on his lance, holds a thunderbolt (emblem of Zeus) in his right hand. His head is turned aside, so that the two ends of his cloth diadem are visible. The monogram below may be an abbreviation of 'Babylon', the metropolis of his Kingdom of Asia. He is represented here as King of Asia in Macedonian military uniform.

ii   The Porus Medallion, a decadrachm. As in i with the plume on the horseman's helmet more visible / as in i, but with Nike about to place a wreath over the high plume of Alexander's helmet, which is as on Plate 15. The two ends of the cloth diadem hang free between his head and his lance. There is no monogram.

iii   Tetradrachm of Lysimachus, portraying Alexander wearing the royal diadem with the two ends showing and the ram's horn of Zeus Ammon over the ear (a symbol of deification) / Athena at rest, helmeted with a shield alongside and with Nike standing on her hand and extending a wreath towards the space above 'of King Lysimachus'. Minted from c.297 BC. The finest portrait of Alexander as he was in the 320s.

Plate 25b: i   Gold stater of Alexander III the Great. Head of helmeted Athena / Nike (Victory) holding a wreath and a stylis (ship's spar), probably commemorating victory at Issus in 333 BC.

ii   Tetradrachm of Alexander III. Head of a young Heracles / Zeus enthroned, holding a sceptre and an eagle. Issued first in Cilicia.

iii   Bronze of Alexander III. Head of a young Heracles / eagle on a thunderbolt.

iv   Tetradrachm of Philip III, in the tradition of Plate 25b: ii.

v   Drachm of Alexander IV. The diademed head is probably his / rider on a prancing horse.

vi   Bronze of Cassander. Head of a young Heracles / naked rider saluting as in Plate 9a: vii.

vii   Tetradrachm of Demetrius I. Nike on a warship's prow / Poseidon at rest, holding his trident. It commemorates his victory off Cyprus in 306 BC.

viii Tetradrachm of Demetrius I. Diademed head of Demetrius / Poseidon at rest, holding his trident. Records the assumption of kingship after the victory.

	ix	Tetradrachm of Antigonus II Gonatas. Macedonian shield / Athena Alcidemus, holding a shield and hurling a thunderbolt.
Plate 26:	i	Tetradrachm of Antigonus II. Head of Poseidon, garlanded with seaweed / Apollo on the prow of a warship.
	ii	Drachm of Antigonus II. Head of Zeus, oak-wreathed / Athena poising a thunderbolt.
	iii	Tetradrachm of Philip V. Diademed head of Philip / Athena poising a thunderbolt.
	iv	Tetradrachm of Philip V. Macedonian shield with the head of the hero Perseus in the centre / an oak-wreathed club (i.e. of Heracles).
	v	Tetrobol of Makedones Amphaxioi. Macedonian shield with a central ornament of six whorls / an oak-wreathed club.
	vi	Tetrobol of Botteatai. Macedonian shield with a central ornament of six whorls / a warship's stern.
	vii	Tetradrachm of Perseus. Diademed head of Perseus / an eagle on a thunderbolt within an oak-wreath, all being emblems of Zeus.
Plate 30:	i	Gold octadrachm of Ptolemy II. Heads of Ptolemy II and Arsinoe II, both wearing a diadem, 'siblings' / heads of Ptolemy I and Berenice, both wearing a diadem, 'gods'.
	ii	Gold octadrachm of Ptolemy IV. Head of Ptolemy III, wearing a radiate crown, with an aegis round his neck and a trident-sceptre behind his head / a radiate cornucopia (horn of plenty).
	iii	Tetradrachm of Seleucus I. Head of a horned horse above an anchor / an elephant, commemorating his victory at the battle of Ipsus.
	iv	Tetradrachm of Antiochus III 'the Great'. Head of Antiochus III, wearing a diadem / Apollo seated on the omphalos (the naval-stone of the Earth).
	v	Tetradrachm of Philetaerus of Pergamum. Head of Seleucus I, wearing a diadem / helmeted Athena at rest, 'of Philetaerus' (without the title 'king').
	vi	Tetradrachm of Attalus I of Pergamum. Head of Philetaerus / helmeted Athena at rest, 'of Philetaerus' with strung bow to the right.
	vii	Tetradrachm of Diodotus of Bactria. Head of Diodotus, wearing a diadem / Zeus about to hurl a thunderbolt, with an eagle below, 'of king Diodotus'.

Select Bibliography and Abbreviations

The books listed below provide full bibliographies for earlier literature. The collections of papers give references to the many articles which have been written in the last decade. Recent discoveries are reported each year in *Archaelogical Reports*.

Books

Andronicus, M., *Vergina: the Prehistoric Necropolis and the Hellenistic Palace* (Lund, 1964).
——, *Vergina: the Cemetery of the Tumuli* (Athens, 1969; in Greek).
——, *Vergina: the Royal Tombs and the Ancient City* (Athens, 1984).
Bosworth, A.B., *Conquest and Empire: the Reign of Alexander the Great* (Cambridge, 1988).
Cawkwell, G.L., *Philip of Macedon* (London, 1978).
Ellis, J.R., *Philip II and Macedonian Imperialism* (London, 1976).
Errington, R.M., *Geschichte Makedoniens* (Munich, 1986).
Fox, R.L. *Alexander the Great* (London, 1973).
——, *The Search for Alexander* (Boston, 1980).
Green, P.M., *Alexander the Great* (London, 1970).
Hammond, N.G.L., *Migrations and Invasions in Greece and Adjacent Areas (New Jersey, 1976).*
——, A History of Macedonia, I (Oxford, 1972).
——, and Griffith, G.T., *A History of Macedonia*, II (Oxford, 1979).
——, and Walbank, F.W., *A History of Macedonia*, III (Oxford, 1988).
——, *Alexander the Great: King, Commander and Statesman* (New Jersey and London, 1980–81; 2nd edn, Bristol Classical Press, 1989).
——, *The Macedonian State* (Oxford, 1989).
Hatzopoulos, M.B., and Loukopoulos, L. (eds) *Philip of Macedon* (Athens, 1980).
Petsas, Ph., *Pella: Alexander the Great's Capital* (Thessaloniki, 1978).
Sakellariou, M.B. (ed.), *Macedonia: 4,000 Years of Greek History and Civilization* (Athens, 1983).
Wirth, G., *Philip II. Geschichte Makedoniens*, I (Stuttgart, 1985).

Collections of papers at conferences on Macedonian affairs

Adams, W.L., and Borza, E.N. (eds), *Philip II, Alexander the Great and the Macedonian Heritage* (Washington, 1982).
Ancient Macedonia, I (1970), II (1977), III (1983), IV (1986), V (pending) (Thessaloniki).
Barr-Sharrar, B., and Borza, E.N. (eds), *Macedonia and Greece in Late Classical and Early Hellenistic Times* (Washington, 1982).

Abbreviations are used for works by the present author:

AG	=	*Alexander the Great*
HG	=	*A History of Greece*
HM	=	*A History of Macedonia*
Migrations	=	*Migrations and Invasions in Greece and adjacent areas*
MS	=	*The Macedonian State*

Index